Go Forth
and
Do Good

Go Forth
and
Do Good

Memorable Notre Dame
Commencement Addresses

—◈—

Selected, Edited, and Introduced by
Wilson D. Miscamble, C.S.C.

—◈—

Foreword by
Theodore M. Hesburgh, C.S.C.

Reflection by
Edward A. Malloy, C.S.C.

University of Notre Dame Press
Notre Dame, Indiana

University of Notre Dame Press
Notre Dame, Indiana 46556
www.undpress.nd.edu
All Rights Reserved

Published in the United States of America

Library of Congress Cataloging-in-Publication Data
Go forth and do good : memorable Notre Dame commencement addresses/
selected, edited and introduced by Wilson D. Miscamble ; foreword by
Theodore M. Hesburgh ; reflection on commencement by Edward A.
Malloy.
     p.   cm.
   ISBN 0-268-02956-3 (cloth : alk. paper)
   ISBN 13: 978-0-268-03525-9 (pbk : alk. paper)
   ISBN 10: 0-268-03525-3 (pbk : alk. paper)
     1. Speeches, addresses, etc., American—Indiana—Notre Dame.
2. University of Notre Dame—History—Sources.   3. Baccalaureate
addresses.   I. Miscamble, Wilson D., 1954–
PS664.153 G6   2003
815.008'0977289—dc21
                                                2003000814

∞ *This book is printed on acid-free paper*

To My Brothers in Holy Cross
Their Blood Is in the Bricks

CONTENTS

viii *Contents*

Contents   ix

FOREWORD

Theodore M. Hesburgh, C.S.C.

Commencement at the University of Notre Dame is an important and wonderful experience for those graduating and for their family members and friends. It marks the successful conclusion of a rigorous course of study and the sending forth of the new graduates onward to the next stage of their lives. Commencement is also an important occasion for the institution itself—an opportunity for the university to consider its collective purpose and to benefit from the ideas shared by distinguished commencement speakers.

During my tenure as president of Notre Dame I was privileged to preside over thirty-five commencements at which a diverse group of speakers graced the commencement podium. I welcomed three American presidents—Dwight Eisenhower, Jimmy Carter, and Ronald Reagan—along with a number of foreign leaders, of whom one was my own former student—Jose Napoleon Duarte. I introduced noted jurists, scientists, diplomats, scholars, university presidents, military officers, and government and church officials. Each and every speaker took his or her task seriously. They offered substantial and significant remarks which surely reflected their respect and regard for the university at which they spoke.

Father Bill Miscamble has included a good number of these speeches in this excellent collection, which gathers together memorable addresses drawn from commencements across the whole one hundred and sixty years of Notre Dame's existence. He also has provided a fascinating and thoughtful introduction to this book which allows one to trace Notre Dame's development in conjunction with events in the society and world around it. This book can be read with profit by Notre Dame graduates of all ages and by all those interested in the special place of Notre Dame in American Catholic life and in American higher education.

These Notre Dame speeches provide a valuable prism through which to view some of the great issues which concerned Americans and especially American Catholics since the university's foundation in 1842. They provide an entree, if you will, into the mind and mood of America and its Catholic community. Some of the addresses are firmly rooted in the time in which they were written, revealing the concerns and interests of those living in a different time and circumstance. Others illustrate the university's development, and its special contribution to the nation and the society around it. And still others allude to the special role and obligations of not only Notre Dame graduates, but also of Catholics in general, both in their public and private lives.

As you read these well-chosen addresses, you will discover words that challenge the intellect, inspire the spirit, and rouse the conscience. Taken as a whole these speeches manifest the treasured principles which guide Notre Dame—the quest for truth in the light of faith and the commitment to service not only in the church but also in the nation and world. It is my hope that the readers of this book may benefit from the wisdom dispensed in these speeches. It is my prayer that the book will serve to encourage its readers to go forth and to do good.

REFLECTION ON COMMENCEMENT

Edward A. Malloy, C.S.C.

Father Bill Miscamble's book, *Go Forth and Do Good,* gathers together for the first time a representative cross-section of Notre Dame commencement addresses. Even more importantly, Father Miscamble provides an insightful history of the issues of the day, both inside and outside the academy, which helps us appreciate the significance of these discourses as commentary and as exhortation. In this sense, the book is an important contribution to the study of Notre Dame history as well as the history of American higher education.

Reading this collection of memorable addresses has led me to reflect further on the nature of a commencement address and on the way that Notre Dame as an institution goes about selecting its speakers. The commencement address itself is intended to contribute to the splendor and special nature of the ceremony in which we send forth our most recent graduates for service of society and the Church. The people offered this honor have garnered distinction in various areas of professional and personal responsibility. Their presence is intended to enliven the ceremony and to provide the graduates and assembled guests an opportunity to hear well-known individuals, ones whose message is timely and inspiring.

I always say to our commencement speakers, as well as to our other honorary degree recipients, that to appreciate fully the commencement weekend, it is desirable to attend the baccalaureate Mass on Saturday and the celebratory dinner that follows, as well as the actual ceremony on Sunday. They thereby receive a first-hand impression of what is most distinctive about Notre Dame as a Catholic university—that we celebrate academic achievement as well as gather to give thanks and praise to God for all that has taken place during the time of residence and study at this institution. The crowd that fills the arena for the baccalaureate Mass and, on the following day, for the commencement exercises is a dramatic testimony to the full nature and mission of this university.

The process by which we choose our commencement speakers can be quite complicated. In the end, the president has the final voice. Over time I receive numerous recommendations from members of the Board of Trustees, fellow officers, faculty, students, alumni, and other interested parties. The process of selection begins in the fall, after the opening of the academic year. One factor that influences the university's choice is the type and variety of speakers we have had in recent years. We seek a mix of men and women, members of different ethnic and racial groups, and representatives of different professions and areas of competence and responsibility. Because some of our speakers are or have been heads of state, the negotiations to secure their commitment can often be quite complicated, and crises of one kind or another may interfere, despite the best intentions of everyone.

I always hope that our speakers will be concerned primarily with addressing the graduates and their families. However, we do not dictate what the topic of their reflections should be, although we provide some suggestions about the structure of the address. In the end, we hope that our speakers have something memorable to say, that their address is delivered in an engaging and focused way, that they draw upon their unique experiences and interpretations of reality, and that they help our graduates realize the responsibilities they bear as Notre Dame alumni and as citizens of the national and world community.

PREFACE

Benjamin R. Civiletti, then serving as attorney general of the
United States, delivered the commencement address at the University of Notre Dame graduation exercises in 1980. He opened his remarks by revealing the results of his own private "survey" of commencement addresses. He found that "86.2 percent of them were too
long. Of those, 19.8 percent were *far* too long. In addition, over 70 percent of the audiences remembered the subject of the address for as
much as an hour following commencement. But less than 10 percent
recalled the subject one week after the address was delivered. By the
time one month had elapsed, that figure had dropped below 1 percent."[1] His lighthearted observation reflects well the usual complaints
one hears from those forced to endure a lengthy commencement address—namely that the seemingly interminable speaker delivered little
worth commending to memory.

Fortunately for graduates of Notre Dame, the "Civiletti statistics"
are greatly exaggerated. While there surely have been long addresses
delivered at Notre Dame commencements, and certainly some may
be fairly judged as being less than memorable, taken as a whole the
quality of the addresses delivered has been quite impressive. Indeed,
a survey of the commencement addresses given over the course of
Notre Dame's one-hundred-and-sixty year history reveals many as
memorable, challenging, and truly inspirational. It is the contention of
this book that they merit reading and even re-reading, including by the
very graduates who may have heard them delivered in person.

This book gathers together twenty-four Notre Dame commencement addresses, along with a letter sent to the 1986 graduates by
Mother Teresa of Calcutta, as well as Father Theodore M. Hesburgh's

1. Benjamin R. Civiletti, Commencement Address, May 18, 1980, *Notre Dame
Report*, vol. 9, no. 18 (June 6, 1980), 400.

final charge to the graduating class of 1987. The speeches range from that of General William Tecumseh Sherman in 1865 to the address delivered by President George W. Bush in 2001.

Needless to say, selecting the speeches to include in this volume was not an easy task. Certainly, some fine speeches have been left out, including one by a former president. I take full responsibility for the selections and would like to convey that the addresses included are the ones which in my judgment are of the most value and interest to the contemporary reader. My introduction provides further clarification regarding the importance of the selected speeches. It also offers, hopefully, a useful context for the speeches by placing them within the contemporaneous history of both Notre Dame and the world around it. In addition, a brief biographical introduction for each speaker precedes the addresses.

Most of the speeches have been printed in their entirety, with the exception of some modest editing of the introductory comments. (The one exception is the address by General Sherman, which has been reconstructed from newspaper reports.) The reader should appreciate that virtually all of the speakers expressed their gratitude for the invitation to speak at Notre Dame and their pleasure and honor in doing so, although their testimonies to that effect have been eliminated to avoid repetition. Of course, these speeches were delivered to an audience and prepared to be orated rather than read privately, but I have found little need to edit the speeches to make them more readable. Some of the speakers gave a title to their address. I have supplied titles, mostly drawn from the addresses, for those who did not.

I would like to thank all those who assisted me to make this book possible. First, I express my deep gratitude for their graciousness to the contributors whose speeches are published here. Similarly, I thank the literary executors of those commencement speakers who are deceased for their kindness and assistance. I am deeply indebted to Father Theodore Hesburgh not only for providing his foreword but also for orchestrating the delivery of so many of the speeches included in this volume. I also thank Father Edward Malloy for his thoughtful reflection and for continuing the tradition of bringing excellent commencement speakers to the campus. Father Timothy Scully, C.S.C., Notre Dame's executive vice-president, supported this project with his customary enthusiasm. I am also grateful to Daniel and Mary Ann Rogers for their practical support and their friendship.

My brothers in Holy Cross, Thomas E. Blantz and James B. King, along with my valued colleagues, Joseph White and Robert Schmuhl, read my introductory essay and offered thoughtful suggestions. They are not responsible for the final product. Jeffrey Hurd, as a candidate at Moreau Seminary, edited the words of his religious superior with notable vigor. Carolyn D'Amore read over the biographical introductions with care. Judy Kuzmich offered valuable assistance with tracking down contributors and literary executors.

The staff of the University Archives at Notre Dame facilitated my access to the speeches and photos housed in its collections. I am especially grateful to Sharon Sumpter and Marlene Wasikowski for their kindness and assistance. At Notre Dame Press I received valued encouragement on this project from Director Barbara Hanrahan and Associate Director Jeff Gainey, which I deeply appreciate. I also am grateful for the professional assistance at the Press of Christina Catanzarite, Rebecca DeBoer, John de Roo, Margaret Gloster, Wendy McMillen, and Julie Beckwith, who ably contributed to bringing this book to fruition.

I prepared this book while serving as superior of the Moreau Seminary religious community. I am indebted to all the community members for their encouragement and support, just as I am for the constant support of my immediate family. I have dedicated this book to my brothers in the Congregation of Holy Cross. I did not imagine when I first came to Notre Dame over a quarter century ago that I would eventually join the order that serves here. But doing so has shaped my life and I give thanks for the privilege of walking in the company of that band of faith-filled men.

A powerful theme that runs through many of the speeches included here is that a Notre Dame education should prompt its recipients to serve well and effectively in the world. As Notre Dame graduates and others sympathetic to Notre Dame's ideals and mission journey forth in the twentieth-first century, it is my hope that this collection might serve to encourage and challenge them to make their distinct mark by doing good.

Wilson D. Miscamble, C.S.C
Notre Dame, Feast of Our Lady of Sorrows, 2002

INTRODUCTION

Commencement Speeches
and Speakers at Notre Dame

A Humble Beginning

The University of Notre Dame celebrated its first commencement in August of 1844.[1] Not even two years before, on November 26,
1842, to be precise, the extraordinary French priest Edward F. Sorin
and a small band of religious brothers—all members of the Congregation of Holy Cross—had arrived at what the French missionaries who
had earlier ministered to the Potawatomi Indians called Ste. Marie
des Lacs. Sorin christened the place Notre Dame du Lac, and there
he and his *confreres* began the work of transforming a small log
chapel–cabin combination into a college.[2] The young priest aimed to
fulfill the promise he made to Bishop Célestine de la Hailandière of
Vincennes by establishing what he believed would be "one of the
most powerful means for good in this country."[3]

The cornerstone of the first real college building was laid in
August of 1843, but even before this construction Sorin had accepted
students—Charles Reckers and Thomas Alexis Coquillard, the boy
who first had led him to the site of Notre Dame.[4] Other students followed and, at least according to Father Arthur Hope's entertaining
centennial history, "every effort was made to engage the attention
of the student on his studies," including the monthly award of prizes.[5]
At the end of the school year more ceremony was called for, and in
1844 Sorin organized a commencement of a sort, no doubt eager that
his fledgling institution should conform to the pattern already well-
established in more prestigious American colleges.[6] Of course there
were no degrees to present, but certain prizes and certificates were

distributed. One may speculate that Father Sorin spoke some words of encouragement as he bade farewell to the students, but such impromptu remarks hardly can be deemed Notre Dame's first commencement address.

The following year—with his tiny school having been granted a charter by the Indiana Legislature empowering it to grant all professional, academic, and scientific degrees—Sorin emphasized the commencement celebration. Never one to neglect an opportunity to demonstrate his commitment to his new land, Sorin chose July 4 to close the academic year.[7] He invited all the "more important personages" of the area to attend. In the largest room of the first main building these local worthies witnessed the reading of the Declaration of Independence, an address by a professor (whom is not clear), and a play entitled *Procida* as well as the distribution of prizes and certificates. Apparently the evening was a great success and Sorin gushingly wrote his superior, Father Basil Moreau, that "everybody in South Bend is talking about that night at the College."[8] Notre Dame's commencement quickly became the center of July 4 entertainment for the surrounding populace and helped strengthen what would later be termed "town-gown" relations.

In 1849, Notre Dame's first proper commencement took place, with two candidates actually receiving the degree of Bachelor of Arts and Letters. "Not only the records of the time," Father Arthur Hope later explained, "but also subsequent events, prove that those degrees were really earned."[9] So it was that Neal Gillespie and Richard Shortis became Notre Dame's first graduates. Each went on to become a priest of Holy Cross, and to serve notably in the order and in the university. By this point Sorin and his collaborators at Notre Dame had conformed the school to the general practices of American college commencements whereby select students addressed the gathered assemblage. With the reverend superior appropriately presiding, a number of younger students gave addresses on a variety of topics ranging from "a comic piece in French" to a "soul-stirring" hour-long address on Ireland before Richard Shortis spoke on "Peace" and Neal Gillespie gave a "Latin Discourse on General History." Following the speeches two plays were performed. The first, entitled *Joseph and his brethren,* was a "moral piece" according to an anonymous observer, while the second was a comedy entitled *The Wandering Minstrel.* After this showcasing of the thespian talents of his students, Father Sorin somehow managed to confer the degrees on Gillespie and Shortis. He followed that privileged responsibility with "a few appropriate remarks on the nature and progress of the institution," and then distributed the premiums (prizes) to the continuing students. During the day's events a band played at various intervals, and such was the interest of the audience assembled that few left their seats during the entire six hours of proceedings! (Obviously there was less concern in those days for brief speeches.) The day culminated with all present partaking in "the hospitality of the college" and so, our unnamed reporter gladly noted, "the people, having enjoyed an intellectual feast above, and a substantial one below, separated, highly pleased and delighted with the entertainments at Notre Dame du Lac."[10]

The template which would guide Notre Dame's commencements for the next decade had been fashioned, but additions and improvements continued in subsequent years. A catalogue (program) for the exercises was now prepared—the one in 1850 printed for the college by future vice-president of the United States Schuyler Colfax.[11] These programs reveal that commencement proved a time for various student groups such as the Philharmonic Society and the St. Aloysius Literary Society to present the "musical, literary and dramatic genius of the students of Notre Dame."[12] The need for such entertainment at commencement was compounded by the fact that from these early days the graduation exercises were also the occasion for the annual alumni reunion, a practice that continued well into the twentieth century. At a meeting of the St. Aloysius Literary Society in 1850, David Gregg, M.A., offered an address. He appears to have been the first person outside of the students and faculty to speak formally at the Notre Dame exercises, although his remarks hardly constituted what we now understand as a commencement address.

David Gregg certainly was not the last of the speakers from be - yond the university. Others were attracted by the opportunity to speak at Notre Dame du Lac, whose reputation developed despite the horrendous trials and tribulations of its initial years. Damaging fires, a terrible cholera outbreak, and a series of financial crises would have tested the commitment of a person without Sorin's iron will and deep faith. But with him at the helm they failed to halt the onward march of the school. Dare one suggest that there is truth in the deeply felt observation of James E. Armstrong, the long-time director of Notre Dame's alumni association, "that the University of Notre Dame, from its origin, reflects a supernatural influence, an arrangement of large and small miracles, a common denominator among its peoples of a destiny beyond the academic."[13]

A sense of Notre Dame's special and distinct quality as a Catholic college and one obviously sympathetic to the Irish cause drew speakers to it. In 1854 Thomas Dale McGee, "a young man, but extensively known in this country as a zealous and talented Catholic layman and editor of the *Celt*," addressed the alumni and the literary and religious societies of the college, which now boasted eighty students.[14] In 1858 the Literary Society of St. Aloysius heard Dr. T. L. Nichols of New York wax at some length on "The Religious Element in Education," a topic which rightly would receive regular attention at Notre Dame. Along with Dr. Nichols's learning, the fourteenth annual commencement held on June 30 (in close proximity to but not exactly on America's national day) consisted of "the usual orations by the students, music by the College Band, the representation of Shakespeare's Play of Henry IV, and distribution of honors and premiums."[15]

In 1861 Notre Dame's commencement, held in conjunction with that of its sister school Saint Mary's College, attracted a fine attendance. Bishop John Henry Luers of Ft. Wayne attended along with a notable representation of clergy from the immediate region and beyond. One of the latter, Rev. Dr. John McMullen of Chicago, accepted Sorin's invitation to address the whole assembly. He delivered "an eloquent appeal to young men to live active lives with the great purpose of doing good ever before them."[16] Little more is known of McMullen's address, but he obviously mined a rich vein of thematic ore which provided content and inspiration for many future speakers. He also was probably the first invited guest to address the whole assembly and to target his remarks primarily at the students. Certainly he was not the last.

The special character of McMullen's address hardly occupied the thoughts of his listeners in 1861. Surely most of their attention was focused on the attempted secession of several southern states, and the determination of President Abraham Lincoln to preserve the Union. Notre Dame as an institution certainly did its part during the Civil War, which served to put what one writer has termed "an indelible stamp of patriotism on the University and its alumni."[17] Seven Holy

Cross priests served as chaplains in the Union Army. The Holy Cross sisters from Saint Mary's won special acclaim for their nursing services. Alumni Union Generals Robert Healy and William Lynch led the way in securing the fighting reputation of the Notre Dame men. Ironically, the war proved to be of some significant direct benefit to Notre Dame, as it received such an influx of students from border states that in 1863 a special dinner was held to celebrate the school's enrollment passing the two hundred mark![18]

Among the students attracted to Notre Dame were the sons of Union General William Tecumseh Sherman, Willie and Tommy, who enrolled in the minims department, which catered to lads age six to thirteen. Sherman's sons visited him in Memphis late in the summer of 1863 following the Confederate surrender to Ulysses S. Grant at Vicksburg. There Willie contracted a fever and died, causing, so Sherman's authoritative biographer John F. Marszalek records, "a wound that never healed." Despite his sorrow Sherman powered forward in his effort to defeat the Southern rebellion by utilizing his brutally effective strategy of "psychological warfare and property destruction." As Marszalek explains it, Sherman saw pillage as preferable to continued "slaughter on the battlefield."[19] The general gained enormous acclaim after his capture of Atlanta and for his marches first from the Georgia capital to the sea and then through the Carolinas which helped break the Southern will to fight. Only Grant surpassed Sherman's popularity and renown in the North at the war's end. The remarkable soldier attended the Notre Dame commencement in 1865—just months after accepting the surrender of General Joseph E. Johnston's Confederate army.

Sherman was Notre Dame's first commencement speaker with a truly national reputation. In reality he visited the campus less to give an address than to utter words of thanks for the kindness shown to his family who had found refuge in the area during the war. The visit made vivid the memories of his dead son, and it was an emotionally taxing experience for him. When prevailed upon to speak, he offered some extemporaneous remarks calling on the Notre Dame graduates and students to "be ready at all times to perform bravely the battle of life." Nothing in Sherman's speech had either any of the pithy quality of his dictum that "War is Hell" or drew anything of the public attention accorded his comment in 1884 that "I will not accept if nominated and will not serve if elected" when he refused entreaties that he run for president. But his speech (which has been recast here in the first person from newspaper reports) belongs in this volume, as it allows us to gain some insight into the thinking of this brilliant soldier at the end of America's greatest conflagration.

Eighteen sixty-five saw the conclusion of the Civil War, and it also saw Father Sorin's service as president of the university end—at least in a formal sense—as he accepted the call to serve first as U.S. Provincial and three years later as Superior-General of the Holy Cross Order. He relinquished his title, if not his power, to Father Patrick Dillon, who guided Notre Dame along well-established paths. The university continued to celebrate its accomplishments and the achievements of its students at its annual commencements. The post–Civil War program still featured student orations, musical interludes, the conferring of degrees, and the distribution of premiums, but it also gave special attention to the valedictory address. Additionally it began to list specifically the person who would address the graduates or who would deliver what was termed the "Oration of the Day." Other significant speeches were given, especially that termed the "Alumni oration," but it becomes easier to identify who delivered what eventually became known as the commencement address.

To the Great Test and Beyond

As it entered the second quarter century of its existence, Notre Dame more often called upon Catholic bishops to speak at commencement than it did upon laymen. Among the latter, Senator A. C. Dodge of Iowa was an obvious choice in 1871, as his son Charles was a student. The good senator solemnly warned his audience that "there is no excellence without great labor; this is the fiat of fate, from which no power of genius can absolve you."[20] (One assumes that at least some of his student listeners took these words to heart!) The most substantial address delivered by a layman during this time was that of William J. Onahan, a prominent Chicago Catholic activist and businessman. In 1876, the centennial year of the nation's foundation, Onahan tackled the subject of "The Catholic and the Citizen." The issue concerning the place of Catholics in American life would bedevil Catholic politicians like Al Smith and John F. Kennedy well into the next century, when many largely sidestepped the question by mov-

ing to "privatize" their religion. Onahan faced the issue head-on and asked if in light of the "widespread distrust of the power and influence of the Catholic Church" whether there existed "a natural incompatibility between the Catholic church and the well-being of the State." Not surprisingly, he argued against such an allegation and eventually argued that "the true greatness as well as the surest hope for America is in the spread and acceptance of Catholic truth, and that no necessary antagonism exists between the one and the other." In the process he issued a healthy warning concerning "the unqualified power of the state," the prescience of which is evident when one reflects for a moment on the ghastly totalitarian experiments of the twentieth
century. He also mounted an energetic defense of "Catholic civilization."[21] His speech is a period piece of sorts, but it addresses issues that future commencement speakers from Charles Bonaparte at the beginning of the twentieth century to Mary Ann Glendon at its end would engage. It warrants reading by those who seek to duly meet their obligations to both church and state.

In the twentieth century bishops regularly graced the official dais at Notre Dame commencements, but with relatively rare exception—two of which are included here—they failed to reach the speaker's podium. They usually were accorded the opportunity to preach at the solemn Mass, eventually termed the baccalaureate Mass, which also became an important part of the commencement exercises. In the latter part of the nineteenth century, however, members of the hierarchy dominated the speaker list. In the 1870s Bishop Joseph Dwenger of Fort Wayne spoke several times while Bishop John A. Watterson of Columbus addressed the graduates in 1883 and 1894. Other bishop-speakers of this era included Francis Chatard of Vincennes in 1882, Ignacio Montes De Oca y Obregon of Linares, Mexico, in 1884, John S. Foley of Detroit in 1892, and Maurice F. Burke (himself a Notre Dame alumnus) of St. Joseph, Missouri, in 1898. But Notre Dame's clear favorite among the hierarchy was the brilliant bishop of Peoria, Illinois, John Lancaster Spalding. He addressed the Notre Dame graduation six times—in 1878, 1886, 1890, 1891, 1895, and 1899—as well as other special assemblies and convocations such as Notre Dame's delayed golden jubilee celebrations of 1895.

Spalding was an outstanding orator and an accomplished writer and thinker, once deemed by a generous observer as "Emerson's equal for keenness of mind and pointed style."[22] He sought an active role in

ecclesiastical, civil, and national affairs. Revealing the views that would see him labelled an "Americanist," he spoke positively of the compatibility between the American form of government and the Catholic faith. Spalding displayed his range and intellectual prowess in his first address, which argued against choosing politics as a profession. Included here, however, is his striking 1886 address entitled "Growth and Duty," in which he developed his ideas not only on the aims and purposes of education but also on a life well lived. Writing at the high point of the Gilded Age when Andrew Carnegie and John D. Rockefeller amassed vast fortunes and when Thomas Edison and George Westinghouse thrilled the world with their scientific and technological discoveries, Spalding initially paid tribute to America's "industrial and commercial miracles." He then moved to the heart of the matter and asked "what is the good of all this money and machinery" were it not to result in "some nobler and better sort of man." He proceeded to contest the notion of "success" as defined by money and offered a different approach to making "money and its equivalents a life-purpose." His thoughtful counsel is apposite in these early years of the twenty-first century when the accumulation of wealth and the range of scientific and technological discoveries easily outdoes that of the Gilded Age. Perhaps now, more than in the 1880s, we need to be reminded that "what we have is not what we are; and the all-important thing is to be, and not to have." Perhaps now, more than in the 1880s, Notre Dame men and women need to appreciate better that "we work not to have more, but to be more; not for a higher place, but for greater worth; not for fame but for knowledge."[23]

In the years between Bishop Spalding's first and second commencement addresses Notre Dame underwent its greatest test. It occurred on April 23, 1879, when the "big fire" swept over the campus and in three hours left much of the work of the previous three decades in ashes. The great fire forced Father William Corby, Notre Dame's president, to close the school. After consultation with his faculty, the heroic veteran of the Battle of Gettysburg decided to grant degrees to all candidates whose work thus far was satisfactory. Fully two months before the scheduled end of classes bachelor's degrees in arts, science, and law were conferred, with diplomas in the commercial courses being awarded as well.[24] These graduates were not treated to a commencement address of any sort. Yet the terrible destruction provoked the most important address ever delivered at Notre Dame. On April 27 Father Sorin, recalled from Montreal, trudged through the still-smoldering ruins of the venture to which he had devoted his life. He then called the entire community into the campus church, somehow miraculously saved from the fierce blaze. There he spoke what Judge Timothy Howard, at the time a student, recalled as "the most sublime words I ever listened to." With absolute faith and con-fidence Sorin looked forward and told his anxious band of followers: "If it were ALL gone, I should not give up." Judge Howard observed that "the effect was electric." Thereafter, "there was never a shadow of a doubt as to the future of Notre Dame."[25] Sorin's resolute speech assured that there would be many commencement addresses in the future.

The growth of Notre Dame after the day of the great fire was impressive. The destroyed building was soon replaced so that by 1882 the present magnificent administration building was crowned with its famed Golden Dome. Six years later Notre Dame's church, a beau-tiful Gothic structure dedicated to Our Lady of the Sacred Heart of Jesus, finally was completed.[26] Notre Dame's signature buildings provided the heart of the campus, but Sorin was eager to keep Notre Dame current with the spirit of the age of industrialism, invention, and impressive technological development. In the 1880s the university became the first American college to be lit by electricity. The follow-ing decade it would be the scene of the first wireless telegraphic message sent in the United States. Yet Sorin's school remained mod-est in size, enrolling only 540 students at the time of the founder's death in 1893 (of whom over half were registered in the preparatory department [high school] and the minims [elementary school]). The school also remained rather modest in ambition. It hardly emerged as a center of Catholic intellectual life or as a place where original re-search and scholarship were highly valued, despite the efforts of the brilliant polymath Father John A. Zahm and his talented engineer brother Albert.[27] Father Hope correctly argued that "Father Sorin's idea of Notre Dame's purpose was to produce, not Catholic scholars, but good Catholic men for the ordinary walks of life."[28]

Notre Dame's graduates left their treasured college in the 1880s and 1890s to enter a society in the midst of a gigantic transformation. Enormous industrial expansion saw the United States emerge as the world's preeminent economic power. An increasingly centralized, urban-industrial society replaced the predominantly rural society that still prevailed when Sorin first arrived in northern Indiana. Teeming cities, a flood of new immigrants, the rise of huge corporations, mass production and consumption, labor's efforts to organize, and increased social conflict all characterized the period. The response of workers to the new industrializing economy and the debate over the respective roles of labor, capital, and government in the new American system proved major issues well into the twentieth century. In 1893, when memories of the bloody strike at Carnegie's Homestead Steel Mill remained vivid, Monsignor Robert Seton, the grandson of Elizabeth Ann Seton, addressed Notre Dame's graduating class on "The Dignity of Labor." Monsignor Seton largely skirted controversial issues like the rights of workers to organize and the role of trade unions such as those gathered in the recently formed American Federation of Labor. He said little of the labor disputes and violence but focused instead on a sympathetic tribute to the value of work. But speaking just two years after Pope Leo XIII issued his important encyclical *Rerum Novarum,* which outlined Catholic social principles and lent some support to the organization of labor unions, Seton did not avoid the contentious matters completely. Predictably he cautioned that "the dignity of labor does not stoop to petty jealousy, or descend to the leveling tendencies of European radicals and socialists." He praised Leo's encyclical and warned of "desperate risks, quick returns [and] the greed for sudden wealth" that degraded labor and demoralized the laborer. Whatever its limitations, Seton's speech reflects Catholic concern for workers and for the dignity of work that can be traced down to Pope John Paul II's encyclical *Laborem Exercens.* Reaffirming this concern and dignity is just as important in these days of the globalized economy, when labor is on the defensive and prominent companies exploit sweatshop labor abroad, as it was when Seton spoke at Notre Dame.

Notre Dame combined its 1895 commencement exercises with the university's golden jubilee celebrations, the latter having been delayed from 1893—the year of "great sorrow" caused by Sorin's death. The festivities ranged over a full week in mid-June and attracted a fine representation of alumni who presumably benefited much from hearing Bishop Spalding speak on "The Making of Oneself." They also heard the governor of Indiana, Claude Matthews, pay a handsome tribute to their school, which had emerged from such "small beginnings to great result."[29] Notre Dame's emergence from a small provincial school to a college of national reputation was aided dramatically by the attention it gave to athletics, especially football, under the firm hand of the president, Father Andrew Morrissey. Denied entry into the regional association (which eventually became the "Big Ten"), Notre Dame's teams ventured beyond the Midwest in search of opponents—garnering devoted followers and favorable publicity for the school along the way. The name of the university was spread far and wide by the superiority of its football team—and the best was still to come in the next century.

The University of Notre Dame entered the twentieth century confidently. Under the leadership of Morrissey and his successor, Father John Cavanaugh, the institution flourished, at least in terms of its own modest criteria. Notre Dame also benefited from the renewal of Catholic thought, especially philosophy and theology, sparked by Pope Leo XIII's encyclical *Aeterni Patris* (1879). The rediscovery of the teaching and method of St. Thomas Aquinas had "opened a world of intellectual discourse and source-material which proved enormously fruitful" for Catholic scholarship.[30] It also led to some rather exaggerated claims in commencement addresses at Notre Dame as speakers sought to demonstrate, in the words of Bishop Burke in 1898, that "the Catholic Church has ever been pre-eminent in the advancement of learning and in the development and culture of the human mind."[31] Eloquent defenses of the "Middle Ages" and their contribution to knowledge became rather *de rigueur*. Painfully, however, the first de - cades of the twentieth century also proved a difficult period for certain Catholic intellectuals in America and beyond (including Notre Dame's own John Zahm), as the Americanist and Modernist crises and the papal condemnations which they prompted served to restrict the creativity of Catholic scholarship and its engagement with the culture of the day.[32]

In the first half of the twentieth century, and especially after World War I, Catholic philosophical and theological scholarship in America, firmly rooted in Thomism, developed on a rather separate track. It stood over and against the dominant culture of a Protestant - ism now undergoing a profound challenge from science and skepticism. Ironically, the certainty about intellectual assumptions and beliefs provided by Thomism helped preserve a distinct Catholic in - tellectual culture which withstood the bewildering array of new and radical ideas that so deepened the religious doubts and intellectual confusion of "mainstream" America at the time. Catholics firmly with - stood the challenge of secularism, skepticism, and relativism, all the while affirming their own deep commitment to America and its prom- ise.[33] Notre Dame encapsulated these dual loyalties in classic fashion. Chicago's Archbishop George Mundelein captured this reality per- fectly in his sermon on the occasion of the university's seventy-fifth anniversary, when he declared of Notre Dame that "I know of no other institution which, while it is so thoroughly Roman in its doc- trine, is so completely American in its spirit."[34]

Paying due obeisance to church and nation led to expressions of both confidence in America and Catholicism and to a certain defen- siveness regarding the dominant culture in many of the commence- ment addresses given in the first decade of the twentieth century. In 1901 Bishop John Shanley of Fargo argued that "religion must not be divorced from secular instruction" and sallied forth into battle against Herbert Spencer's naturalism.[35] The following year William P. Breen, a distinguished layman from Fort Wayne and the valedictorian at Notre Dame a quarter century before, sanguinely assured the gradu- ating class of the benefits of "education, in this day of progress" and affirmed it as "the indispensable requisite for station and place." (Both before and since such positive thinking has served as a reassur- ance to parents who met the tuition bills.) Few speakers missed the opportunity to emphasize the importance of patriotism and service to country. This included laymen like John M. Gearin, U.S. senator from Oregon and a Notre Dame alumnus (1903), and Charles P. Neill, the U.S. commissioner of labor (1909), as well as clerics like the priest- author and lecturer John Talbot Smith (1907).

But Charles Bonaparte, a leading progressive who would soon join Theodore Roosevelt's cabinet as secretary of the navy, treated this broad subject of the obligations of the Catholic citizen best in his 1904 address. Like William Onahan before him, Bonaparte began by posing the question of whether there was an "incompatibility" be- tween American institutions and the Catholic Church. He quickly observed that such a view could only be held by "a Catholic who is not an American, or by an American who is not a Catholic" and proceeded to pay tribute to the growth of both his church and nation. The sheer growth of the church when joined to its vitality proved conclusively for Bonaparte that Catholicism could indeed "live in the United States" and that "liberty is good for the Church." With that matter settled Bonaparte moved on to discuss "the full burden of duty and consequent responsibility cast upon [Catholics] by the Church's growing greatness." His exploration of this subject, particularly his emphasis on immigrants surrendering identification with their homelands and becoming "Americans first, last and all the time," might grate on sensibilities formed in the era of cultural diversity. But his reflections should prompt fruitful discussion of religion and politics and of faith and patriotism.[36]

The activist presidents Theodore Roosevelt and Woodrow Wilson dominated the first decades of the century. These were years of rapid and anxiety-producing change in which America not only witnessed the full emergence of its corporate economy but also saw the development of a new and positive vision of government charged with regulating corporate excesses and abuses and promoting the public welfare. It was an era that emphasized honest government, public service, managerial skills, organizational regularity, and reform of all sorts.

Notre Dame came to terms with the increasing importance of those in public life and enlisted them more regularly as speakers in the second decade of the century. The governor of Indiana, Thomas Riley Marshall spoke in 1910 but nothing he said proved as memorable as his later quip that "what this country needs is a really good five-cent cigar." (He was serving as Wilson's vice-president at the time.) Other notable public officials who addressed the graduates included Ohio governor (and 1920 Democratic presidential candidate) James M. Cox (1913), Louisiana's U.S. Senator Joseph E. Ransdell (1914), and Boston's mayor John F. "Honey Fitz" Fitzgerald, the grandfather of John F. Kennedy (1915). Notre Dame also began the practice of inviting public officials from other nations to address the graduates. In 1911 Sir Charles Fitzpatrick, the chief justice of the Dominion of Canada, gave a lengthy discourse on his country's many virtues.

In 1916 Father Cavanaugh introduced Judge Martin J. Wade as the commencement speaker, and that exemplary jurist reflected on "The Final Test of the Republic." He rightly observed that "over the entire world hangs the pall of human warfare and bloodshed and death." The ghastly conflict which we know as World War I had begun two years before, and as the good judge observed, by June of 1916 "rivers of human blood [had] fertilized the fields of the most cultured and Christian nations of Europe." Not surprisingly, he asked why the United States had not been drawn into the bloody contest and inquired as to "the source of [its] cherished exemption from this world of woe." Judge Wade attributed America's peaceful state to "the spirit of the Constitution" and developed his argument at considerable length.[37] But neither the Constitution nor anything else prevented American entry into the war after Germany resumed unrestricted submarine warfare on American shipping early in 1917. By the commencement of 1917, the United States toiled at the demanding task of mobilization so it might, in the words of President Woodrow Wilson, make the world "safe for democracy."[38]

Long before Congress's declaration of war on April 4, 1917, preparations had begun for the 1917 commencement, which was to be the occasion for the celebration of Notre Dame's seventy-fifth jubilee. In view of the war declaration it was decided that seniors who left to enlist in the armed forces before finishing the academic year would be granted their degrees. The jubilee celebrations from June 8 to 11 proved memorable. They were graced with the presence of the great American prelate Cardinal James Gibbons of Baltimore, and many other members of the hierarchy. One of them, Archbishop (later Cardinal) George Mundelein of Chicago, read the apostolic letter of congratulation and benediction from Pope Benedict XV. In keeping with Notre Dame's well-developed talent for demonstrating its pa-triotic fervor, the Laetare Medal—Notre Dame's annual award to a distinguished Catholic—was presented to Admiral William Shepherd Benson, the chief of naval operations, whose congratulatory telegrams from President Wilson and Navy Secretary Josephus Daniels were read publicly to warm approval. At the conclusion of the solemn Mass at which Cardinal Gibbons presided, eight seniors bearing the Ameri-can flag marched slowly to the altar where Father Cavanaugh blessed the striking banner. Notre Dame already had enshrined this practice, which continues to this day, but as Father Hope observed, "due to the magnificence of the ceremony and the fact that we were at war, there was an added touch of solemnity."[39] After the Mass the distinguished company proceeded to the dedication of Notre Dame's splendid new library (now the Bond School of Architecture) amid much fanfare and celebration.

Delivering the commencement address during these days of celebratory fervor presented a formidable task, which fell to the coadjutor Bishop of Indianapolis, Joseph Chartrand. He responded well to the challenge. Speaking to an audience that included twenty-five or thirty enlisted men who had come from Fort Benjamin Harrison to receive their degrees, Chartrand resisted the temptation to focus his remarks on either the war or America's likely part in it. Instead, he concentrated on education and on the purposes of Catholic education. "The highest purpose of true education," he argued, "is to unfold, to safeguard, to strengthen, and to beautify God's precious masterpiece here—human character." This constituted "education's grandest work," and he paid tribute to Sorin and his collaborators and their successors who had devoted their labors to it, sustained by "their faith, their self-sacrifice, their love of God and man."[40] One trusts similar remarks will not appear antiquated if offered at future significant jubilee celebrations at Notre Dame.

The United States participated in World War I in a limited but important fashion. By the time of the 1918 commencement the country was still about the challenging task of mobilizing an army of 2 million men and transporting it to Europe. This army eventually included nearly three hundred Notre Dame men and eight priest-chaplains, including Vice-President Matthew Walsh. At Notre Dame's commencement exercises, Edward N. Hurley, chairman of the U.S. Shipping Board, reported on the contribution of the merchant marine in this mobilization effort. He also took the opportunity to assure his audience that "time as well as righteousness fights on the side of America and the Allies." One assumes that there were few present who seriously doubted this assurance. Hurley also looked forward beyond the war's end and argued that America "must play the role of protector to honorable nations whose fault is weakness."[41] This pointed in the direction of the enhanced role which Woodrow Wilson proposed for the United States through its participation in his brainchild, the League of Nations. Wilson's dream foundered, however, on the twin shoals of Senate recalcitrance and his own maddening refusal to compromise. His successor, Warren G. Harding, quietly shelved the issue of

American participation in the league and encouraged the nation to return to what he termed "normalcy."

TRIUMPHS AND TRIALS IN PROSPERITY, DEPRESSION, AND WAR

The 1920s proved a crucial decade for Notre Dame. Under the brief but brilliant leadership of Father James A. Burns, measures were initiated which finally transformed Notre Dame into a true institution of higher education.[42] By the decade's end both the high school department and Sorin's treasured minims were gone. Burns created five distinct colleges and a committee on graduate study. He paid serious attention to fund-raising and organized a lay board of trustees to help manage the newly established endowment. Such measures represented important steps for the long-term academic credibility and financial security of the university. The university also expanded its physical plant during this decade, which saw the construction of some of the campus's most beautiful buildings—among them Howard, Morrissey, and Lyons Halls and the magnificent South Dining Hall.[43] At the time such developments were overshadowed completely by Notre Dame's extraordinary football success under the legendary coach Knute Rockne.[44]

In this sports-crazed era the renowned exploits of Rockne's teams generated more attention in a single game than the cumulative efforts of all the earnest commencement speakers during the decade. The majority of these speakers served as judges or attorneys, and they offered in the main appropriately measured and eminently forgettable words of advice and admonition. They failed to engage the major so - cial issues and movements of the decade and remained largely silent on matters such as the rise of nativism, the experiment with prohibition, the severe restrictions on immigration, and the changing role of women in the society. The remembered words uttered at or about Notre Dame during the twenties all focused on football such as Grantland Rice's lead to his report on the 1924 Notre Dame–Army game, which began: "Outlined against a blue-gray October sky, the Four Horsemen rode again. In dramatic lore they are known as Famine, Pestilence, Destruction, and Death. These are only aliases. Their real names are Stuhldreher, Miller, Crowley and Layden."[45] Of course the most famous and oft-quoted Notre Dame speech of this decade—or for that matter of any other—was far shorter than any commencement address. As all familiar with Notre Dame lore know well, Knute Rockne told his 1928 team at halftime in the bruising encounter with Army at Yankee Stadium to "go out and win one for the Gipper," and that they did.[46] "Winning one for the Gipper," however, would make its way into subsequent commencement speeches.

Senator David I. Walsh of Massachusetts gave the decade's liveliest address at the 1921 commencement. With the turbulent aftermath of the war with its wave of strikes, bombings, the Red Scare, and race riots clearly still on his mind, Walsh attacked not only the ideas of political and social radicals (bolshevism, communism, etc.), but the attitudes of organized wealth as well. "Shun as you would a hissing serpent the false teachings of the revolutionists and the money worshippers," he thundered.[47] His counsel that the "Domers" seated before him "avoid both these camps of destructive and faulty philosophy" illustrates well the political outlook of one of the nation's leading Catholic politicians at the time.

But more revelatory of the temper and outlook of the decade as a whole is William J. Donovan's 1929 speech included in this volume. Decorated for bravery during World War I, "Wild Bill" Donovan divided his time in the twenties between the private and public practice of law—he served as assistant attorney general in 1924–25—while occasionally and unsuccessfully mounting campaigns for statewide political office in New York. This lawyer-soldier focused his Notre Dame address on science and contemporary civilization. Speaking at the end of a period of remarkable economic growth in which new technology and mass production had allowed for enormous expansion in industries like automobiles, steel, rubber, glass, chemicals, and communications, Donovan acknowledged the tremendously important place which "science" had won for itself in modern American life. He readily noted the material benefits that science and technology had brought but astutely observed that "our great problem is while making the fullest use of these new forces that we should not be dominated by them." Donovan's modest little speech hardly provided a clear solution to the problem, but reading it might prompt further reflection on his question today as quite different and even more powerful scientific and technological forces influence contemporary society for both good and ill. Donovan concluded his remarks with the optimistic assurance to the graduating class that "the years ahead for you are glorious if you will make them so." Events later in 1929, beginning with the stock market crash in October, removed much of the possibility of easy "glory" as the nation plunged relentlessly into a deep depression.

The disaster of the Great Depression dominated American life until the outbreak of World War II. The devastating collapse of the economy caused widespread unemployment and immense social hardship. It broke the presidency of Herbert Hoover and eventually brought Franklin D. Roosevelt and his New Deal to Washington. Given the immensity of human suffering in the nation as a whole, Notre Dame navigated its way through the Depression relatively well. Naturally, belts were tightened and some annual contracts were not renewed.[48] Enrollment declined a little, but President Charles O'Donnell, a poet and wartime chaplain, managed to keep the institution operating in a fairly normal manner and maintained an impressive building program. Alumni and Dillon Halls opened in 1931 and provided more opportunities for students to benefit from Notre Dame's hallmark residential experience. The Hurley College of Business Administration (1932) and the Cushing Hall of Engineering (1933) added considerably to Notre Dame's academic facilities. And of course, in 1930, at the very outset of the depression, the famous and long-planned "house that Rock built," the new football stadium, swung its gates open to welcome Notre Dame's myriad fans. Rockne's championship seasons in 1929 and 1930 had buoyed spirits, but the great coach's death in a plane crash in March of 1931 caused enormous grief both on campus and beyond.

Angus McDonald, an alumnus and the treasurer of the United States Railroad Commission, paid a handsome tribute to Knute Rockne in his 1931 commencement address. He then proceeded to reassure the graduates that, the depression notwithstanding, life was "full of promise" for them.[49] Not all of the decade's speakers proved quite so blithe, but few had anything to contribute that is of lasting consequence. Such prominent figures as the leading corporate executive Owen D. Young (1932), Indiana's talented Governor Paul V. McNutt (1933), and Notre Dame alumnus and chair of the Council on Emergency Relief, Frank Walker (1934), all identified the enormous economic challenge constituted by the depression but had little to offer on how it should be confronted. This should hardly surprise us, as uncertainty prevailed generally. Even the New Deal constantly changed its policies as it sought to ameliorate the economic ills which beset the country. Roosevelt pragmatically steered a course between the extremes of *laissez-faire* and socialism, at times allowing for significant government expenditures while at others enforcing budget restraint.[50]

Father Charles O'Donnell could not preside at the commencement of 1934 due to grave illness. He died the day after commencement. Father John O'Hara, who was well known for his service on campus as prefect of religion, succeeded him and proved deft at attracting notable scholars and speakers to campus, such as the leading Christian philosophers Jacques Maritain and Etienne Gilson. O'Hara also presided over the first visit to Notre Dame of a sitting president when Franklin Roosevelt visited the campus in December of 1935 to participate in a special convocation honoring the establishment of the new Commonwealth of the Philippines and its founding president, Manuel Quezon.[51] O'Hara also hosted a future pope, the then Vatican secretary of state, Cardinal Eugenio Pacelli, on a visit to Notre Dame in the fall of 1936. Like President Roosevelt the cardinal received an honorary degree from the university, and he won special gratitude from the assembled students by awarding them a holiday.[52] O'Hara failed to attract such renowned figures to the annual commencement exercises over which he presided, although the speakers in 1935 and 1936—the Irish author Shane Leslie and the respected physician (and cofounder of the Mayo Clinic) Dr. William Mayo—delivered thoughtful talks.

President O'Hara's emphasis in his ministry on frequent attendance at Mass and reception of communion and his preparation of the daily *Religious Bulletin* had earned him the nickname of "the Pope" among the students.[53] His talents for ecclesial leadership were obvious, and in 1939 he moved to serve the church beyond Notre Dame when he accepted appointment as auxiliary bishop of the Military Ordinariate—thereby becoming the only president of Notre Dame to be appointed to the church hierarchy. (He later served as bishop of Buffalo and as cardinal-archbishop of Philadelphia.)[54] Father J. Hugh O'Donnell succeeded to the presidency of Notre Dame early in 1940.

Hugh O'Donnell's tenure in office was dominated by the approach of and American participation in World War II. In the 1940 presidential election Franklin Roosevelt was returned to the White House for an unprecedented third term. He quickly declared in an end-of-year fireside chat that the United States must become "the arsenal of democracy," and he made no attempt to hide his sympathies for the British and the French now engaged in all-out war with Hitler's Germany. In January of 1941 he asked the Congress to fund Lend-Lease aid to the Allies in their fight against the Axis powers and began to lend significant naval support to the British in the Atlantic as they sought to combat the German U-boats. In May he issued a proclamation declaring that a state of unlimited emergency existed. Under such circumstances Notre Dame's selection of Joseph P. Kennedy as its commencement speaker in June of 1941 was rather controversial. Kennedy had resigned as ambassador to Great Britain in the fall of 1940 and was known to be less than enthusiastic about entering the war on the side of the British. The possibility existed that he would use the platform at Notre Dame to openly dissent from Roosevelt's policies. This he chose not to do, although he notably gave no endorsement to them. Referring to Roosevelt's recent proclamation of an unlimited national emergency, Kennedy declared that "what is important to everybody, even to all of us who feel strongly that our country should keep out of war is this—that your President and my president . . . has announced that the threat to our national security demands from all of us an unlimited loyalty, a cessation of personal antagonism which the defense and protection of this nation require." Kennedy tried to outline a formula for the proper exercise of freedom of speech in this period of developing national crisis. He proposed "no criticism or complaint that primarily gives aid, comfort, or information to the enemy, actual or potential, only criticism or complaint when, by the standard of judgment or experience or both, the actions or inactions of government are imperiling the success of its defense."[55] This speech by an opponent of Roosevelt's policies reveals well the restraints placed upon those who wanted to avoid a complete break with the president while retaining some political viability in opposing his actions.

The Japanese attack on Pearl Harbor on December 7 ended any serious opposition to American entry into the war and broke the back of the American isolationist sentiment. America's mobilization for the war transformed the Notre Dame campus into something approaching a training base for the U.S. Navy, as the university again demonstrated its patriotic commitment. As early as the fall of 1941 O'Donnell allowed the Naval R.O.T.C. to organize on campus. In February of 1942 the navy announced that Notre Dame had been selected for a thirty-day training program for one thousand V-7 (deck officer) candidates. Four V-7 classes passed through before the navy decided to use the Notre Dame campus to train midshipmen (the V-12 program). From 1942 until the war's end the navy dominated Notre Dame but did not control it. O'Donnell demonstrated political savvy in maintaining Notre Dame's independence. Student numbers were decimated and, as in past wars, priests and other faculty members left to serve in the armed forces, but O'Donnell kept the university running, although students were graduated on an accelerated basis.

In difficult circumstances this patriotic president also maintained the tradition of regular commencements for the awarding of degrees. In 1942 he brought J. Edgar Hoover, the director of the Federal Bureau of Investigation, to campus. Much had changed in the year since Joseph Kennedy addressed the graduates, and the FBI director now solemnly intoned that "red-blooded Americanism, typified by the valorous men of Notre Dame, will not permit our Nation to bow in defeat."[56] In predictably excessive patriotic rhetoric Hoover warned that "appeasement must forever be quarantined in America." The other wartime commencements were modest affairs with Holy Cross priests serving as speakers. The exception occurred in October 1943 when the university held its one hundredth commencement for the small accelerated class of 1944. Harry Kelly, past president of the Notre Dame Alumni Association, veteran of World War I, and then governor of Michigan, gave the address. He proceeded to tell his small audience that strong local government would serve as "the best bulwark against socialism and autocracy."[57] Perhaps some of his audience paid attention, but their thoughts were likely more focused on American military progress in the great battles of Europe and the Pacific.

In the spring of 1945 the university announced the closure of the midshipmen school through which over 8,500 navy officers had passed since October of 1942. The Navy R.O.T.C. program remained, but by

August of 1945, when the atomic bombing of Hiroshima and Nagasaki brought the war to an end, student enrollment of civilians exceeded that of the curtailed navy programs at Notre Dame. By the fall of the following year Notre Dame's enrollment reached a record of over 4,400 students. The accelerated program of studies concluded and the campus returned to its regular schedule of two eighteen-week semesters along with an eight-week summer session. In June of 1946 the university also returned to the combined commencement and alumni reunion program. That same year Hugh O'Donnell retired from the presidency. His patriotism and a certain pomposity in dealing with naval officers had served Notre Dame well during the war. Providence proved particularly kind to the university in providing the leaders who followed him.

Postwar Expansion

Father John J. Cavanaugh led Notre Dame into the postwar era, a time when the campus experienced dramatic growth and development. A debonair and gracious man, he raised academic standards and established the Notre Dame Foundation in order to expand the university's development capabilities. Under his guidance Notre Dame took full advantage of the G.I. Bill of Rights, which paid a veteran's tuition and incidental educational costs as well as providing a modest stipend. The university even purchased thirty-nine prisoner-of-war barracks from the U.S. government to house the families of married veterans attending Notre Dame—campus housing soon christened "Vetville." Cavanaugh also had the pleasure of watching Coach Frank Leahy's football teams of hardened veterans and former players from the war years rack up impressive seasons in 1946, 1947, 1948, and 1949. Arguably Cavanaugh's most important contribution to Notre Dame involved the nurturing and training of his successor, the one-time "Vetville" chaplain and chair of the religion department, Theodore Martin Hesburgh. Father Hesburgh served as executive vice-president for three years, and at age thirty-five he took over the keys of the president's office on the third floor of the Administration Building.

Hesburgh's dynamic leadership transformed Notre Dame from a mainly undergraduate and somewhat provincial institution known best for its winning football program to the leading American Catholic university and an important national teaching and research institution. He proved an extraordinary fund-raiser and effectively used the support of foundations and private individuals to almost double student enrollment and to dramatically enhance not only faculty size and quality but also the physical facilities, financial resources, graduate programs, and academic prestige of the institution. He aimed to shape Notre Dame as a beacon, bridge, and crossroads "where all the intellectual and moral currents of our times meet and are thoughtfully considered."[58] He would certainly utilize the commencement exercises as part of his effort to bring major figures in politics, science, culture, and education to the campus.

Cavanaugh and Hesburgh led Notre Dame during an extraordinary period in American history. The United States emerged from World War II the preeminent military and economic power in the world. The sole possessor of the atomic bomb, it also led the world in international trade and in the export of its culture. American capitalism seemed triumphant. Yet, the quick development of the Cold War and the long political, military, and ideological contest between the United States and the Soviet Union forced the United States to remain fully engaged in international affairs. There could be no retreat into prewar isolationism. Containing the spread of communist influence around the world became the guiding rationale for American foreign policy. The influence of the Cold War flowed over into many aspects of American life—both for good and for ill. American higher education certainly benefited through the 1950s as the national government channeled substantial funding into scientific and technological research. The era of the "Cold War University" had arrived. Notre Dame hardly benefited from this largesse in the same order as institutions like MIT and Stanford, but under Father Hesburgh the university clearly indicated a willingness to use its laboratories to serve the nation through government-funded research.

The onset of the Cold War clearly influenced the themes of the addresses delivered at commencement ceremonies over which Cavanaugh presided. In 1946 (actually O'Donnell's last commencement), the well-known newspaper columnist George Sokolsky spoke on "the clash of civilizations" and warned of the dangers inherent in the Rus - sian system.[59] In 1947, just months after President Harry S. Truman

outlined his doctrine "to support free peoples who are resisting attempted subjugation by armed minorities or by outside pressures," Air
Force General George C. Kenney posed the question to Notre Dame's
graduating class: "Are we to survive as free citizens of a free country or
as soulless cogs in a state machine, paying allegiance to an alien philosophy administered by an alien dictator?" General Kenney promised
survival to the graduates if they would "continue to uphold the fundamental ideals and principles for which this university and this country
stand."[60] Nineteen forty-eight brought Paul Hoffman, the newly appointed director of the European Recovery Program (the Marshall
Plan), to Notre Dame as commencement speaker. He recently had resigned as president of South Bend's Studebaker Corporation to accept his new duties. Amidst the background of a deepening Cold War
and a recently imposed Soviet blockade of West Berlin, he painted a
stark portrait of "the clear-cut division between the barbaric dictatorship of Stalin, aggressive, expanding, insatiable, and the free Western
civilization developed through twenty centuries of Christianity on the
broad foundation of classical Greece and Rome." Eager to enlist support for his efforts to facilitate the reconstruction of western Europe,
Hoffman pleaded that "our concern about free institutions and the
freedoms of peoples must extend beyond our shores."[61]

The Cold War provided the background for the last address delivered during Cavanaugh's tenure as president, although the speaker
did not focus on the great East-West confrontation. Instead Charles
Malik, the Lebanese minister to the U.S. and the chairman of the
United Nations Commission on Human Rights, lucidly and sympa-
thetically explored "the issue of America: her destiny and her meaning
for the rest of the world."[62] He proceeded to identify some essential
features of the United States which he warned should not be com-
promised. In addition he called upon the United States to rise to the
challenge of world leadership. His speech bears re-reading in a different time and international climate when intelligent American global
leadership is as essential as ever.

The earliest commencement speakers of the Hesburgh era testify
to the new president's great interest in networking amidst and con-
necting his university to the elite circles of American higher education. He brought the presidents of Johns Hopkins University and of
MIT to campus in 1953 and 1954. His developing connections in Wash-

ington, D.C., also helped bring notable speakers to campus through the fifties, including Attorney General Herbert Brownell (1955), Chief of Naval Operations Admiral Arleigh Burke (1956), and Chief Justice of the Supreme Court Earl Warren (1957). Hesburgh's keen interest in scientific matters following upon his appointment by President Dwight D. Eisenhower to the National Science Board in 1954 and his specific interest in nuclear matters manifested by his service as Vatican representative on the International Atomic Energy Agency after 1957 undoubtedly led to his inviting John McCone, who chaired the U.S. Atomic Energy Commission (AEC), to speak at the 1959 commencement. McCone, a devout Catholic, chose to highlight the work of the agency he headed. Without any apparent inhibition he proudly announced that he headed the "nation's nuclear armorer." He also explained, however, that the AEC worked to facilitate "the use of the atom for peaceful purposes."[63] His speech fleshed out the integral relationship between this government institution and the nation's research universities, and still serves to cast light on this broad subject. McCone promised to fund a new laboratory facility to allow Notre Dame to expand its basic research in radiation chemistry. A few years later Notre Dame's Radiation Research Building was completed, and it proceeded to operate with federal funds. This development probably makes McCone's the commencement speech with the most obvious tangible "payoff" for the university.

Hesburgh might have felt well-satisfied that the visit of Chairman McCone had allowed the planting of seeds for a significant research facility at Notre Dame. But in 1960 he executed an exquisite coup in attracting the sitting president of the United States, Dwight Eisenhower, to campus. It was the university's first presidential commencement speech, and it brought the school much national attention. It was established as a place where presidents came to deliver the commencement address, and four of his successors have followed Ike's lead. The 1960 event gained further repute because Eisenhower shared the dais with Cardinal Giovanni Battista Montini, Archbishop of Milan and later Pope Paul VI, who had traveled to Notre Dame to preach at the baccalaureate Mass.[64] As if a sitting president and future pope were not enough, Notre Dame's commencement gained further luster by the presence among the honorary degree recipients of Tom Dooley, the famed Southeast Asian jungle doctor whom literally millions of Americans considered a hero.[65] Little wonder that Hesburgh considers this the most notable of all the commencements over which he presided during his long tenure at the helm of Notre Dame.

President Eisenhower's speech at Notre Dame gained little of the notoriety that surrounded his final address in office when he warned of the increasing power of a military-industrial complex, but it still warrants a careful reading today. Eisenhower put forth his predictable case for limited government, arguing that it should assure "the security and general welfare of the nation in concord with the philosophy of Abraham Lincoln, who insisted that government should do, and do only, the things that people cannot do for themselves." Then, and rather surprisingly, the president launched a strong appeal for citizens to commit themselves—at least for a time—to politics and public service.

In January 1961, Eisenhower passed the baton of the presidency to John F. Kennedy, the youngest person ever elected to the office, and so the decade of the sixties effectively began. This decade exercises a hold over the American imagination like few others. One need merely to list a series of major developments—Kennedy's New Frontier and Lyndon Johnson's Great Society programs, the achievement of the civil rights movement, the racial turmoil and urban violence, the continued Cold War and the Cuban Missile Crisis, America's deepening involvement in the Vietnam War and the growing antiwar movement at home, the social turbulence and the sexual revolution, the women's movement, the emergence of the youth movement and counterculture, the upheaval on college campuses, the terrible assassinations of John and Robert Kennedy and Martin Luther King, Jr., and the Apollo space program and moon landing—in order to recall some sense of the triumphs and tragedies of this traumatic decade. Interestingly, important aspects of the decade can be tracked through the commencement speeches given at Notre Dame.

The decade began with a burst of optimism. The handsome and intelligent president aimed to "get the country moving again" after the seeming somnolence of the fifties. Burdens were to be borne, hardships met, and problems solved by an administration that would adopt a tough, pragmatic, and vigorous approach to world affairs. R. Sargent Shriver, the president's brother-in-law and founding director of the Peace Corps, exhibited the "can-do" spirit of the New Frontier in his commencement address at Notre Dame in 1961. Hesburgh and Notre Dame played an important role in launching the Peace Corps, and Shriver acknowledged this contribution in his address. He also provided a clear rationale for this effort to send American volunteers abroad, noting that it would serve to combat the communist challenge and even suggesting that it fulfilled a Christian obligation. Fundamentally, however, Shriver explained that the Peace Corps aimed to liberate the world's peoples from the bonds of hunger, ignorance, and poverty.

By mid-decade the optimistic mood was tempered. President Johnson still pursued his Great Society goals and initiated major federal efforts in civil rights, education, and health care, but the nation's attention increasingly gravitated toward Southeast Asia. Notre Dame's 1965 commencement speaker, National Security Adviser McGeorge Bundy, played an important part in the Johnson administration's decisions that year to enlarge the air and ground war in Vietnam and to commit American combat forces there.[66] Among the very brightest of "the best and the brightest," this former Harvard professor and dean studiously avoided a justification of American policy in Vietnam.[67] Instead he focused on 1940 "as a turning point in the international affairs of the United States" and proceeded from there to outline the international obligations of the United States in the following quarter century. His listeners, however, needed little help to make the connections.[68] For him the American commitment in Vietnam constituted a further American obligation to contain communism, and it fell in line behind the Truman Doctrine, the Marshall Plan, the North Atlantic Treaty, and the Korean War. Those who would seek to understand the sixties will benefit from reading Bundy's calm and measured speech, however much they might disagree with his conclusions.

The American willingness and capacity to confront major problems at home and abroad waned in the latter half of the decade. In 1966 the noted British Catholic writer and economist Barbara Ward fought a rearguard action in her commencement address to defend foreign assistance to poorer nations. Her fine speech was the first commencement address delivered to the all-male undergraduate graduating class by a woman, a sure sign of things to come. American campuses during this turbulent period hardly proved bastions of good sense capable of generating constructive solutions on problems like world development. Instead they became the prime locations for the full-fledged youth revolt which emerged from the civil rights and antiwar struggles. On elite campuses across the country privileged babyboomers charged that something was fundamentally wrong with America's political system and its institutions, indeed with the entire structure of American life and values. Campus unrest at Notre Dame was relatively modest compared to institutions like the University of California at Berkeley and Columbia University, a reality helped along by Hesburgh's firm hand at the institution's tiller. He held to a vision of the university as an institution for genuine academic freedom characterized by civility and real respect for differing views.

Many of the commencement addresses delivered in the late sixties and early seventies concentrated on matters related to higher education and its place in American society. The most notable, which can still be read with profit, were delivered by Minnesota Senator Eugene McCarthy in 1967 and Daniel Patrick Moynihan, then serving as domestic policy advisor in the Nixon administration, in 1969. McCarthy, who would challenge Lyndon Johnson for the Democratic Party's presidential nomination the following year, told his audience that "education, educators and the educated are always on trial, but they are on trial in a very special and clear way today." He outlined the nature of this "trial" and then offered some counsel that stands the test of time. Moynihan brought the powers of his considerable intellect to bear in a speech he conspicuously titled, "Politics as the Art of the Impossible." He courageously refused to pander to his student listeners and declared that "nothing like the present pattern of threats to and actual assault on university institutions and university members has ever yet occurred." He defined the proper role of the university in society in modest terms and went on to discern many of the contemporary problems on campuses as resulting from secular intellectuals channeling their spiritual quest for meaning into the political realm. Moynihan concluded that "if politics in America is not to become the art of the impossible, the limits of politics must be perceived and the province of moral philosophy greatly expanded." Moynihan's astute observations are just as apposite today, and his witness of an intellectual who courageously kept his senses during a time of turmoil is one that warrants emulation.

BUILDING A GREAT CATHOZIC UNIVERSITY

Notre Dame changed considerably during the late sixties and early seventies. In 1967 at Hesburgh's initiative and in conformity with what he took to be the spirit of the Second Vatican Council, the ownership and governance of Notre Dame were transferred from the Congregation of Holy Cross to a predominately lay board of trustees and a board of fellows equally divided between Holy Cross and lay members. To his everlasting credit, in 1972 Hesburgh oversaw the admission of undergraduate women to the university—a move with immediate and far-reaching benefits for the institution. The growth of the institution continued apace, with new programs and buildings being regularly opened. While the university changed in important ways the pattern for its commencement exercises now became well established. The completion of the Athletic and Convocation Center (ACC) allowed the 124th commencement in 1969 to be held indoors for the first time in almost two decades. Gone were the days of praying for sunshine for ceremonies in either the stadium or on the main quad. Now both the sacred rites of the baccalaureate Mass on the Saturday and the graduation rites on the Sunday could be held in the impressive all-purpose edifice, which invariably accommodated its capacity of almost twelve thousand people.

While Notre Dame advanced impressively in the 1970s, the nation struggled in the years immediately prior to its bicentennial celebrations. The long and costly withdrawal from Vietnam, the constitutional crisis of Watergate, Nixon's resignation with its attendant disillusionment with politics, the tattered social fabric, the economic malaise manifested in "stagflation" and high oil prices all combined to make this a testing time for the country. Such circumstances provided the context for a relatively unknown and inexperienced southern governor, Georgia's Jimmy Carter, to win the presidency in 1976.

Hesburgh had lent some (appropriately nonpartisan) assistance to Carter during his election campaign and quickly established a fine rapport with the new president. He eventually accepted an appointment from Carter to lead the American delegation to the U.N. Conference on Science and Technology for Development, holding the rank of ambassador. He used his influence to persuade the president not only to deliver the commencement address at Notre Dame, but to deliver a speech of substance. Carter chose to outline his administration's new approach to foreign policy by calling for a "foreign policy that is democratic, that is based on our fundamental values, and uses power and influence for humane purposes." Carter argued for a new foreign policy that would move beyond containment. He memorably proclaimed—in words he regretted after the Soviet invasion of Afghanistan two years later—that Americans were "now free of that inordinate fear of communism which once led us to embrace any dictator who joined us in our fear." Most notably Carter declared that a cardinal premise of American foreign policy must be a "basic commitment to promote the cause of human rights."[69] Carter's convincing affirmation of human rights as a "fundamental tenet of foreign policy" warrants him regard and respect whatever the other limitations of his foreign policy and his presidency.

In historical terms, Carter's address is probably the most politically significant of the various commencement addresses delivered at Notre Dame. It set out the broad directions of his foreign policy and is referenced in standard American history texts. It attracted much discussion and debate and even attracted a direct rebuttal at the following year's commencement when William F. Buckley, Jr., the renowned conservative and editor of *The National Review*, contested Carter's rather benign view of communism.[70] Buckley's essential view was repeated just three years later, although in a more optimistic and upbeat temper, when another president graced the graduation ceremonies.

Ronald Reagan, the Hollywood actor turned California governor, political commentator, and committed advocate of conservative principles, defeated Jimmy Carter in the 1980 election with promises to restore American pride and prosperity. After just two months in office Reagan was seriously wounded in an attempted assassination. In May of that year, two short months after the attempt on his life, Reagan journeyed to Notre Dame—his first visit outside the nation's capital since John Hinckley fired upon him. With protesters of his domestic and foreign policies gathered outside the ACC, and with tough security measures applied to all those who ventured into it, Reagan arrived to a rousing reception. He delivered a speech that was classic Reagan and which revealed well why he earned his label as the "Great Communicator." The president played his Notre Dame connections to the hilt, which was facilitated by the presence among the other honorary degree recipients of Pat O'Brien, who had played Knute Rockne to his George Gipp in the film *Knute Rockne: All American*.

Reagan initially evoked the life and legend of Rockne and his "win one for the Gipper" speech to draw the moral of men who "joined together in a common cause and attained the unattainable." After his sentimental but characteristically effective lead-in the president deftly moved to address the two great overarching themes of his presidency—the need to correct the excessive government intervention in people's lives and in the economy as well as the obligation to overcome the communist challenge. It was on the latter topic that Reagan uttered the memorable lines: "The years ahead will be great ones for our country, for the cause of freedom and for the spread of civilization. The West will not contain communism; it will transcend communism. We will not bother to denounce it; we'll dismiss it as a sad, bizarre chapter in human history whose last pages are even now being written."[71] The events at the end of the decade confirmed the remarkable prescience of his comments. The Reagan era remains fodder for comtemporary partisan debate, but whatever one's attitudes towards his presidency, it is indisputable that Reagan's ideas and actions set a tone for the decade which continues to affect American political and economic life.

It might be said that subsequent speakers reacted to Reagan and his policies. In 1982 Canadian Prime Minister Pierre Trudeau asked for greater East-West understanding and appealed for the renewal of arms-control negotiations.[72] The next year, Chicago's Cardinal Joseph Bernardin spoke to similar themes. Bernardin headed the bishops committee charged with drafting a statement on the issue of nuclear war and peace that had been established in the very month of Reagan's inauguration. The committee's final draft, titled *The Challenge of Peace: God's Promise and Our Response*, which won overwhelming approval from the American bishops in May of 1983, provided the substance for Bernardin's address.[73] The document, like the cardinal's remarks at Notre Dame published here, declared that America's reliance on nuclear deterrence was tolerable if, and only if, it was used as a stage in serious negotiations for arms control and disarmament.[74]

The bishops' pastoral letter on war and peace and speeches like Bernardin's signified the new place which Catholics occupied in American society. Unlike their predecessors who conscientiously strove to demonstrate their patriotism, the bishops held no fear whatsoever of being labeled un-American if they challenged government policy. The Jesuit historian Gerald P. Fogarty, judged at the time that "the recent pastoral is more significant than Kennedy's election, for Catholics are not only accepted as Americans but are also exercising their full rights as Americans."[75] Perhaps Fogarty engaged in some hyperbole here, yet the leaders of the largest single religious body in the United States had confronted the government on a fundamental issue of national policy. And it was not an issue directly concerned with the institutional interests of the church, as in previous skirmishes, but involved basic elements of American nuclear strategy. The pastoral letter truly marked a genuine milestone in Catholic assimilation. Bernardin's speech should be read in this light. Circumstances had changed for Catholics since the time when William Onahan and Charles Bonaparte spoke at Notre Dame.

Whatever the significance of the bishops' peace pastoral for the American Catholic community, it had limited immediate impact on the Reagan administration, which launched a nuclear arms buildup and put serious arms-control negotiations on hold. Similarly, the bishops' criticism of the Reagan administration's hard-line policy in Central America produced little of a positive nature. Reagan viewed this region primarily through the lens of the global East-West conflict and judged military pressure and force as the best means to deal with the Marxist governments and movements of the area, especially the Sandinista regime in Nicaragua. Notre Dame's 1985 commencement brought a distinctive Central American leader to campus, Jose Napoleon Duarte, president of El Salvador. He happened to be the first graduate of the university to become a head of state and was also the first elected civilian president of his country in half a century. Although some protesters identified him as too close to Reagan's Manichaean approach to the region, Duarte was a brave Christian Democrat who believed that his "obligation lay in freeing [his] country from the two totalitarian extremes: the Marxists and the fascists."[76] His speech is a moving testament to his efforts and is a tribute to the importance of his Notre Dame education and specifically to the influence of Father Hesburgh upon him.

Hesburgh had exercised his influence for the good in the lives of literally thousands of Notre Dame men and women during an extraordinary period as Notre Dame's leader. In 1987 his presidency came to an end after thirty-five years. Harvard's president, Derek Bok, was on hand to deliver a commencement address in which he rightly paid tribute to Hesburgh as a leader in American higher education and as a "virtuous man."[77] Bok's thoughtful but ponderous words on the place of education in international cooperation were swallowed up by the emotion surrounding Hesburgh's departure and his reception of Notre Dame's highest honor, the Laetare Medal. He was lauded for having "given testimony in word and deed to the centuries-long tradition of the Catholic university, to the dedication of this country to establishing justice, and to the two great commandments, love of God and love of neighbor."[78] Some of his old friends were on hand to receive honorary degrees—among them Rosalyn Carter, Joan Kroc, and Coretta Scott King—their very presence a further testament to his great career of service at Notre Dame and far beyond. The outgoing president had been feted extensively over the previous months and had delivered a variety of speeches and sermons of varying lengths. As the 1987 commencement drew to a close he approached the podium and delivered his final charge to a graduating class. His heartfelt words are included here in hopes that they will be read by Notre Dame graduates long into the future.

The daunting task of following Hesburgh in the presidency of Notre Dame fell to Father Edward A. Malloy, a moral theologian and a man of steady and determined disposition. Under his leadership Notre Dame continued to grow in stature and quality. Notable achievements in areas such as faculty quality and size, student selectivity, size of endowment, and new construction on campus all combined to earn the university a regular ranking among the top twenty schools on the much noted (if somewhat dubious) *U.S. News and World Report* annual listing. During the Malloy years the university increased the presence of women at all levels from students to senior administrators and it doubled its minority student population. It also undertook a major effort in international programs and emphasized the importance of campus ministry, social outreach, and volunteer service. While Notre Dame's place as America's leading Catholic university remained unchallenged, the issue of preserving and fostering the Catholic character of the university remained perhaps the most challenging issue. Would Notre Dame fulfill its true promise as a Catholic university and reject the easy temptation of the secularism which characterizes most American universities? Would it live in accord with its treasured heritage from Sorin to Hesburgh and pursue its distinct mission, thereby avoiding the uniformity accepted by most American private and public universities? These remained pertinent questions as Notre Dame celebrated its sesquicentennial in 1992 and they remain so a decade later, although they are rarely evident to short-term visitors like commencement speakers.

The first commencement of the Malloy presidency brought to campus the noted civil and human rights leader and then mayor of Atlanta, Andrew Young. He gave a stirring address befitting an ordained minister in the United Church of Christ which focused on his own life story and his work with Martin Luther King, Jr., in the civil rights movement. Calling the students forth to public service and com - mitment, Young counseled that "it ought to be possible with all of the technology at our disposal to see to it that the hungry are fed and that the naked are clothed and that people learn somehow to live in peace."[79] To any naysayers in the audience Young testified that "if the things could happen in my lifetime that have happened, God working with you can make much more happen in your lifetime through you." This testimony serves to remind any who would commit themselves to do good not to set their ambitions too low.

The speakers who followed Andrew Young—Peter Ueberroth and Bill Cosby—offered addresses rather lighter in content. In 1991 the thoughtful editor of *Commonweal* magazine, Margaret O'Brien Steinfels, passed on to her student audience some helpful counsel on work, friendship, and faith.[80] Her instruction to the graduates to "do something truly difficult: Do good," is incorporated in this volume's title. In the election year of 1992 the first President George Bush journeyed to Notre Dame no doubt eager to use the national platform it supposedly provided to address Catholic voters. He focused on the decline in the American family and called on the graduates to do their part to rebuild and restore America "from the ground up, family by family, home by home, community by community."[81] The president's concern with family life and values undoubtedly was genuinely felt, but the public perceived him as somehow out of touch and he lost to the dual challenge of Bill Clinton and Ross Perot later in the year. Notre Dame's platform proved of little political benefit to him.

During the rest of the nineties the commencement speakers were drawn from the worlds of journalism, politics, and academe. Tom Brokaw, the NBC *Nightly News* anchor, came in 1993 and identified a long compendium of issues deserving attention in an appropriately authoritative tone.[82] The lively political commentator and Notre Dame graduate Mark Shields delivered an entertaining address in 1997 filled with pungent quips including the observation that "life is not like college. Life is a lot more like high school."[83] Albert Reynolds, the taoiseach [prime minister] of Ireland, came in 1994 and provided a well-meaning but overly lengthy appraisal of where matters stood in the Irish peace process.[84] Indiana's lieutenant governor and Notre Dame alumnus Joseph Kernan spoke in 1998 in a humorous manner and gently countered those who had considered him not significant enough to serve as commencement speaker at Notre Dame. He offered the insightful counsel to "do good things by doing the right thing—always."[85] Elizabeth Dole journeyed to the campus in 1999 testing the waters and laying the groundwork to bid for the Republican nomination for the presidency the following year. With the embarrassing scandals of the Clinton presidency still fresh in the minds of her listeners, she aimed to counter the cynicism of many young people regarding the nation's political, economic, and other institutions.[86] Her speech did not exhaust the need for authentic words on this subject.

The speeches delivered by the denizens of academe held the most lasting value and are both included in this collection. Condoleezza Rice, in 1995 serving as provost of Stanford University, noted that with the end of the Cold War the United States was "in the midst of another great and challenging transition," but she did not address her remarks to her specialization in international relations to chart a course for the post–Cold War world. Instead, she attended to the proper place of the university in society and to the role of the educated person. In contrast to many speakers who charge graduates with sallying forth to change the world, Rice asked the soon-to-be-domers to "reflect, then, not on transforming the world, but on how truly transformed you are by the experience and the privilege of higher education."[87] One hopes that Notre Dame graduates might draw some satisfaction from such reflection.

Mary Ann Glendon, the Learned Hand Professor of Law at Harvard University, delivered the address the following year. Her talk was relatively brief, contained flashes of humor, and was filled with wisdom—a veritable model for a contemporary commencement address. Glendon recently had returned from leading the Vatican delegation to the U.N. Conference on Women in Beijing. She exemplified a committed Catholic unafraid to venture into the public square. Initially, she spoke favorably of an education that integrates faith and reason and criticized the idea that religion should be sequestered in some private sphere. Her deft exposure of the "way of the turtle" and "the way of the chameleon" in regard to Catholic involvement in public life provided the launching point for her to call for the graduates to bring their religious perspectives into public debate and discussion, but in terms meant to persuade "men and women of good will—of all faiths, and of no faith."[88]

The first years of the new millennium brought two successive speakers to campus who were concerned about poverty. One concerned himself primarily with the extreme poverty that afflicts almost half of the world's population. The other focused on new and creative ways in which poverty at home might be successfully confronted. Kofi A. Annan, the secretary general of the United Nations, spoke in 2000. He outlined the details of extreme poverty, which he rightly deemed "an affront to our common humanity." But he did not stop there. He proceeded to outline measures which might allow the poorer half of the world's population to enjoy a great share of the largesse of the new global economy. In a manner which bears some resonance of Sargent Shriver's Peace Corps appeal, he called on a new generation of Notre Dame graduates to volunteer their service—especially in the area of information technology—in ways that would benefit the development of poor countries.

The second speaker was the second President George Bush, who delivered his first commencement address as the nation's chief executive at Notre Dame in 2001, even before he spoke at his *alma mater,* Yale University. Bush came with the purpose of promoting his newly established White House Office of Faith-based and Community Initiatives and with the intention of courting Catholic voters, whom he appreciates will be decisive in any second-term bid. He gave an eloquent and in some ways audacious speech on the need to create "a caring society" if the United States would be a great society. Bush clearly sought to emphasize the compassion that he links to his undoubted conservatism. He even praised two Democratic presidents, Lyndon Johnson and Bill Clinton, and surprisingly quoted the co-founder of the Catholic Worker Movement, Dorothy Day, saying that an effective war on poverty must deploy "the weapons of the spirit." Much has changed in America since the terrible terrorist attacks of September 11, 2001, but one hopes that President Bush's call for American citizens to engage in the war against poverty will not be forgotten. It is not too much to hope that some of Bush's listeners might have been inspired by his address such that they find themselves inspired to fight poverty and to address the harsh inequalities of wealth that prevail in the nation and the world.

Notre Dame had expected Mexican president Vicente Fox to deliver the commencement address in 2002, its 160th year, but the vagaries of Mexico's internal politics prevented his participation. Tim Russert, the moderator of NBC's *Meet the Press* and chief of the network's Washington bureau, stepped into the breach and delivered a lively address. He touched on a wide range of matters, including the clergy sexual abuse scandal in the Catholic church, the responsibilities of the media in the aftermath of September 11, the importance of care for children and of traditional family structures, and the special obligations placed on those who receive a Notre Dame degree.

The best of commencement addresses always have served to enlarge the vision and inspire the actions of the graduates. They have called Notre Dame men and women to go forth and do good. They have challenged the graduates to live truly good lives—lives in which faith is not sequestered in some private domain. Certainly, this is what Mother Teresa of Calcutta did in the powerful letter (also included in this volume) which she wrote to the graduates of 1986 asking them to "be wholehearted, fully committed Christians, dedicated to Truth, Integrity and Justice."[89] One trusts Notre Dame graduates will continue to respond to such calls long into the future. Ultimately the university's success in fulfilling Father Sorin's dream of being a powerful force for good depends upon it.

NOTES

1. My account relies on Arthur J. Hope, *Notre Dame One Hundred Years*, rev. ed. (Notre Dame: University of Notre Dame, 1950), 77.

2. On Sorin see the splendid biography by Marvin R. O'Connell, *Edward Sorin* (Notre Dame: University of Notre Dame Press, 2001).

3. Letter from Edward Sorin to Basil Moreau, December 5, 1842, cited in Edward L. Heston, trans., *Circular Letters of the Very Reverend Basil Anthony Mary Moreau*, 2 vols. (Notre Dame: Ave Maria Press, 1943), vol. 1, 58–60.

4. Hope, *Notre Dame One Hundred Years,* 54.

5. Hope, *Notre Dame One Hundred Years,* 76.

6. On the history of commencement see John S. Brubacher, "Introduction: The Traditions of Commencement," in Francis H. Horn, *Go Forth and Be Strong* (Carbondale: Southern Illinois University Press, 1978), xxv–xxxiii.

7. Sorin's love for and commitment to the United States was evident even before he left France to come to Indiana. Before his departure he wrote Bishop Hailandière: "My body is in France; but my mind and heart are with you . . . I live only for my dear brethren of America. That is my country, the center of all my affections and the object of all my pious thoughts." Sorin to Hailandière, undated, quoted in James T. Connelly, C.S.C., "Editor's Preface," in Edward Sorin, C.S.C., *Chronicles of Notre Dame Du Lac,* ed. James T. Connelly, C.S.C. (Notre Dame, University of Notre Dame Press, 1992), xv.

8. Hope, *Notre Dame One Hundred Years,* 77.

9. Hope, *Notre Dame One Hundred Years,* 79. There is no question that Neal Gillespie completed all requirements for his degree. There is some question concerning Richard Shortis. His entry in the silver jubilee booklet compiled by Joseph A. Lyons in 1869 reads: "In 1849, after passing a creditable examination, though not a student proper in the College, he received the degree of B.A. at the University of Notre Dame, in company of Rev. N. H. Gillespie." Joseph A. Lyons, *Silver Jubilee of the University of Notre Dame* (Chicago: E. B. Myers and Company, 1869), 85.

10. Letter to the Editor, "Annual Exhibition of the University of Notre Dame Du Lac, Indiana," *The Catholic Advocate,* (Louisville, KY), July 21, 1849, Commencement Collection, University of Notre Dame Archives, Notre Dame (hereafter UNDA).

11. Timothy E. Howard, *A History of St. Joseph County, Indiana,* 2 vols. (Chicago: The Lewis Publishing Co., 1907), vol. 2, 630.

12. Howard, *A History of St. Joseph County,* vol. 2, 630.

13. James E. Armstrong, *Onward to Victory: A Chronicle of the Alumni of the University of Notre Dame Du Lac, 1842–1973* (Notre Dame: University of Notre Dame Press, 1974), 3.

14. "The 4th at Notre Dame," *The St. Joseph County Forum,* July 8, 1854, Commencement Collection, UNDA.

15. "University of Notre Dame," *The Catholic Telegraph,* July 3, 1858, Commencement Collection, UNDA.

16. "Commencement at Notre Dame University and St. Mary's Academy, Indiana," *New York Tablet,* May 13, 1861, Commencement Collection, UNDA.

17. Armstrong, *Onward to Victory,* 12.

18. See "The Meaning of Notre Dame," *The Notre Dame Scholastic,* vol. 54, no. 30 (Endowment Number, June 1921), 7.

19. John F. Marszalek, *Sherman: A Soldier's Passion for Order* (New York: The Free Press, 1993), 294.

20. Sen. A. C. Dodge, "Oration of the Day," *The Notre Dame Scholastic*, vol. 4, no. 23 (June 28, 1871), 3.

21. William J. Onahan, "The Catholic and the Citizen," *The Notre Dame Scholastic*, vol. 9, no. 43 (June 24, 1876), 672–75.

22. Quoted from "The Meaning of Notre Dame," *The Notre Dame Scholastic*, vol. 54, no. 30 (Endowment Number, June 1921), 15.

23. J. Lancaster Spalding, "Growth and Duty," in *The Notre Dame Scholastic*, vol. 19, no. 42 (June 30, 1886), 673–78.

24. On the great fire and Notre Dame's response to it see Hope, *Notre Dame One Hundred Years*, 183–87. Also see "Our Great Calamity: The University Destroyed by Fire," *The Notre Dame Scholastic*, vol. 12, no. 34 (April 26, 1879), 532–35.

25. Timothy Howard quoted in Hope, *Notre Dame One Hundred Years*, 186.

26. On the construction and naming of the new church see Joseph M. White, *Sacred Heart Parish at Notre Dame: A Heritage and History* (Notre Dame: Sacred Heart Parish, 1992), 45–48.

27. On the contribution of the Zahm brothers see Hope, *Notre Dame One Hundred Years*, 260; and Ralph Weber, *Notre Dame's John Zahm* (Notre Dame: University of Notre Dame Press, 1961).

28. Hope, *Notre Dame One Hundred Years*, 181. In Hope's critical portrayal, the founder "countenanced no moves that might make Notre Dame a real university."

29. On the golden jubilee celebrations see Hope, *Notre Dame One Hundred Years*, 262–63.

30. Eamon Duffy, *Saints and Sinners: A History of the Popes* (New Haven: Yale University Press, 1997), 241.

31. Maurice F. Burke, Commencement Oration, *The Notre Dame Scholastic*, vol. 31, no. 36 (July 2, 1893), 628–29.

32. For a balanced summary of this complex episode see Duffy, *Saints and Sinners*, 241, 249–51. On the Modernist crisis see Marvin R. O'Connell, *Critics on Trial: An Introduction to the Catholic Modernist Crisis* (Washington, D.C.: The Catholic University of America Press, 1994). On the American branch of the movement see R. Scott Appleby, *"Church and Age Unite!" The Modernist Impulse in American Catholicism* (Notre Dame: University of Notre Dame Press, 1992).

33. On these complex intellectual developments see Philip Gleason, *Contending with Modernity: Catholic Higher Education in the Twentieth Century* (New York: Oxford University Press, 1995); and William M. Halsey, *The Survival of American Innocence: Catholicism in an Era of Disillusionment, 1920–1940* (Notre Dame: University of Notre Dame Press, 1980).

34. Archbishop George Mundelein quoted in Hope, *Notre Dame One Hundred Years*, 321.

35. Bishop John Shanley, Commencement Address, *The Notre Dame Scholastic*, vol. 34, no. 36 (June 22, 1901), 617–20.

36. Charles J. Bonaparte, "Some Thoughts for American Catholics," June 15, 1904, *The Notre Dame Scholastic*, vol. 37, no. 36 (Commencement Number, June 1904), 606–13.

37. Martin Joseph Wade, "The Final Test of the Republic," *The Notre Dame Scholastic*, vol. 49, no. 37 (June 24, 1916), 596–604.

38. Woodrow Wilson's Address to Congress, April 2, 1917, *The Papers of Woodrow Wilson*, ed. Arthur Link et al. (Princeton: Princeton University Press, 1983), vol. 41, 525.

39. Hope, *Notre Dame One Hundred Years*, 323.

40. Address by Rt. Rev. Joseph Chartrand, *The Notre Dame Scholastic*, vol. 50, no. 35 (Diamond Jubilee Number, June 1917), 652–55.

41. Address by Edward N. Hurley, *The Notre Dame Scholastic*, vol. 51, no. 33 (Commencement Number, June 1918), 561–67.

42. On Burns's extraordinary contribution at Notre Dame see Anna Rose Kearney, "James A. Burns, C.S.C.—Educator," Ph.D. dissertation, University of Notre Dame, 1975.

43. On the development of the campus I rely on the wonderful study by Thomas J. Schlereth, *The University of Notre Dame: A Portrait of Its History and Campus* (Notre Dame: University of Notre Dame Press, 1976).

44. For a good overview of the Notre Dame coach see Ray Robinson, *Rockne of Notre Dame: The Making of a Football Legend* (New York: Oxford University Press, 1999); and Murray Sperber, *Shake Down the Thunder: The Creation of Notre Dame Football* (New York: Henry Holt, 1993).

45. Grantland Rice quoted in Hope, *Notre Dame One Hundred Years*, 387.

46. Robinson, *Rockne of Notre Dame*, 211–12. The full text of the speech went: "Before he died, Gipp said to me, 'I've got to go, Rock. It's all right. I'm not afraid. Sometimes, when things are going wrong, when the breaks are beating the boys, tell them to go out and win one for the Gipper. I don't know where I'll be then, Rock. But I'll know about it and I'll be happy.'"

47. Sen. David I. Walsh, Commencement Address, *The Notre Dame Scholastic*, vol. 54, no. 30 (Commencement Number, June 1921), 544–47.

48. For details on Notre Dame in the depression years see Robert E. Burns, *Being Catholic, Being American: The Notre Dame Story, 1842–1934* (Notre Dame: University of Notre Dame Press, 1999), 495–99.

49. Angus McDonald, Commencement Address, *The Notre Dame Alumnus*, vol. 9, no. 10 (June 1931), 355–57, 371.

50. On the changing economic approaches of the New Deal see the classic work by Ellis Hawley, *The New Deal and the Problem of Monopoly* (Princeton: Princeton University Press, 1966).

51. For details of Roosevelt's visit see Hope, *Notre Dame One Hundred Years*, 461–62.

52. Hope, *Notre Dame One Hundred Years*, 463–64.

53. Armstrong, *Onward to Victory*, 291.

54. Thomas T. McAvoy, *Father O'Hara of Notre Dame, the Cardinal Archbishop of Philadelphia* (Notre Dame: University of Notre Dame Press, 1967).

55. Joseph P. Kennedy, Commencement Address, *The Notre Dame Alumnus*, vol. 19, no. 8 (June 1941), 5–6, 22–23. On Kennedy's disagreements with FDR see Michael R. Beschloss, *Kennedy and Roosevelt: The Uneasy Alliance* (New York: W. W. Norton, 1980).

56. J. Edgar Hoover, Commencement Address, *The Notre Dame Alumnus*, vol. 20, no. 7 (May 1942), 7–8, 18.

57. Harry F. Kelly, Commencement Address, *The Notre Dame Alumnus*, vol. 22, no. 2 (December 1943), 9, 23.

58. Theodore M. Hesburgh, "Introduction," *The University of Notre Dame Faculty Manual* (Notre Dame, 1967). This article is more accessible as "The Challenge and Promise of a Catholic University," in Theodore M. Hesburgh, C.S.C., ed., *The Challenge and Promise of a Catholic University* (Notre Dame: University of Notre Dame Press, 1994), 1–12.

59. George E. Sokolsky, "The Clash of Civilizations," *The Notre Dame Alumnus*, vol. 24, no. 4 (August 1946), 7–8, 20.

60. General George C. Kenney, Commencement Address, *The Notre Dame Alumnus*, vol. 25, no. 3 (June 1947), 20–21, 23.

61. Paul Hoffman, Commencement Address, *The Notre Dame Alumnus*, vol. 26, no. 4 (July–August 1948), 4, 7.

62. Charles Malik, "The American Question," *The Notre Dame Alumnus*, vol. 30, no. 3 (August–September 1952), 9–11.

63. John A. McCone, "The Atomic Energy Commission and the University," *The Notre Dame Alumnus*, vol. 37, no. 3 (September 1959), 21–22.

64. On the circumstances surrounding his inviting both Cardinal Montini and President Eisenhower see Theodore M. Hesburgh, *God, Country and Notre Dame* (New York: Doubleday, 1990), 249–51.

65. On Dooley see James T. Fisher, *Dr. America: The Lives of Thomas A. Dooley, 1927–1961* (Amherst: University of Massachusetts Press, 1997).

66. Kai Bird, *The Color of Truth: McGeorge Bundy and William Bundy—Brothers in Arms* (New York: Simon and Schuster 1998), 270–349.

67. David Halberstam, *The Best and the Brightest* (New York: Random House, 1972).

68. McGeorge Bundy, Commencement Address, June 6, 1965, Commencement Files, UNDA.

69. Jimmy Carter, Commencement Address, May 22, 1977, *Notre Dame Report*, vol. 6, no. 18 (June 3, 1977), 435–39.

70. William F. Buckley, Jr., Commencement Address, May 21, 1978, *Notre Dame Report*, vol. 7, no. 18 (June 2, 1978), 420–23.

71. Ronald W. Reagan, Commencement Address, May 17, 1981, *Notre Dame Report*, vol. 10, no. 18 (June 12, 1981), 489–92.

72. Pierre Elliott Trudeau, Commencement Address, May 16, 1982, *Notre Dame Report*, vol. 11, no. 18 (June 11, 1982), 480–83.

73. National Conference of Catholic Bishops, *The Challenge of Peace: God's Promise and Our Response* (Washington, D.C.: U.S. Catholic Conference, 1983).

74. Cardinal Joseph Bernardin, Commencement Address, May 15, 1983, *Notre Dame Report*, vol. 12, no. 18 (June 10, 1983), 473–76.

75. Gerald P. Fogarty, "Why the Pastoral Is Shocking," *Commonweal*, vol. 110 (June 3, 1983), 335–39.

76. Jose Napoleon Duarte, Commencement Address, May 19, 1985, *Notre Dame Report*, vol. 14, no. 18 (June 14, 1985), 588–92.

77. Derek Bok, Commencement Address, May 17, 1987, *Notre Dame Report*, vol. 16, no. 18 (June 19, 1987), 353–57.

78. Laetare Medal citation, May 17, 1987, *Notre Dame Report*, vol. 16, no. 18 (June 19, 1987), 359.

79. Andrew Young, Commencement Address, May 15, 1988, *Notre Dame Report*, vol. 17, no. 18 (June 10, 1988), 400–403.

80. Margaret O'Brien Steinfels, Commencement Address, May 19, 1991, *Notre Dame Report*, Vol. 20, No. 18 (June 14, 1991), 396–99.

81. George H. W. Bush, Commencement Address, May 17, 1992, *Notre Dame Report*, vol. 21, no. 18 (June 12, 1992), 451–53.

82. Tom Brokaw, Commencement Address, May 16, 1993, *Notre Dame Report*, vol. 22, no. 18 (June 11, 1993), 436–39.

83. Mark Shields, Commencement Address, May 18, 1997, *Notre Dame Report*, vol. 26, no. 18 (June 13, 1997), 448–50.

84. Albert Reynolds, Commencement Address, May 15, 1994, *Notre Dame Report*, vol. 23, no. 18 (June 10, 1994), 403–6.

85. Joseph E. Kernan, Commencement Address, May 17, 1998, *Notre Dame Report*, vol. 27, no. 18 (June 12, 1998), 391–93.

86. Elizabeth Hanford Dole, Commencement Address, May 16, 1999, *Notre Dame Report*, vol. 28, no. 18 (July 22, 1999), 429–32.

87. Condoleezza Rice, Commencement Address, May 21, 1995, *Notre Dame Report*, vol. 24, no. 18 (June 16, 1995), 531–33.

88. Mary Ann Glendon, Commencement Address, May 19, 1996, *Notre Dame Report*, vol. 25, no. 18 (June 14, 1996), 471–73.

89. Letter from Mother Teresa to the Graduating Class of 1986, April 3, 1986, *Notre Dame Report*, vol. 15, no. 18 (June 13, 1986), 350–51.

COMMENCEMENT SPEECHES
AND SPEAKERS
AT NOTRE DAME

WILLIAM TECUMSEH SHERMAN

William Tecumseh Sherman (1820–1891) ranks among America's most notable soldiers. West Point alumnus and veteran of the Mexican War, Sherman eventually left the army and tried banking and business without either success or satisfaction. By contrast, he enjoyed his duties as superintendent of a military college in Louisiana. When the Civil War broke out in the spring of 1861, Sherman reluctantly left the South and accepted an appointment as an infantry colonel in the Union Army.

After several initial wartime disappointments, Sherman rebounded following his association with General Ulysses S. Grant. Their partnership was to bring the Union great military success in the years to come. Although wounded at the battle of Shiloh, Sherman recovered and collaborated with Grant to take the Confederate stronghold of Vicksburg, Mississippi, in July of 1863. Sherman's capture of Atlanta in 1864 helped turn the tide for Lincoln's reelection. His devastating march from Atlanta to the sea and the subsequent march through the Carolinas ravaged both the Southern economy and its psyche—weakening its resolve and hastening the Confederate defeat.

When Grant became president in 1869, Sherman succeeded him as commanding general. He firmly resisted later entreaties, however, that he seek to succeed Grant as president.

Perform Bravely the Battle of Life

(1865)

I am called upon to take a novel part here today. I don't pretend to be a speaker, nor have I prepared a speech for this occasion. But it is clear that you expect me to say something and I don't want to disappoint you.

I can sympathize with all the parties present on this occasion. I can remember what it was like to be a schoolboy. I can sympathize with both the parents and the boys. The former have come to hear and see what the latter are ambitious and joyful to show them, namely the progress they have made during this past session. I am happy to learn from the professors present that the boys have not spent their time and labors in vain. I empathize also with the professors. Nothing could be more interesting to you than to watch the first coming of the light of the intellect—to see it bursting forth from the aboriginal darkness of nature, like order from chaos, like light at the feet of God. It is like the creation of God.

Let me not forget that I was once a young man like those who have appeared before the audience on this day and occasion. You should be grateful that you are under such good instruction and guidance. You now have a pilot on board ship to guide you, but the time will come, and soon, when you will have to go forth into the great, dark seas alone, under your own guidance. Happy are those who know how to navigate the ship!

You must see to it that the ship is strong, the pilot true and the compass unerring. . . . No one can tell when the ship might be wanted, when it will be required to go into action and even to do American fighting for America. God knows there has been enough of fighting for a long spell, but it is the highest wisdom and the best

46

policy both of the individual and the States to be ready for that encounter at any moment. The great deep pit of politics is full of contending monsters which might cast up such strife that we might be compelled to deal with it for our own safety.

Who could have foretold five years ago that the terrible and tremendous war, now happily ended, would ever, or could ever, have begun on this continent, in these flourishing commercial States, in this grand America? I confess that I was cowed at first before the lurking dangers and terrors which were ahead of us all at that time. I knew the landscape and the horizon and I knew what the first little cloud, no bigger than a man's hand, meant when it began to loom there. I still tremble at the appalling consequences of its development and growth.

But I ask you all to remember that, although I have no more than ordinary abilities such as any of you possess, I had not forgotten to take care of the ship and that I trusted in the pilot—in myself. I relied upon my own courage and foresight and in my devotion to the good old cause, to the Union, to truth, to liberty and, above all, to the God of battles. God has brought me all right from and amidst a sea of the direst troubles which ever fell upon a nation.

So I call upon the young men here to be ready at all times to perform bravely the battle of life. We might never have to go to war anymore on this continent but then again we might. War is possible and we must be ready for the contingency. But more than this I want to say that there is a kind of war which is inevitable to all—it is the war of life. A young man should always stand in his armor, with his sword in hand and his buckler on. Life is only another kind of battle and it requires as good a generalship to conduct it to a successful end as it did to conquer a city, or to march through Georgia.

I assure you young men and your parents that I will always regard you and your pursuits with interest and will note your careers if circumstances permit. I know that each of you will try to make your careers honorable as well as successful. You must not forget the instructions which you have received in this College from your preceptors. I heartily wish you Godspeed. This may be the last time you will hear my voice for I intend to leave these parts tomorrow, so let me bid you good-bye.

—⟋⟍—

WILLIAM J. ONAHAN

William J. Onahan (1836–1919) was a leading Catholic layman in the last third of the nineteenth century. Born in Carlow, Ireland, in 1836, he joined millions of his fellow countrymen and women in escaping the deprivation and horror of the Great Famine. After working briefly in England, he emigrated to America and eventually settled in Chicago. He worked initially as an office clerk and became active in politics and public affairs—serving as both a city tax collector and a member of the Chicago Board of Education. During the Civil War he recruited for the Union Army and served as civilian secretary for the famous Irish Brigade. Following the Civil War he achieved success as president of a savings bank.

Self-educated and a prodigiously talented organizer, Onahan devoted much of his time, labor, and money to Catholic causes such as the Irish Colonization project in Minnesota sponsored by Archbishop John Ireland. He also helped organize the first Catholic Congress in Baltimore in 1889, and served as chairman of the second Catholic Congress in Chicago in 1893, which met in conjunction with the Columbia Exposition and World Parliament of Religions. Onahan also authored a number of books, including The Influence of the Catholic Layman. *In addition to serving as Notre Dame's commencement speaker in 1876, Onahan was awarded the Laetare Medal by the university in 1890 in recognition of his exemplary contributions to the Catholic community in the United States.*

The Catholic Citizen and the State

(1876)

When I yielded to the request and invitation, with which I was honored by the esteemed President of Notre Dame University, to deliver a brief address on the occasion of the Annual Commencement, it was not without an effort on my part to persuade him that his heart or his judgment were at fault in the selection. Assuredly I would feel proud and honored were I able to justify the wisdom and discreteness of his choice by presenting to you an address that would be worthy of the occasion, and interesting to the large and distinguished audience assembled around me. I would indeed be deterred from attempting so responsible a task were I not persuaded in advance that my poor effort would be received with the most kindly and generous indulgence.

I am, moreover, encouraged by the reflection that however imperfectly I may be qualified to assume the role and office of teacher or mentor in the halls of this University, I yet may be enabled to draw from the lessons acquired in the broader school of the world and of history, some reflections which may serve to engage and interest my audience. An ancient philosopher remarked, and the observation has since become trite, that education does not end with the termination of a school or college career. The great world which now opens its portals to the many young, eager-bounding hearts and ambitious intellects who today surround me, is only a larger and broader school than the one whose hospitable roof and generous tutelage they are now about to depart from. I need hardly say that in this school of the world the tasks will often be found far more irksome than those allotted in these academic halls, the task-masters far less indulgent, and the applause and rewards for their efforts vastly less generous and certain than those hitherto enjoyed in these benignant surroundings.

It is not my purpose, however, to philosophize on the problem of life, nor on the duties and responsibilities which now devolve upon those who are about to enter into competition for the prize or goal which duty or ambition sets before those who now vault into the arena of the world. I have mapped out for myself a less comprehensive but perhaps more congenial task.

The influence and the teaching of a Catholic college must of necessity impress itself on the character and future of its students and graduates. In the classroom and the lecture hall they have acquired a knowledge of the arts and sciences from professors able and accomplished: in the sacred aisles of yonder church they have been imbued with the more valuable lessons of faith and of duty.

I do not fear to be misunderstood. I speak as a Catholic—albeit an unworthy one—to Catholics. I do not seek to awaken or wound any just religious sensibilities. I would be unworthy to occupy the honorable position in which I now stand before you, were I to do so; but facts should not be ignored, nor is it wise to be silent when duty demands of us to speak out. There is everywhere a jealousy and widespread distrust of the power and influence of the Catholic Church. We see her oppressed and trampled upon in Germany and in Poland, her priests and religious exiled or imprisoned, her churches closed or violated, and the sacred offices and functions prohibited. In Italy, once the proud center of faith and unity, the Church is curbed and fettered, her possessions—consecrated by ten centuries of almost undisturbed tenure—confiscated, and her venerable Pontiff a virtual prisoner in that capital of which it may be truly said every stone in its churches and palaces belongs of right not to Italy but to the Catholic world, which has contributed of its blood and treasure to their erection and preservation. Switzerland imitates its Russian exemplar, and even Catholic France, under the influence of infidel zealots, seeks to curb and restrain the just influence of the Catholic Church. England, too, has lately been filled with clamorous outcries on the subject. Nor has our own land wholly escaped the infection. It becomes a serious question, therefore, for Catholics—Why this outcry against us? Is there, then, a natural incompatibility between the Catholic Church and the well-being of the State? Is there in the relations which must necessarily exist betwixt the one and the other a peril or a danger for which the Catholic Church or its teachings is responsible?

This is the inquiry which I shall now briefly attempt to answer. I do not propose, it would be presumption in me to attempt, to enter into the domain of theology, and discuss faith and dogma. I shall deal with the question of the Catholic and the citizen, or, if you please, the Catholic citizen and the State purely in their secular relations.

John Stuart Mill, in his essay on representative government, says that "Community of language and community of religion is of importance as contributing to an enduring nationality." Another distinguished writer, whose thoughts and opinions on American institutions have been in many respects remarkable for their prescience and sagacity— De Tocqueville—remarks, referring to the future of this country:

> The time will come when 150 millions of men will be living in North America, equal in condition, the progeny of one race, owing their origin to the same cause, and preserving the same civilization, the same language, *the same religion*, the same habits, the same manners, and imbued with the same opinions propagated under the same forms.

Time and the logic of events have given new force and significance to his prophecy. The jealousy and distrust of the power and influence of the Church is not a new or latter-day suspicion. It is as old as Christianity itself, and found a notable example in the public teaching of our Divine Savior; and in every succeeding age, in almost every country, there have arisen similar fears, conflicts and divergences. That these fears of the power and ecclesiastical authority of the Church, whether entertained in good faith, or arising from interested motives, are ill-founded and have no just basis, I think can be clearly shown.

The Catholic Church inculcates the duty and obligation upon all her children of unreserved loyalty and fealty to the State and the constituted authorities thereof, with only this qualification that they shall "render to Caesar the things that are Caesar's, and to God the things that are God's." The Church does indeed enforce the obligation of primary obedience to a law which is of necessity higher and more authoritative than any which may be enacted or enforced by any merely human authority or government, but common sense and Christian teaching alike combine to convince and satisfy us that between the legitimate political domain of the sovereign or the State and the ecclesiastical or spiritual authority of the Church, there is not and in the nature of things cannot be any just conflict. Unhappily, these antagonisms have occurred in all ages and probably will not cease until the end of time.

Among the legacies and promises left to the Church by her Divine Founder was the assurance that her existence would be an unceasing conflict, and the final triumph would come only at the end. I have said that we owe our first and highest allegiance to God and His laws. We owe a subsidiary obedience to the State. God gave us existence, a soul, faculties, and a destiny. The State, which is our own creation, protects us in our material interests and property, and is the agency by which we seek to promote and protect our temporal wants and aspirations. It can exact allegiance from us only in affairs of purely temporal concern. It is entitled to demand of us obedience to its laws and authority, but when it enters the sanctified domain which is consecrated to God, when it attempts to regulate and restrain the Christian in the free exercise of those duties which God and nature impose as primary obligations, it becomes in fact an usurper and trespasser. The Church in her theology, by the mouth and pen of her great doctors, has very clearly defined the doctrine of the obedience due from the subject or citizen to the sovereign and State, and no Protestant writer or authority has ventured to advocate doctrines and principles so broad and liberal in the interest of human freedom.

The theory now so widely prevalent and enforced of the unqualified supremacy of the State, makes of the latter an earthly deity and requires of us to bow down and worship it. It demands an acceptance for itself of that dogma which it so scoffs at when claimed by the Church, namely, Infallibility!

History, that philosophy which teaches by example, is a witness to the glory and development which is compatible with the highest Catholic civilization.

In what regard has this not been demonstrated? It is attested in the genius and the piety which has covered Europe with monuments of architectural grandeur that are now the marvel and wonder of the traveler; and in the arts by which Catholic talent has adorned and embellished the cathedrals and palaces of the Continent and which have consecrated to religion the loftiest inspirations of the human intellect.

Has the Church been a curb to material progress or to national renown? What States have attained the glory or surpassed in opulence France and Spain when their destinies were controlled and their laws administered by a Cardinal Richelieu and Ximenes? Is it commercial greatness [that] is in question? Then let the enterprise and maritime renown of the Catholic republics of the Adriatic and of Holland tell the story! In what regard have they been successfully rivaled? Their decay has been due to natural, not to religious causes. Or if the latter was in question, it will be found that they have deteriorated because of their denial or departure from well-known Catholic principles. Empires have risen and fallen, have reached the zenith of human power and greatness even before the advent of Christianity, and the now deserted and lonely ruins of Thebes and Palmyra, and others which abound on the borders of the Mediterranean, admonish us that wealth and opulence is peculiar to no condition of modern civilization; it can be attained under the auspices of a barbaric regime, as well as under the splendor and glare of modern enlightenment. History, and its lessons and teachings for the past three centuries, has been for the most part presented to us in a false guise and perverted by reckless or foolish pens so as to bring the Church into dishonor and disrepute. De Maistre says "history has been an unvarying conspiracy against truth," but, despite the adverse combination of false pens, truth in the long run will inevitably prevail. It has indeed often seemed, as Macaulay suggested, that the power of the Church's long dominion approached a close, but ever and anon that supernatural agency, which has never failed her, appeared to intervene in her behalf and safely carry her through every peril; time and again that power and supremacy has seemed to be beyond human salvation and rescue, but it has as often triumphed over all adverse influences. Do I need to appeal to the American writers who have sometimes reluctantly spoken her eulogies? To Bancroft, to Prescott, to Parkman, and a long chain of others whose prejudices have given way to their sense of justice. Let us recall, too, that while many sectarian writers have sought to prove that the Popes attempted to destroy civil monarchy by confiscating it to their profit, it is a great Protestant historian, Müller, who says that "The Father of the Faithful was during the barbarous ages a tutor and a guide sent by God to the European Nations."

Do you need a proof and striking example of the character and influence of Protestantism as opposed to Catholicity? Then mark the successive religious revolutions which desolated Germany after the subversion of catholicity: maxims and theories destructive of all society were propagated; upon the field of battle and upon the scaffold blood flowed in torrents; towns and cities were desolated or destroyed. Life was without safety, and property without security. The infidel disorders and revolution of a later century nearly brought down the whole European superstructure and civilization in total wreck. And the young Catholic intellect of this and of other lands should never forget the debt of gratitude due to the first of Frenchmen and the grandest of modern Catholic writers when he challenged modern infidelity to the combat in a memorable speech in the French house of Peers, when he proudly said: "*We are the sons of the Crusaders, and we will never draw back before the sons of Voltaire.*" But if you want a less defiant utterance and exclamation, then I tell you in the language of Tertullian and the gentle Fenelon: "You have nothing to fear from us, but we do not fear you." It is alleged that Catholic teaching favors despotism, and would maintain the doctrine of the divine right of kings! Even the most casual student and writer needs only to consult the pages of Suarez, of Bellarmine, and of the Angelic Doctor, Thomas Aquinas, in refutation of this assertion. Never was [a] charge more ill-founded. I repeat again here, the greatest doctors and most honored theologians have always spoken and written on the side of the largest and widest popular liberty.

A great French bishop has lately answered in a characteristically clever book the charge that the Church is inimical to progress, to civilization and to human dignity; let me ask what existing institution has done for civilization what the Church has accomplished? What other human institution or sect has labored without ceasing for the establishment and maintenance of hospitals for the infirm, of asylums for the insane and afflicted, of refuges for the Magdalene and the outcast, and of homes for the poor and the orphan? Tell me the Church or denomination that makes similar sacrifices to maintain and support the widest and most generous system of schools, and that presents today so liberal and munificent a scheme of higher training in colleges and institutions.

But perhaps I am departing from my theme, which is to prove that the true greatness as well as the surest hope for America is in the spread and acceptance of Catholic truth, and that no necessary antagonism exists between the one and the other. America is Catholic in her earliest traditions, as she should still be in her faith. Why should we not hold our heads erect, we the inheritors of the faith of a Columbus, of De Soto, of Calvert and of Champlain? Are we not the spiritual children of a Marquette, a Breboeuf, a Carroll? And are we not animated by the same patriotic spirit and love of country which moved in the breasts and stirred the hearts of the Sullivans, the Fitzgeralds, and the Montgomerys, the Moylans, and the Barrys, of Revolutionary fame and memory?

There is on all the wide earth no more broad and generous field for the spread and development of Catholic truth than exists in this great Republic, nor is there any people more calculated to adorn and distinguish the annals of that Church. One of the great missionaries with whom America is favored, a member of the distinguished Order of Jesuits, in a notable address at a recent gathering in Philadelphia said that "the surest guarantee for the peace, the purity, and prosperity of American institutions, of good government and of free government, lay in the acceptance of Catholic truth." It was a Pagan philosopher who said that "the destruction of piety towards the gods would be the destruction also of good faith, of human society, and of the most excellent of virtues—justice"—and a modern French writer observes: "People talk of the danger of theocracy: but in what warlike nation did a priest ever lead men into slavery?" There is no cry raised against the Church that does not arise either from false or interested motives. She alone, when all else in human society was in confusion, preserved to us the semblance and the fact of order, in law and in government. When dynasties gave way, and empires and kingdoms were wrecked and deposed, the Church stood proudly erect amidst the general downfall—as she will always stand—unmoved and undismayed.

Great writers have written magnificent perorations on the marvelous fertility of her resources and the apparent indestructibility of her power. In the presence of the distinguished professors and the young gentlemen to whom these studies are so familiar, I need not attempt to repeat, still less echo in my own poor language, their majestic utterances. But this much I may venture to say, that in the general wreck and upheaval of empires in Europe, which the complications of the times show us to be inevitable, there is given to us in this favored land a great and a grand destiny. Exempt from foreign complications, we can now pursue unobstructed the great mission for which America was destined.

And for the Church, no greater arena exists the wide world over. Let me not be misunderstood or misinterpreted. The missionaries of the Church seek only to extend her spiritual dominion by those peaceful agencies and persuasive utterances which have invariably characterized her teachings, and in no land more conspicuously than in this. Now, as ever before, her priests and religious have in their hearts that beautiful motto which is inscribed on the banners of all her devoted children and servants: "*Ad majorem Dei gloriam.*" It is this spirit and this holy zeal which has won and redeemed by the labor of these devoted religious and their predecessors in the Faith, this once wild tract, until now it blossoms with the gifts and fruits of the earth, and greater boon still abounds in those institutions of charity, of learning and religion which are a gift and a blessing to humanity. Do you ask to know what is the ambition of the Church and these her too often maligned servants? It is to dot the land with institutions of Christian grace and benevolence similar to those which surround us here on every side. To wean men from vice to the practice of the exalted virtues—those virtues which adorn and beautify the human character, and in the acceptance and practice of which is the highest hope and surest security for the future of these States.

It is for you, gentlemen, who today go forth from these hallowed precincts to your various homes in different States to carry with you into all the chequered pursuits of that active career which is before you the constant lessons of the teaching which I am sure you have wisely learned in the halls of your *Alma Mater*. I am but a poor and unworthy monitor, but I do assure you in the struggles which are inevitably before you that no experience which you may acquire will stand you in so great stead as those lessons which have been inculcated by your reverend professors and teachers at Notre Dame. Be true to them, and in their possession you will have an enduring and unfailing joy.

One word more and I shall close. In this centenary year, America claims much and expects great things of her sons, and especially from those who bring to her ranks, in whatever sphere, the service of young hearts and uncontaminated intellects. We should seek to restore the purity and the virtue which these centennial days recall. Be it yours the duty and the glory to give to this land your loyal and most devoted services, and by bringing about that much-needed restoration of purity in public life, thereby recall and renew the era of the better days of this Republic.

JOHN LANCASTER
SPALDING

A Kentucky native, John Lancaster Spalding (1840–1916) trained for the priesthood in Belgium at the American College of the Catholic University of Louvain. Ordained in 1863, he served first in Louisville before moving to New York City in the 1870s. There he pursued his interest in education, ran a school, and published a biography of his distinguished uncle, Archbishop Martin J. Spalding. A brilliant Catholic spokesman and public intellectual, Spalding was named the first bishop of Peoria, Illinois, in 1877 and served there for the next thirty-one years.

Coincident with his duties in his diocese, Spalding played an active role in civil, national, and church affairs. He emphasized the distinctive qualities and important contributions of Catholic education in America and wrote extensively on the subject. Spalding's concern to provide graduate training for American Catholic clergy led him to play an important role in the establishment of the Catholic University of America. His stature as a national figure—with influence that extended beyond the Church— was confirmed in 1902 when President Theodore Roosevelt appointed him to the Anthracite Coal Commission at the behest of striking miners.

Growth and Duty

(1886)

What life is in itself we do not know, any more than we know what matter is in itself; but we know something of the properties of matter, and we also have some knowledge of the laws of life. Here it is sufficient to call attention to the law of growth, through which the living receive the power of self-development—of bringing their endowments into act, of building up the being which they are. Whatever living thing is strong or beautiful has been made so by growth, since life begins in darkness and impotence. To grow is to be fresh and joyous. Hence the spring is the glad time; for the earth itself then seems to renew its youth, and enter on a fairer life. The growing grass, the budding leaves, the sprouting corn, coming as with unheard shout from regions of the dead, fill us with happy thoughts, because in them we behold the vigor of life, bringing promise of higher things.

Nature herself seems to rejoice in this vital energy; for the insects hum, the birds sing, the lambs skip, and the very brooks give forth a merry sound. Growth leads us through Wonderland. It touches the germs lying in darkness, and the myriad forms of life spring to view; the mists are lifted from the valleys of death, and flowers bloom and shed fragrance through the air. Only the growing—those who each moment are becoming something more than they were—feel the worth and joyousness of life. Upon the youth nothing palls, for he is himself day by day rising into higher and wider worlds. To grow is to have faith, hope, courage. The boy who has become able to do what a while ago was impossible to him, easily believes that nothing is impossible; and as his powers unfold, his self-confidence is nourished; he exults in the consciousness of increasing strength and cannot in any way be made to understand the doubts and faint-heartedness of men who have ceased to grow. Each hour he puts off some impotence, and why shall he not have faith in his destiny, and feel that he shall yet grow to be poet, orator, hero, or what you will that is great and noble? And as he delights in life, we take delight in him.

In the same way a young race of people possesses a magic charm. Homer's heroes are barbarians, but they are inspiring, because they belong to a growing race, and we see in them the budding promise of the day when Alexander's sword shall conquer the world; when Plato shall teach the philosophy which all men who think must know; and when Pericles shall bid the arts blossom in a perfection which is the despair of succeeding generations. And so in the Middle Ages there is barbarism enough, with its lawlessness and ignorance; but there are also faith, courage, strength, which tell of youth, and point to a time of mature faculty and high achievement. There is the rich purple dawn, which shall grow into the full day of our modern life.

And here in this New World we are the new people, in whose growth what highest hopes, what heavenly promises lie! All the nations which are moving forward are moving in directions in which we have gone before them—to larger political and religious liberty; to wider and more general education; to the destroying of privilege, and the disestablishment of State churches; to the recognition of the equal rights not only of all men, but of all men and women.

We also lead the way in the revolution which has been set in motion by the application of science to mechanical purposes, one of the results of which is seen in the industrial and commercial miracles of the present century. It is our vigorous growth which makes us the most interesting and attractive of the modern peoples. For whether men love us, or whether they hate us, they find it impossible to ignore us, unless they wish to argue themselves unknown; and the millions who yearn for freedom and opportunity, turn first of all to us.

But observant minds, however much they may love America, however great their faith in popular government may be, cannot contemplate our actual condition without a sense of disquietude; for there are aspects of our social evolution which sadden and depress even the most patriotic and loyal hearts. It would seem, for instance, that with us, while the multitude are made comfortable and keen-witted, the individual remains commonplace and weak; so that on all sides people are beginning to ask themselves what is the good of all this money and machinery, if the race of godlike men is to die out, or indeed if the result is not to be some nobler and better sort of man than the one with whom we have all along been familiar. Is not the yearning for divine men inborn? In the heroic ages such men were worshipped as gods, and one of the calamities of times of degeneracy is the dying out of faith in the worth of true manhood through the disappearance of superior men. Such men alone are memorable, and give to history its inspiring and educating power. The ruins of Athens and Rome, the cathedrals and castles of Europe, uplift and strengthen the heart, because they bid us reflect what thoughts and hopes were theirs who thus could build. How quickly kings and peasants, millionaires and paupers become a common, undistinguished herd! But the hero, the poet, the saint defy the ages, and remain luminous and separate, like stars. They

> Waged contention with their time's decay,
> And of the past are all that cannot pass away.

The soul, which makes man immortal, has alone the power to make him beneficent and beautiful.

But in this highest kind of man, in whom soul—that is, faith, hope, love, courage, intellect—is supreme, we Americans, who are on the crest of topmost waves of the stream of tendency, are not rich. We have our popular heroes; but so has every petty people, every tribe its heroes. The dithyrambic prose in which it is the fashion to celebrate our conspicuous men has a hollow sound, very like cant. A marvelous development of wealth and numbers has taken place in America; but what American—poet, philosopher, scientist, warrior, ruler, saint—is there who can take his place with the foremost men of all this world? The American people seem still to be somewhat in the position of our new millionaires. Their fortune is above them, overshadows and oppresses them. They live in fine houses, and have common thoughts;

they have costly libraries, and cheap culture; and their rich clothing poorly hides their coarse feeling. Nor does the tendency seem to be towards a nobler type of manhood.

The leaders of the Revolution, the framers of the Federal Constitution, the men who contended for State-rights, and still more those who led in the great struggle for human rights, were of stronger and nobler mold than the politicians who now crowd the halls of Congress. Were it not for the Pension Office, one might cherish the belief that in our civilization the soldier is doomed to extinction, and that the military hero will be known only to those who study the remains of a past geologic era. Even as things are, what a blessed country is not this, where generals, not to be idle, are reduced to the necessity of fighting their battles in the pages of sensational magazines—powder magazines being no longer needed, except for purpose of blasting! The promise of a literature which a generation ago, budded forth in New England was, it appears, delusive. What a sad book is not that recently issued from the press on the poets of America! It is the chapter on snakes in Ireland which we have all read—there are none. And are not our literary men whom it is possible to admire and love either dead, or old enough to die?

All this, however, need not be cause for discouragement, if, in the generations which are springing up around us, and which are soon to enter upon the scene of active life, we could discover the boundless confidence, the high courage, the noble sentiments, which make the faults of youth more attractive than the formal virtues of a maturer age. But youth seems only to disappear from human life, to leave only children and men. For a true youth the age of chivalry has not passed, nor has the age of faith, nor the age of poetry, nor the age of aught that is godlike and ideal. To our young men, however, high thoughts and heroic sentiments are what they are to a railroad president or a bank cashier—mere nonsense. Life for them is wholly prosaic, and without illusions. They transform ideas into interests, faith into a speculation and love into a financial transaction. They have no vague yearnings for what cannot be; hardly have they any passions. They are cold and calculating. They deny themselves, and do not believe in self-denial; they are active, and do not love labor; they are energetic, and have no enthusiasm. They approach life with the hard, mechanical thoughts with which a scientist studies matter. Their one idea is success, and success for them is money. Money means power; it means leisure, it means self-indulgence; it means display; it means, in a word, the thousand comforts and luxuries which, in their opinion, constitute the good life.

In aristocratic societies, the young have had a passion for distinction. They have held it to be an excellent thing to belong to a noble family, to occupy an elevated position, to wear the glittering badges of birth and of office. In ages of religious faith they have been smitten with the love of divine ideals; they have yearned for God, and given all the strength of their hearts to make His will prevail. But to our youth, distinction of birth is fictitious, and God is problematic; and so they are left face to face with material aims and ends, and of such aims and ends money is the universal equivalent.

Now, it could not ever occur to me to think of denying that the basis of human life, individual and social, is material. Matter is part of our nature; we are bedded in it, and by it are nourished. It is the instrument we must use even when we think and love, when we hope and pray. Upon this foundation our spiritual being is built; upon this foundation our social welfare rests. Concern for material interests is one of the chief causes of human progress; since nothing else so stimulates to effort, and effort is the law of growth. The savage, who has no conception of money, but is satisfied with what nature provides, remains forever a savage. Habits of industry, of order, of punctuality, of economy and thrift, are, to a great extent, the result of our money-getting propensities. Our material wants are more urgent, more irresistible; they press more constantly upon us than any other; and those whom they fail to rouse to exertion are, as a rule, hopelessly given over to indolence and sloth. In the stimulus of these lower needs, then, is found the providential impulse which drives man to labor, and without labor welfare is not possible.

The poor must work, if they would drink and eat;
  The weak must work, if they in strength would grow;
  The ignorant must work, if they would know;
The sad must work, if they sweet joy would meet.

The strong must work, if they would shun defeat;
    The rich must work, if they would flee from woe;
    The proud must work, if they would upward go;
The brave must work, if they would not retreat.

So on all men this law of work is lain:
    It gives them food, strength, knowledge, victory, peace;
It makes joy possible, and lessens pain;
    From passion's lawless power it wins release,
Confirms the heart, and widens reason's reign;
    Makes men like God, whose work can never cease.

Whatever enables man to overcome his inborn love of ease is, in so far, the source of good. Now, money represents what more than anything else has this stimulating power. It is the equivalent of what we eat and drink, of the homes we live in, of the comforts with which we surround ourselves; of the independence which makes us free to go here or there, to do this or that—to spend the winter where orange blossoms perfume the soft air, and the summer where ocean breezes quicken the pulse of life. It unlocks for us the treasures of the world, opens to our gaze whatever is sublime or beautiful; introduces us to the master-minds, who live in their works; it leads us where orators declaim, and singers thrill the soul with ecstasy. Nay, more, with it we build churches, endow schools, and provide hospitals and asylums for the weak and helpless. It is, indeed, like a god of this nether world, holding dominion over many spheres of life, and receiving the heart-worship of millions.

And yet if we make money and its equivalents a life-purpose—the aim and end of our earthly hopes—our service becomes idolatry, and a blight falls upon our nobler self. Money is the equivalent of what is venal—of all that may be bought or sold: but the best, the godlike, the distinctively human, cannot be bought or sold. A rich man can buy a wife, but not a woman's love; he can buy books, but not an appreciative mind; he can buy a pew, but not a pure conscience; he can buy men's votes and flattery, but not their respect. The money-world is visible, material, mechanical, external; the world of the soul, of the better self, is invisible, spiritual, vital. God's kingdom is within. What we have is not what we are; and the all-important thing is to be, and not to have. Our possessions belong to us only in a mechanical way. The poet's soul owns the stars and the moonlit heavens, the mountains and rivers, the flowers and the birds more truly than a millionaire owns his bonds. What I know is mine, and what I love is mine; and as my knowledge widens and my love deepens, my life is enlarged and intensified. But, since all human knowledge is imperfect and narrow, the soul stretches forth the tendrils of faith and hope. Looking upon shadows, we believe in realities; possessing what is vain and empty, we trust to the future to bring what is full and complete.

All noble literature and life has its origin in regions where the mind sees but darkly; where faith is more potent than knowledge; where hope is larger than possession, and love mightier than sensation. The soul is dwarfed whenever it clings to what is palpable and plain, fixed and bounded. Its home is in worlds which cannot be measured and weighed. It has infinite hopes, and longings, and fears; lives in the conflux of immensities; bathes on shores where waves of boundless yearning break. Borne on the wings of time, it still feels that only what is eternal is real—that what death can destroy is even now but a shadow. To it all outward things are formal, and what is less than God is hardly anything. In this mysterious, supersensible world all true ideals originate; and such ideals are to human life as rain and sunshine to the corn, by which it is nourished.

What hope for the future is there, then, when the young have no enthusiasm, no heavenly illusions, no divine aspirations, no faith that man may become godlike, more than poets have ever imagined, or philosophers dreamed—when money, and what money buys, is the highest they know, and therefore the highest they are able to love—when even the ambitious among them set out with the deliberate purpose of becoming the beggars of men's votes; of winning an office, the chief worth of which, in their eyes, lies in its emoluments—when even the glorious and far-sounding voice of fame for them means only the gabble and cackle of notoriety?

The only example, which I can call to mind, of a historic people, whose ideals are altogether material and mechanical, is that of China. Are we, then, destined to become a sort of Chinese Empire, with three hundred millions of human beings, and not a divine man or woman?

Is what Carlyle says is hitherto our sole achievement—the bringing into existence of an almost incredible number of bores—is this to be the final outcome of our national life? Is the commonest man the only type which in a democratic society will in the end survive? Does universal equality mean universal inferiority? Are republican institutions fatal to noble personality? Are the people as little friendly to men of moral and intellectual superiority as they are to men of great wealth? Is their dislike of the millionaires but a symptom of their aversion to all who in any way are distinguished from the crowd? And is this the explanation of the blight which falls upon the imagination and the hearts of the young?

Ah! Surely, we, who have faith in human nature, who believe in freedom and in popular government, can never doubt what answer must be given to all these questions. A society which inevitably represses what is highest in the best sort of men is an evil society. A civilization which destroys faith in genius, in heroism, in sanctity, is the forerunner of barbarism. Individuality is man's noblest triumph over fate, his most heavenly assertion of the freedom of the soul; and a world in which individuality is made impossible is a slavish world. There man dwindles, becomes one of a multitude, the impersonal product of a general law, and all his godlike strength and beauty are lost. Is not one true poet more precious than a whole generation of millionaires; one philosopher of more worth than ten thousand members of Congress; one man who sees and loves God dearer than an army of able editors?

The greater our control of nature becomes, the more its treasures are explored and utilized, the greater the need of strong personality to counteract the fatal force of matter. Just as men in tropical countries are overwhelmed and dwarfed by nature's rich profusion, so in this age, in which industry and science have produced resources far beyond the power of unassisted nature, only strong characters, marked individualities, can resist the influence of wealth and machinery, which end to make man of less importance than what he eats and wears, to make him subordinate to the tools he uses.

From many sides personality, which is the fountain-head of worth, genius and power, is menaced. The spirit of the time would deny that God is a person, and holds man's personality in slight esteem, as not rooted in the soul, but in aggregated atoms. And the whole social network, in whose meshes we are all caught, cripples and paralyzes individuality. We must belong to a party, to a society, to a ring, to a clique, and deliver up our living thought to these soulless entities. Or, if we remain aloof from such affiliation, we must have no honest convictions, no fixed principles, but fit our words to business and professional interests, and conform to the exigencies of the prevailing whim. The minister is hired to preach not what he believes, but what the people wish to hear; the congressman is elected to vote not in the light of his own mind, but in obedience to the dictates of those who send him; the newspaper circulates not because it is filled with words of truth and wisdom, but because it panders to the pruriency and prejudice of its patrons; and a book is popular in inverse ratio to its individuality and worth. Our national library is filled with books which have copyright, but no other right, human or divine, to exist at all. And when one of us does succeed in asserting his personality, he usually only makes himself odd and ridiculous. He rushes into polygamous Mormonism, or buffoon revivalism, or shallow-minded atheism; nay, he will even become an anarchist, because a few men have too much money and too little soul. What we need is neither the absence of individuality or a morbid individuality, but high and strong personalities.

If our country is to be great, and forever memorable, something quite other than wealth and numbers will make it so. Were there but question of countless millions of dollars and people then indeed the victory would already have been gained. If we are to serve the highest interests of mankind and to mark an advance in human history, we must do more than establish universal suffrage, and teach every child to read and write. As true criticism deals only with men of genius or of the best talent, and takes no serious notice of mechanical writers and bookmakers, so true history loses sight of nations whose only distinction lies in their riches and populousness. The noblest and most gifted men and women are alone supremely interesting and abidingly memorable. We have already reached a point where we perceive the unreality of the importance which the chronicles have sought to give to mere kings and captains. If the king was a hero, we love him; but if he was a sot or a coward, his jeweled crown and purple robes leave him as unconsidered by us as the beggar in his rags. Whatever influence, favorable or unfavorable, democracy may exert to make easy or difficult the advent of the noblest kind of man, an age, in which the people think and rule, will strip from all sham greatness its trappings and tinsel. The parade hero and windy orator will be gazed at and applauded, but they are all the while transparent and contemptible. The scientific spirit, too, which now prevails is the foe of all pretense; it looks at things in their naked reality, is concerned to get a view of the fact as it is in itself without a care whether it be a beautiful or an ugly, a sweet or a bitter truth. The fact is what it is and nothing can be gained by believing it to be what it is not.

This is a most wise and human way of looking at things, if men will only not forget that the mind sees farther than the eye, that the heart feels deeper than the hand; and that where knowledge fails, faith is left; where possession is denied, hope remains. The young must enter upon their lifework with the conviction that only what is real is true, good and beautiful, and that the unreal is altogether futile and vain.

Now, the most real thing for every man, if he is a man, is his own soul. His thought, his love, his faith, his hope are but his soul thinking, loving, believing, hoping. His joy and misery are but his soul glad or sad. Hence, so far as we are able to see or argue, the essence of reality is spiritual; and since the soul is conscious that it is not the supreme reality, but is dependent, illumined by a truth higher than itself, nourished by a love larger than its own, it has a dim vision of the Infinite Being as essentially real and essentially spiritual. Allowing faith in this infinite spiritual reality is the fountainhead not only of religion, but of noble life. All wavering here is a symptom of psychic paralysis. When the infinite reality becomes questionable, then all things become material and vile. The world becomes a world of sight and sound, of taste and touch. The soul is poured through the senses and dissipated; the current of life stagnates, and grows fetid in sloughs and marshes. Minds for whom God is the Unknowable have no faith in knowledge at all, except as the equivalent of weight and measure, of taste and touch and smell.

Now, if all that may be known and desired is reduced to this material expression, how dull and beggarly does not life become— mere atomic integration and disintegration, the poor human pneumatic machine puffing along the dusty road of matter, bound and helpless and soulless as a clanking engine! No high life, in individuals or nations, is to be hoped for, unless it is enrooted in the infinite spiritual reality—in God. It is forever indubitable that the highest is not material, and no argument is therefore needed to show that when spiritual ideals lose their power of attraction, life sinks to lower beds.

Sight is the noblest sense, and the starlit sky is the most sublime object we can behold. But what do we in reality see there? Only a kind of large tent dimly lighted with gas-jets. This is the noblest thing the noblest sense reveals. But let the soul appear, and the tent flies into invisible shreds: the heavens break open from abyss to abyss, still widening into limitless expanse, until imagination reels. The gas-jets grow into suns, blazing since innumerable ages with unendurable light, and binding whole planetary systems into harmony and life. So infinitely does the soul transcend the senses! The world it lives in is boundless, eternal, sublime. This is its home; this the sphere in which it grows, and awakens to consciousness of kinship with God. This is the fathomless, shoreless abyss of being wherein it is plunged, from which it draws its life, its yearning for the absolute, its undying hope, its love of the best, its craving for immortality, its instinct for eternal things. To condemn it to work merely for money, for position, for applause, for pleasure, is to degrade it to the condition of a slave. It is as though we should take some supreme poet or hero and bid him break stones or grind corn—he who has the faculty to give to truth its divinest form, and to lift the hearts of nations to the love of heavenly things.

Whatever our lot on earth may be—whether we toil with the hand, with the brain, or with the heart—we may not bind the soul to any slavish service. Let us do our work like men—till the soil, build homes, refine brute matter, be learned in law, in medicine, in theology; but let us never chain our souls to what they work in. No earthly work can lay claim to the whole life of man; for every man is born for God, for the Universe, and may not narrow his mind. We must have some practical thing to do in the world—some way of living which will place us in harmony with the requirements and needs of earthly life; and what this daily business of ours shall be each one, in view of his endowments and surroundings, must decide for himself.

And it is well to bear in mind that every kind of life has its advantages, except an immoral life. Whatever we make of ourselves, then—whether farmers, mechanics, lawyers, doctors, or priests—let us above all things first have a care that we are men; and if we are to be men, our special business work must form only a part of our lifework. The aim—at least in this way alone can I look at human life—is not to make rich and successful bankers, merchants, farmers, lawyers and doctors, but to make noble and enlightened men. Hence the final thought in all work is that we work not to have more, but to be more; not for higher place, but for greater worth; not for fame, but for knowledge. In a word, the final thought is that we labor to upbuild the being which we are, and not merely to build round our real self with marble and gold and precious stones. This is but the Christian teaching which has transformed the world, which declares that it is the business of slaves even, of beggars and outcasts, to work first of all for God and the soul. The end is infinite, the aim must be the highest. Not to know this, not to hear the heavenly invitation, is to be shut out from communion with the best, is to be cut off from the source of growth, is to be given over to modes of thought which fatally lead to mediocrity and vulgarity of life.

> To live for common ends is to be common;
> The highest faith makes still the highest man;
> For we grow like the things our souls believe,
> And rise or sink as we aim high or low.
> No mirror shows such likeness of the face
> As faith we live by of the heart and mind.
> We are in very truth that which we love;
> And love, like noblest deeds, is born of faith.
> The lover and the hero reason not,

But they believe in what they love and do.
All else is accident—this is the soul
Of life, and lifts the whole man to itself,
Like a key-note, which, running through all sounds,
Upbears them all in perfect harmony.

We cannot set a limit to the knowledge and love of man because they spring from God, and move forever towards Him, who is without limit. That we have been made capable of this ceaseless approach to an infinite ideal is the radical fact in our nature. Through this we are human, through this we are immortal; through this we are lifted above matter, look through the rippling stream of time on the calm ocean of eternity, and beyond the utmost bounds of space, see simple being, life and thought, and love, deathless, imageless, absolute. This ideal creates the law of duty, for it makes the distinction between right and wrong. Hence the first duty of man is to make himself like God, through knowledge ever-widening, through love ever-deepening, through life ever-growing.

So only can we serve God, so only can we love Him. To be content with ignorance is infidelity to His infinite truth. To rest in a lesser love is to deny the boundless charity which holds the heavens together, and makes them beautiful; which to every creature gives its fellow; which for the young bird makes the nest; for the child, the mother's breast; and in the heart of man sows the seed of faith and hope and heavenly pity.

Ceaseless growth toward God—this is the ideal, this is the law of human life, proposed and sanctioned alike by Religion, Philosophy, and Poetry. *Dulcissima vita sentire in dies se fieri meliorem.*

Upward to move along a Godward way,
  Where love and knowledge still increase,
And clouds and darkness yield to growing day,
  Is more than wealth or fame or peace.

No other blessing shall I ever ask;
  This is the best that life can give;

This only is the soul's immortal task,
For which 'tis worth the pain to live.

It is man's chief blessedness that there lie in his nature infinite possibilities of growth. The growth of animals comes quickly to an end, and when they cease to grow they cease to be joyful; but man, whose bodily development even is slow, is capable of rising to wider knowledge and purer love through unending ages. Hence even when he is old, if he has lived for what is great and exalted, his mind is clear, his heart is tender, and his soul is glad. Only those races are noble, only those individuals are worthy, who yield without reserve to the power of this impulse to ceaseless progress. Behold how the race from which we have sprung—the Aryan—breaks forth into ever new developments of strength and beauty in Greece, in Italy, in France, in England, in Germany, in America; creating literature, philosophy, science, art; receiving Christian truth, and through its aid rising to diviner heights of wisdom, power, freedom, love and knowledge.

And so there are individuals—and they are born to teach and to rule—for whom to live is to grow; who, forgetting what they have been, and what they are, think ever only of becoming more and more. Their education is never finished, their development is never complete, their work is never done. From victories won they look to other battle-fields; from every height of knowledge they peer into the widening nescience; from all achievements and possessions they turn away towards the unapproachable Infinite, to whom they are drawn. Walking in the shadow of the too great light of God, they are illumined and they are darkened. This makes Newton think his knowledge ignorance; this makes St. Paul think his heroic virtue nought. O blessed men! Who make us feel that we are of the race of God, who measure and weigh the heavens, who love with boundless love, who toil and are patient; who teach us that workers can wait. They are in love with life, they yearn for fuller life. Life is good, and the highest life is God; and wherever man grows in knowledge, wisdom and strength, in faith, hope and love, he walks in the way of Heaven.

And to you, young gentlemen, who are about to quit these halls, to continue amid other surroundings the work of education which

here has but begun, what words shall I more directly speak? If hitherto you have wrought to any purpose, you will go forth into the world
filled with resolute will and noble enthusiasm to labor even unto the
end in building up the being which is yourself, that you may unceas-
ingly approach the type of perfect manhood. This deep-glowing fervor
of enthusiasm for what is highest and best is worth more to you, and
to any man, than all that may be learned in colleges. If ambition is
akin to pride, and therefore to folly, it is none the less a mighty spur to
noble action; and where it is not found in youth budding and
blossoming like the leaves and flowers in spring, what promise is
there of the ripe fruit which nourishes life? The love of excellence
bears us up on the swift wing and plumes of high desire.

> Without which whosoe'er consumes his days
> Leaveth such vestige of himself on earth
> As smoke in air or foam upon the wave.

Do not place before your eyes the standard of vulgar success.
Do not say: I will study, labor, exercise myself that I may become able
to get wealth of office; for to this kind of work the necessities of
life and the tendency of the age will drive you; whereas, if you hope
to be true and high, it is your business to hold yourself above the spirit
of the age. It is our worst misfortune that we have no ideals. Our very
religion, it would seem, is not able to give us a living faith in the reality
of ideals; for we are no longer wholly convinced that souls live in the
atmosphere of God as truly as lungs breathe the air of earth. And we
find it difficult even to think of striving for what is eternal, all-holy and
perfect, so unreal, so delusive do such thoughts seem.

Who will understand that to be is better than to have and that in
truth a man is worth only what he is? Who will believe that the kingdom of the world, not less than the kingdom of Heaven lies within?
Who, even in thinking of the worth of a pious and righteous life, is not
swayed by some sort of honesty-best-policy principle? We love knowledge because we think it is power; and virtue, because we are told,
as a rule, it succeeds. Ah! do you love knowledge for itself—for it
is good; it is godlike to know? Do you love virtue for its own sake—
for it's eternally and absolutely right to be virtuous? Instead of giv-

ing your thoughts and desires to wealth and position, learn to know how little of such things a true and wise man needs for the secret of a happy life does not lie in the means and opportunities of indulging our weaknesses, but in knowing how to be content with what is reasonable, that time and strength may remain for the cultivation of our nobler nature. Ask God to inspire you with some noble thought, some abiding love of what is excellent, which may fill you with gladness and courage, and in the midst of the labors, the trials, and the disappointments of life, keep you still strong and serene.

ROBERT SETON

*The grandson of St. Elizabeth Ann Seton, Robert Seton (1839–1927)
was born in Pisa, Italy. He studied at several schools in Europe before
transferring to the Pontifical North American College in Rome as
its first student. Ordained in 1866, he returned to the United States
and served as a priest in the diocese of Newark, New Jersey. In the
years that followed, he edited Mother Seton's writings and served as
chief notary at the third Plenary Council of Baltimore. He returned
to Rome in 1901, where he acted as an informal intermediary between
the papacy and the American people, even serving for a
time as a New York Times correspondent. He was named the
titular archbishop of Heliopolis in 1903, and he remained
active in ecclesiastical circles until his retirement and
departure from Rome in 1914.*

The Dignity of Labor

(1893)

The dignity of labor appeals to us immediately, because its origin is in the mind itself of God. The history of creation begins with a record of work. In Genesis we read: "So the heavens and the earth were finished and all their host. And on the seventh day God ended His work which He had made." Hence the title of St. Gregory of Nyssa's exegetical treatise in the Latin translation from the original Greek is *De Opere Sex Dierum*. Man, the noblest of God's works here below, was not ever to be idle. His Creator, the Scriptures tell us, "put him in the paradise of pleasure, to dress it and to keep it." Thus occupation of some kind was assigned to man from the very beginning. Even in a state of innocence he was not inactive. God gave him work to do, and his employment contributed to his happiness. Even in Eden a law of labor was imposed:

> God hath set
> Labor and rest, as day and night to men
> Successive; and the timely dew of sleep,
> Now falling with soft, slumberous weight, inclines
> Our eyelids; other creatures all day long
> Rove idle, unemploy'd, and less need rest;
> Man hath his daily work of body or mind
> Appointed, which declares his dignity
> And the regard of Heaven on all his ways.[1]

Cain and Abel are represented in the Bible as a shepherd and a husbandman.

78

The discovery of different arts, doubtless the offspring, for the most part, of necessity—which is the mother of invention—dates from the earliest ages of the world. Even before the Deluge many arts were known and practiced. The building of cities must have had a favorable effect upon the advancement of the arts; for then men could readily get assistance in their work, could profit by the experience of others, and could find employment by which to earn their daily bread. Moses testifies that Tubal-Cain "was an artificer in every kind of copper and iron work." This name resembles that of Vulcan, and it is probable that the fables concerning the Roman god of fire arose from traditions regarding the famous biblical workman. The scholar will here recall to mind Virgil's description of the subterranean furnace of the Cyclops in the 8th Book of the Aeneid, in which the poet's imagination seems to have anticipated the busy scenes in one of our own great founderies, ending with

> *Illi inter sese multa vi brachia tollunt*
> *In numerum, versantque tenaci forcipe massam,*

where we may say, as in the "Essay on Criticism":

The line too labors, and the words move slow.

The celebrated Smithsonian Institute at Washington carries in its name a tribute to the dignity of labor, *Smith* being the oldest and most respectable of all names of occupation. It is derived from the Anglo-Saxon *smitan*, formed in imitation of the sound of smiting, striking, pounding, as of hammer, anvil, and metal. Hence the old English couplet:

> From whence came Smith, whether artisan or squire,
> But from the smith that forgeth at the fire?

The just reproaches which Jacob made to Laban show us that the ancient patriarchs took labor very seriously and were not backward in turning their hands to it. We may judge of how the men worked in that earlier and simpler age, from the way that even the women worked whose fathers were yet men of substance and consideration. Rebecca came from a distance to fetch water from a well and carried the "pitcher on her shoulder"; Rachel fed her father's flock, and took them to water. Their beauty and their station, raised far above necessity, did not lead them to disdain work.

A similar simplicity was then the universal rule. Homer describes kings and princes working with their own hands; and one of the very oldest writings that have come down to us from classical antiquity is a tribute to the dignity of labor. It is the Ἔργα καὶ Ἡμέραι, or "Works and Days" of Hesiod, who was a poet of the plow and of the people, inculcating the peaceful pursuits of agriculture and mechanical labor. Xenophon tells of a citizen of Athens who went out every morning into the country to superintend his workmen and help them with his own hands, thus encouraging the rest and keeping himself in perfect health. Cyrus the Younger had a private garden which it was his recreation to tend unaided. Cicero says that he knew of some Sicilian laborers who, although they moved the ground themselves, pruned the fruit trees, dressed the vines, and engaged in all sorts of manual labor, yet lived in houses adorned with beautiful statues and ate off of plates of silver and gold. It has been a custom for over three thousand years in China—the most industrious country in the world—for the emperor and court officials to go out solemnly towards the end of March every year and begin the agricultural work of the season by putting hand to plow and tracing each a long furrow in the ground.

After the Israelites had occupied the Promised Land, we find manual labor ever held there in the highest estimation. Everyone made his own instruments of husbandry. Women, even matrons of rank and wealth, were employed in spinning, weaving and embroidery, making garments not only for their own family, but also to sell to strangers. We may here remark, as showing the respect of our ancestors for work, that spinster—one who spins—is the English legal designation of a single or unmarried woman. Gedeon engaged in threshing and cleansing wheat when an angel of the Lord appeared to him to declare the deliverance of Israel; Ruth gleaning the ears of corn in her kinsman's field; Saul, although king not changing his manners or pursuits on account of his elevation, but found "following oxen out of the field," when summoned to the relief of Jabes-Galaad; David keeping his father's sheep; Eliseus receiving the holy mantle from

Elias when plowing the soil; Amos called to the prophetical office while a herdsman of the kingdom of Juda, are so many examples among others that might be given, which illustrate the dignity in which labor was held by the chosen people of God. Indeed, after the captivity we find the Talmudists laying it down as a precept to parents not to neglect to teach their children some trade or mechanical art. Then mention is made of several even learned Jews who practiced a manual art. In the New Testament we have St. Joseph a carpenter, Simon of Joppe a tanner, and St. Paul and Aquila tentmakers. It might here be mentioned, as akin to this part of our subject, that it was formerly the rule for every prince of the blood in France to be taught a trade of some kind, and Louis the Sixteenth, who helped the American colonies to independence, was a skillful locksmith. It is still a custom for the sons of Roman princes who count themselves at the head of the European nobility, to be aggregated to one or other of the many guilds or confraternities of mechanics and tradesmen, which the wisdom and liberality of the popes have multiplied in the Eternal City.

Slavery may be likened, wherever introduced, to the fabled upas-tree of the East which gives death to those who rest in its shade. There is an irrepressible conflict between free and slave labor: they cannot long exist under the same government. The innate dignity of free and honest labor would be insulted and finally extinguished if placed in competition with the enforced and degraded labor of the slave. Two salient examples from ancient and modern history confirm the maxim of economics that in all places and at all times and in every circumstance the same effects follow from similar causes. Slavery, introduced among the Romans by war and conquest, gave the first blow to labor among a free people. In course of time the whole country, of which Rome was the capital and center, became covered with vast farms called *Latifundia*, tilled by slave labor; so that the same amount of land which in the time of the Republic had contained from one hundred to one hundred and fifty farmer families, was later occupied (and only occasionally), as a single estate, by one patrician family and perhaps fifty slaves. Pliny denounced this state of things as the ruin of the empire.

With the preaching of Christianity a new principle was introduced, or rather reintroduced: the principle that labor of itself has nothing humiliating, nothing degrading, and is not incompatible with liberty and knowledge. One of the aims of the Church, from the very beginning, was to rehabilitate manual labor in public estimation, and thus to abolish slavery itself in the Roman world. Before the end of the fifth century labor was restored to its original dignity and the economy of work found its proper place once more in the social conditions of mankind. How could it, indeed, be otherwise? Many of the parables of our Lord were taken from subjects of labor. He even deigned to liken His Eternal Father to a husbandman, a vine-dresser; He was Himself called a carpenter—"Is not this the carpenter, the Son of Mary?" The insults and objections of pagans, who turned upon the Christians their own contempt for labor, were commonly directed against the humble and laborious origin of their Founder and His Apostles. It has never been attempted by our apologists to explain away these conditions. On the contrary, they were boldly and gladly accepted and insisted upon. The pagans, being ashamed of manual labor, avoided all mention of it on their tombs. Only the burial urns of slaves and freed-men told of their occupations. On the other hand, the Christians gloried in doing so, and in representing on their burial slabs the instruments of their work. Cicero couples "workman" with "barbarian," using both words as terms of reproach; but among Christians the expressions *operarius, operaria*, were held in honor. Thus in a beautiful inscription of the middle of the fourth century the noble widow of Junianus styles herself *amatrix pauperum et operaria*—"a lover of the poor and a working-woman." To be a breadwinner, a wage-earner, a worker, was to be esteemed mean and contemptible by pagans, but praiseworthy by the Christians; for labor, although in its present aspect a penalty of the Fall, is also a remedy of sin and a condition of future reward.

In the fifth century we behold a complete restoration of the dignity of labor. We can conceive how great has been the moral revolution in the minds and manners of men throughout the ancient world on hearing St. John Chrysostom tell his hearers, the pleasure-loving people, the luxurious nobles, the imperial dignitaries of Constantinople: "When you see a man who cuts the wood, or who, grimy with soot, works the iron with his hammer, do not despise him, but rather for that reason admire him."[2]

In the primitive Church the *Fossores*, or grave-diggers, belonged to the ecclesiastical body although their work was primarily one of manual labor. St. Jerome calls them clerics.[3] They were constantly in familiar intercourse with the priests, and were the devoted, laborious and heroic servants of the Christian community. By them were excavated those stupendous underground cemeteries around Rome and other cities generally called catacombs. Their work required strength, patience, zeal and courage. Their life was one of continual danger and self-sacrifice. In the laws of the fourth and fifth centuries they are styled *Copiatae*, from the Greek, meaning, emphatically, laborers. It was not a mercenary service which these men rendered to the Church, but a work of personal devotion which might, and did, sometimes result in martyrdom. It has been conjectured that they were the *Ostiarii*—Door-keepers—of those times, or, at least, formed a part of that body of Minorists. Hence we derive another illustration of the dignity of labor when we see the laborer raised by the Church to such a degree. In the beginning bishops and priests often gave the example of manual labor, following in this the apostolic tradition, as the Apostles themselves had followed the Jewish custom. It appears to have been contemplated by earlier councils that the clergy should, in part at least, maintain themselves by the work of their hands. The learned, however, regard all canons bearing on this subject as permissive rather than mandatory. Still they are undoubted proofs that manual labor was thought honorable and meritorious.

Epiphanius has recorded that many, while they might live by the altar which they served, preferred from motives of humility—of religion—to support themselves by the work of their own hands. Interesting examples of a later period are given in Cardinal Moran's "Irish Saints in Great Britain." The monastic orders all originally enjoined work of the hands; and St. Augustine, a Doctor of the Church, wrote a treatise entitled *De Opere Monachorum*, about the year 400, in which he condemns certain monks who occupied themselves solely in reading, prayer and meditation, to the exclusion of manual labor. The forty-eighth chapter of the Rule of St. Benedict, patriarch of the monks of the West, is headed "Of Daily Manual Labor." We may truly say that *Laborare et orare*—"To work and to pray"—was the fundamental maxim of the monastic life. After the ravages and devastation of the Barbarian inroads, whole districts of Europe were again cleared and cultivated by the labor and intelligence of monks. They were also the architects and mechanics, the bridge-builders and road-makers, the farmers and gardeners of the early Middle Ages. Among the religious orders, dislike of slavery and serfdom, with a corresponding respect for free labor, were traditions carefully handed down during those long periods of conquest, oppression and social disturbances which preceded, accompanied and followed the formation of Christendom. Perhaps the most touching of our dear poet Longfellow's miscellaneous pieces is "The Norman Baron," in which he shows us the influence exerted in this direction by monks, the keepers of men's consciences. These traditions continued down to the end. While the bishops and prelates of the secular clergy were too often but court favorites, or the younger sons of great families, the list of the Mitred Abbots—who sat as spiritual peers of parliament in England, at the time of the Reformation—shows that the majority of them sprang from the people, and were the sons of those who worked for their living. Their labor received additional dignity from the eminent positions to which their children rose.

Nothing, also, is more democratic than the Papacy. Democracy is the friend and natural ally of Labor; and many are the popes who have honored labor by springing from the laboring classes and wearing high above coronets and crowns the tiara of merit, mind and moral worth.

Do not, however, mistake. The dignity of labor does not stoop to petty jealousy, or descend to the leveling tendencies of European radicals and socialists. Joseph was, indeed, a carpenter: but he was also of the race of King David and kept his genealogy with scrupulous exactitude. There is nothing contradictory between a "long descent" and a genuine respect for labor. The laborer is not a beast of burden. Even the ox that treadeth out the corn was not to be muzzled. The laborer has a right to fixed and limited hours of work, and to stated periods of rest and recreation. This is a principle which the Church laid down in commanding cessation from labor on Sundays and holidays of obligation; for, as said a rigid and censorious Roman:

> *Interpone tuis interdum gaudia curis:*
> *Quod caret alterna requie, durabile non est.*[4]

The example from modern history, showing that contempt for labor brings a nation to ruin, is that of Poland. At the outset Poland—as every people that conformed to the guidance of the Church which converted them and civilized them—was comparatively democratic. It was the bringing in of prisoners of war who became the personal property of their captors which cheapened work and gradually made it impossible for free to compete with slave or serf labor. The Polish peasant, freeman as he was and the owner of a bit of land for which he had no over-lord, fell by degrees into a condition in which he had few social and no political rights. Such grew to be the arrogance and unwisdom of the Polish aristocracy that a man lost caste, who, however poor, engaged in mechanical or industrial labor. This finally brought about the extinction of Polish nationality. In the days preceding this event—a century ago—it was a common saying that Poland was the paradise of idle nobles and the hell of industrious workers.

It is pleasant to turn from such a state of things to the wise imaginations of Sir Thomas More in his *Utopia*. There we see portrayed not only a voluntary communism—an accepted division of labor and profit—such as the Church had ever approved in her religious orders and which, in apostolic times, was occasionally practiced by families while still living in the world, but we have also depicted, to the enhancement of the love and dignity of labor a class of men who of their own volition neglected the softer side of life to "live laborious days." Here follows a description of these men:

> Some of them visit the sick, others mend the highways, cleanse out ditches, repair bridges, or dig turf, gravel or stones. Others fell and cleave timber and bring wood, corn and other necessaries, in carts into their towns. Nor do these serve the public only but even private men, and more faithfully than the slave themselves. If there is anywhere a rough and disagreeable piece of work to be done from which others are deterred by the labor and disagreeable nature of the task, not to say the despair of accomplishing it, they cheerfully and of their own accord, undertake it. These men spend their whole life in hard labor; and yet they do not value themselves upon it, nor lessen other people's credit to raise their own; and by stooping to such servile employment, so far

from being despised, they are the more esteemed by the whole nation.[5]

Every true American will sympathize, one would think, with that generous, enthusiastic and high-souled band which tried to carry on the Brook Farm community, near Boston, some fifty years ago. Hawthorne belonged to it for awhile, and has written in "Blithedale Romance" those noble words:

> We mean to lessen the laboring man's great burden of toil by performing our due share of it at the cost of our thews and sinews. . . . And as the basis of our institution, we propose to offer up the earnest toil of our bodies, as a prayer no less than an effort for the advancement of our race.

It has been said, with more or less truth, that everything in English literature can be referred to the Bible, to Shakespeare, or to Bacon's Essays. One of the longest of the essays is that one "Of the True Greatness of Kingdoms and Estates," and shows the change that came over Europe at the period of and, in some manner, as a consequence of the Protestant Reformation in the setting up of absolute monarchies and the keeping of standing armies which are the two worst enemies of honest, self-respecting labor. How different the estimate of Bacon from that of his Catholic predecessor in the Lord Chancellorship, as to what constitutes we believe the strength and power of a people—the good condition of its laboring classes—is clear from this single sentence: "The principal point of greatness in any State is to have a race of military men." No well-informed American can agree with this; but he will prefer the maxim of the gentle Fenélon inculcating in "Telemachus" the wise advantages of industry and peace. If it be objected that they alone should speak of labor who know from their own experience what labor is, let us answer in the finest line ever penned by Latin scribe:

> *Homo sum: humani nihil a me alienum puto.*

It embodies a sentiment that every American accepts; for if not everyone of us is obliged to labor with his own hands, yet everyone of us is expected to respect and to encourage him who has to do so. A beautiful anecdote of the great Napoleon tells us that one day at St. Helena he met, unexpectedly, a laborer toiling up the path with a heavy load on his shoulders. The poor man would have turned aside and ceded the right of way to the emperor, but Napoleon prevented him and turned aside himself saying to his faithful followers: *Honneur au travail*—"Let us honor labor."

Our Revolution was the dawn of a new era in which the dignity of labor was to be acknowledged in a free citizen enjoying absolute political equality with whomsoever; and by our example and prosperity we now demand a juster recognition of the rights of labor throughout the world. With hardly an exception, the official seals of the states and territories of the Union bear engraved upon them the republican symbols of industry and labor—the plow, the shears, the spade and pick and axe, the grapevines and the bee-hive, the ship-builder's instruments and the miner's tools, telling of an origin and a history far other than that which the feudal towers and heraldic anomalies proclaim upon the shields of monarchical Europe.

Labor is the key to American success. The emigrant privations and pioneer struggles of our people in the making of New England, in the making of the Great West and all the rest of our beloved country; the boyhood difficulties of so many of our eminent men from Clay and Webster to Lincoln, Grant and Garfield, have set a halo of romance on the sacred brow of labor. The ring of the woodman's ax, the cling-clang of hammer and anvil, the thud and sputter of red-hot beaten iron, the buzz of saw, the whiz and whirl of wheels, the shuttle in the loom, the murmur of imprisoned waters, the hiss of escaping steam, the rumble and roar of machinery in motion—the varied sounds of human skill and labor—is the music of America and the industrial harmony of the universe. In our republican country the people have no crests except those of rude toil. Here there is no aristocracy but that of hand and brain. Here all are equal before God and before the law. Here all are assured a chance to rise above their original condition. This is the brotherhood of man through Christian equality:

> Turn, turn, my wheel! The human race,
> Of every tongue, of every place,

Caucasian, Coptic, or Malay,
All that inhabit this great earth,
Whatever be their rank of worth,
Are kindred and allied by birth,
And made of the same clay.[6]

"The sleep of a laboring man is sweet," says the Scripture. It is the effect of healthy exercise. His nights are not disturbed by social ambition. The Catholic laborer learns from his mother the Church how to be happy though poor. This is one of the problems of life whose solution has been hidden from the wise and prudent and revealed to little ones: "Yea, Father; for so it hath seemed good in Thy sight." (Matt. xi, 26.) The Church teaches the lesson of mutual help and sympathy. The Church ignores the so-called barriers between the classes and the masses, holding them to be fictitious obstructions and imaginary lines of demarcation which only pride, prejudice and plutocracy can be so foolish as to prate about. The Church suggests that a divine blessing rests on labor and elevates it to the nobility of nature:

The honest man, though e'er sae poor,
    Is king o' men for a' that.

The "Fair and Happy Milkmaid" in Overbury's *Characters,* the loving couples in the "Cotter's Saturday Night," "Evangeline" at her spinning, "Paul and Virginia" in their island home never knew the misery of wealth which stamps its mysterious mark on the rich and the idle:

—medio de fonte leporum
Surgit amari aliquid quod in ipsis floribus angit.[7]

The contrast between those who ride in carriages and those who go afoot has amused the pencil of the humorist and the thoughts of the philosopher, for both recall the adage: "God shows His contempt for riches by the sort of people He gives them to." Labor is at its best when it believes, with the apostle, that "Piety with sufficiency is great gain." Desperate risks, quick returns, the greed for sudden wealth—*Auri sacra fames*—these degrade labor, demoralize the laborer, and make unwilling workers in the mills of God. Thrice happy they to whom the Encyclical of Pope Leo "On the Condition of Labor" is familiar! Thrice happy they if the Holy Family be their model, and, in the words of the Pope establishing the Confraternity, "They lift up their eyes to Jesus, Mary and Joseph to find in this domestic group cause for rejoicing rather than for repining at their lot."

Such as these would be the hope of America:

Men whose lives glided on like rivers that water the woodlands,
Darkened by shadows of earth, but reflecting an image of
    heaven.

NOTES

1. "Par. Lost," iv.
2. Hom. xx, 12.
3. Epist. Ad Innocent.
4. Cato.
5. Ch. xi.
6. Longfellow, *Kéramos*.
7. "Lucretius."

CHARLES J.
BONAPARTE

A distant relative of Napoleon Bonaparte, Charles J. Bonaparte (1851–1921) grew up in Baltimore amid wealth and prosperity. A graduate of both Harvard College and Harvard Law School, he quickly established a reputation as a capable lawyer in his home city. There he worked tirelessly for civil service reform against the entrenched power of city and state political bosses. Bonaparte's reform work brought him to the attention of Theodore Roosevelt, and the two reformers became friends during the 1890s when Roosevelt served on the U.S. Civil Service Commission.

Upon becoming president in 1901, Roosevelt enlisted Bonaparte to serve on the Board of Indian Commissioners. There, among other things, he arranged more equitable treatment for Catholic schools serving Native Americans. In 1905 Roosevelt appointed Bonaparte to serve as navy secretary, and late in 1906 he was named attorney general. As attorney general Bonaparte vigorously sought to enforce the Sherman Antitrust Act. This active Catholic layman was an important officer in the army of progressive reformers in the United States.

Some Thoughts for American Catholics

(1904)

To consult the Oracle of Delphi was an expensive no less than a solemn proceeding. The Pythoness acted on sound business principles in fixing the price of her services; and, as she also dealt strictly on a spot cash basis, the happy pilgrim who left her august presence may have thought himself the richer in heavenly wisdom, but must have known himself a good deal the poorer in worldly dross. As some compensation he had thrown in, provided he took the trouble to read the inscription over the gate, a piece of good advice which differed widely in value from curbstone opinions and gratuitous counsel in general; it was not only worth more than the nothing he paid for it, but far more than all the obscure warnings and equivocal hints for which he had just paid so handsomely. "Know thyself" was a precept of well-nigh boundless utility for the ancient Greek; it is no whit less suited to the American and, more particularly, to the Catholic American of today. We American Catholics may perhaps spend a few minutes fruitfully in the attempt to practically apply it; or, in other words, to find out, if we can, what we are and why we are here; what work we have to do, and upon what conditions we may hope to do this work well.

"Undoubtedly," said the New York *Nation* in its issue of January 30, 1868, "political equality, free public education under Protestant auspices and a national rule which compels sectarian toleration, are forces which must in time either destroy Catholicism in this country, or essentially change its nature." Is this statement true? Is its probability established or even indicated by our thirty-six years' experience since it was published, or by the Church's history during the entire period since she was first exposed to what the same paper, in the article from which I have quoted, calls "the corroding action of our institutions?"

These questions are not new. I doubt not that you have all heard and read—many of you probably often, some perhaps *ad nauseam*—that there is an "incompatibility" between American institutions and the Catholic Church. You may have heard this not only from enemies but from friends of the Church. In truth it is said sometimes by those who know something of the Catholic Church and nothing of American institutions, although more frequently by those who know something of American institutions and nothing of the Catholic Church, and most frequently of all by those who know nothing, or next to nothing, about either. Were I speaking seventy-five or even fifty years ago, I might ask whether the audience before me believed this; today such an inquiry would be needless. Now such a thought may be, perhaps, entertained by a Catholic who is not an American, or by an American who is not a Catholic; but surely the opinion is no longer shared by any American Catholic sufficiently informed to have an intelligent opinion.

On November 6, 1789, a Bull of Pope Pius VI founded the American hierarchy. At that date the Catholic population of the United States was estimated, probably too liberally, at forty thousand, or about the one-hundredth part of our entire people. There were in all some thirty priests; hardly so many chapels; no edifice which could, with any propriety of language, be called a church; not one asylum or hospital or other benevolent institution, and but a single school or seat of learning of any class—Georgetown College then just founded. When, one hundred years later, the American Catholic Congress met at Baltimore its members represented a Catholic population of probably more than eight millions, constituting between one-eighth and one-seventh of the whole nation. The Church was ruled by thirteen archbishops and seventy-one bishops; commanded the services of over eight thousand priests; possessed some ten thousand five hundred places of public worship, five hundred and twenty hospitals and asylums, twenty-seven seminaries for the education of the clergy exclusively, six hundred and fifty colleges and academies, and, most significant of all, for those who hope or fear much from "the corroding action" of "free public education under Protestant auspices," more than thirty-one hundred parish schools, with, at a low estimate, three-quarters of a million of pupils.

In the fifteen years since that Congress was held the Church's progress has been even more rapid. Without speaking of Puerto Rico or the Philippines, it is safe to say that there are now in the American Union several times as many Catholic bishops as there were priests when our Constitution was adopted; fully as many priests as there were then adult male laymen; more churches than there were Catholic families in the thirteen States; convents and monasteries, schools and colleges, asylums and hospitals, of which the combined means of the entire Catholic population of those days could not have built a tenth. It is true that since the adoption of our Constitution the growth of this country has been marvelous, but the growth of the Catholic Church in this country has been far more marvelous; while the number of American citizens has increased perhaps twenty-fold, the number of American Catholics has increased much more than three hundred fold. If an amazing progress in numbers and wealth were sufficient to prove the Church's vitality, the question suggested by the *Nation's* unlucky prediction would need no further answer. Surely the mustard seed planted on these shores a hundred and fifteen years ago fell on no ungrateful soil; of this fact no better proof can be given or reasonably asked than time has furnished in the stately tree with its deep roots and wide-spreading branches which has grown from that seed.

But this is not enough. For all this might be true, and yet there might be in this very prodigious outward development the germ of a deep inward decay. For one who would judge whether "the action of our institutions" has been or is in truth "corroding" to Catholic faith I deem more worthy of thought the spirit which quickens this mighty frame. To feel as well assured as you and I feel that the Church is here to stay and to prosper, he must, perhaps, believe as you and I believe; but any man able to see things at all as they are, and having some knowledge of the facts, will recognize that nowhere is there greater zeal or greater harmony in the Catholic Church than here; nowhere are the relations of the hierarchy with the Holy See, of the clergy with their superiors, or of the laity with their spiritual advisers, more nearly what Catholics could wish them; and those of the Church with the civil power and of her members with citizens of other faiths marked by less bitterness and less friction. Blind men then may argue whether the Catholic Church can live in the United

States; but for those who have eyes that can see and will open them to the truth, that question is a question no longer; if they see anything, they see that she can live because she has lived and lives today. Lives, too, not as a sickly exotic: she grows and flourishes and waxes strong with a sound and healthy growth; gaining, not in mere size but in vigor, daily; in short, she is and feels herself to be at home. If we apply to the sum of American institutions the vague and much-abused term "liberty," the history of a century and a quarter proves that liberty is good for the Catholic Church: if it has "essentially changed the nature of Catholicism," the change has been but to make the Church more enterprising and aggressive, more than ever full of the missionary, proselytizing spirit which makes a truly living faith, and yet to put asleep the hatred which she once encountered here and still encounters elsewhere.

I have mentioned the *Nation's* prophecy; but I propose to give none of the comparatively little time at my disposal this evening to the more or less gloomy vaticinations of those among our separated brethren who travail in spirit to see the Church so near them and so big, and growing daily the bigger and coming daily the nearer; because, with all possible respect for many among them, I find little to consider, with promise of profit, in their utterances. These are almost invariably either fair words which butter no parsnips, or big words which break no bones; either the expressions of an uneasy, affected optimism which would belittle a danger it secretly fears to face, or tongue-lashings for that very improper character of Babylon who so strongly affects scarlet, and differs so widely in sedentary capacity from Saint Cecilia's cherubs. Time may be trusted to test the merit of the first; as to the second, their object has been little the worse for a very liberal and protracted application of this treatment, and I think she can stand it yet.

There is used, however, one argument against the Catholic Church—or at least an outcry doing duty as an argument—which merits a passing word; if for no other reason, for its antiquity. Pilate was told that his prisoner made himself King of the Jews: we are sometimes told today that the Church aspires to temporal dominion. Pilate asked for and heard the truth and declared the charge groundless; yet he feared the cry: "If thou release this Man thou art no friend to Caesar." There have been men in public life among us as consciously unjust when they cowered before the like clamor. On this subject let us ask but two questions: Were those Jews who thus drove Pilate to shed innocent blood, in truth, friends to Caesar? Is anyone who, in our day and country, would proscribe men for their faith and stir anew the dying embers of sectarian hatred—is he, in truth, a friend to American liberty?

It is more to my purpose that we Catholic Americans should know and feel the full burden of duty and consequent responsibility cast upon us by the Church's growing greatness. To my mind, nothing can be more certain than that the Church has greatly prospered in America precisely because America greatly needed the Church. Recruiting her hierarchy from every rank and class of men, living less with or for the rich or learned than with and for that great mass of humanity whose passions untamed by letters, are fairly goaded by physical wants, her influence is most salutary where *ardor civium prava jubentium* constitutes an ever-present danger. The working of American democracy has no doubt shown some a priori objections to popular government to be exaggerated or groundless, but it has also shown no less clearly that *Demos,* like other sovereigns, is often selfish, shortsighted, lazy and misled by bad advice. He is as ready as any other ruler to grow into a tyrant—and a very bad tyrant he can be.

A self-governing nation, of all others, needs the Catholic Church. She can remind the sovereign people, as one having authority over it as over all monarchs, that right and wrong are things changeless and eternal, not molded by earthly fortune or fixed by its or any royal pleasure; that for her "success" never "sanctifies a fraud"; that for her as for her Founder, one man's guilt is but blackened when he finds to share it thousands of accomplices or dupes.

True, the Church has no politics: she knows nothing of candidates or platforms, of administrations or policies, of tariffs or currencies. She is mute on every question as to which honest men may honestly differ; and no more tells her children what ticket they shall vote than what food they shall eat or what clothes they shall wear. But as she demands that they eat with temperance, that they dress with decency, so she requires of them to vote with an unclouded judgment, with an undrugged conscience, with the good of their country as their motive, with the fear of God before their eyes.

Needed in all times and all countries, she is—or at least, to me, she seems—needed most of all in our day and our country; for today Americans are learning what burdens, what dangers, what temptations wait on national greatness. In our youth of weakness and solitude, set apart from the world by oceans and wildernesses, we looked calmly on the sins and follies of our brethren, wondered sagely at baleful passions which took shape in war and conquest and oppression, and thanked God with unction that we were not as others were.

The time of trial came—the time which should teach us how vain and presumptuous were our daydreams; how little beneath the surface our common human nature is changed by intellectual training or material surroundings, by customs or forms of government; how surely

> . . . . We are the same our fathers have been.
> We drink the same stream and see the same sun,
> And run the same course our fathers have run.

And what in the past befell them, now befalls us: as fruits of war, we face today the labors, the perils, the duties of conquerors.

It is not for us to murmur, still less to shirk the appointed task; we cannot lay down at will these grave responsibilities; and to vainly seek such escape were mere cowardice and folly; but we may well, nay, in reason and conscience, we must, welcome any help which can fit us to fulfill them: and in this work, as in all that concerns man, there is room—which none other can fill—for the Church of Christ.

She can remind us, she indeed, and not another, of the common Fatherhood of God, of the consequent brotherhood of all men, which make empty and trivial differences of race or color of wealth or knowledge, which stamp the just rights of any man, however humble and ignorant, be his skin black or red, brown or yellow, as no less sacred than if he were the wisest, the most learned, the most reasonably honored of an enlightened people. She can tell us, and tell us as one speaking with authority, that if God has given us power over distant lands and strange men, we hold it but to serve those we thus rule; that a government, whatever its shape or name, seeking other ends than the good of the governed, is a tyranny, a tyranny all the more odious and baneful if millions share in its guilt.

Finally she can say to us what too many called to speak yet fear to say or say plainly, that a people ordained of God to uplift brethren who have lagged behind is doubly bound to so guard and order its national life that this may fit its mission. She can warn us that if we suffer blind prejudices, narrow selfishness or unworthy fears to baffle the honest fulfillment of our civic duties, if we tolerate and even reward in our public servants dishonor and breach of trust, perfidy to our organic law and sacrilege in their oaths of office, if, in short, we lazily endure a disgrace and danger to Christian civilization in our government at home, then our sway abroad can bring but wrong and suffering on those we rule, but shame and future vengeance on us and our children.

We must learn to accept these truths; to accept them not as vague, cold fruits of curious speculation, but as vital principles of our national being, as perpetual beacons to guide our thoughts and lives as citizens. It is a matter of life and death to our country that we learn; but who else shall teach us? Does anyone still ask this office of "Culture" or "Progress" or "Humanity," or any other of those fetishes of modern thought in whose names we were once promised so much? They have all been tried; tried and found wanting. We know them now for mere mirrored images of man, fair reflections of his fairer features, gazed on with rapture by the dreamer in love with his kind, but dead idols, with sightless eyes, dumb lips, ears that hear not, hands that do not toil.

Will any yet fancy that the very increase of wealth and material prosperity, the widened knowledge of Nature's secrets, the greater subjugation of natural forces to man's will, may meet our need? In these lie much of our peril. Can any nation remain free and worthy of freedom and yet grow rich as we grow rich? Can time and thought be found for conscience and honor, patriotism and just dealing, when the day and the night have too few hours for our chase of gain? Will self-sacrifice at the call of duty be fostered by our daily deepening luxury? Will the burdens and restraints of political liberty be long tolerated by men softened by indulgence to the pampered fiber of slaves?

That great man who, most of men, gave life to this republic has warned us how, and how only, it may live and deserve to live. "Virtue," says the Farewell Address, "is a necessary spring of popular government. Of all the dispositions and habits which lead to political prosperity, religion and morality are indispensable supports." For Americans, Washington is a safe guide: to light the darkness which shadows our national pathway, to walk scathless amid the dangers clustering angrily about it, we must look for aid, not to man or his words or works, but to the religion of Christ, to the morality of the Gospel.

Whoever believes these things must rejoice to hear the Church say, as she tightens her grasp of American life, "*J'y suis, j'y reste*," and to feel in his heart that she says this truly. But we may know this fact, and not necessarily or immediately appreciate its consequences. This is no less true of Catholic than of other Americans. The notion that the Church is a stranger and a sojourner in our land has not been outgrown by all her children. Some Catholics have but half learned, although they are every day learning more thoroughly and more and more rapidly, that they are Americans, and not Irishmen or Germans, Frenchmen, Italians or Poles. *Not*, understand me well—Americans *first* and some sort of foreigners afterward, but Americans, first, last and all the time; and nothing else *at all*, at least in a sense which would make them any the less Americans. No man can really have two countries, any more than he can faithfully serve two masters: a hybrid type of citizenship will be always and everywhere ephemeral and sterile. A great Nation like ours can tolerate no divided allegiance: those who would be hers at all must be hers altogether. Where a man was born she has, indeed never been over curious to ask. Alexander Hamilton and Albert Gallatin are no more her stepchildren than great (to the *n*th power) grandchildren of the *Mayflower's* passengers. But no one is or can be an American citizen, in the full and true sense of the word, who feels himself an Irishman or a German or anything else, except as George Washington or John Adams might have felt himself an Englishman, or (to compare a very small person to great ones) I may feel myself a Corsican.

I say this, of course, subject to all reasonable qualifications. No civilized man, certainly no Christian, can be indifferent to the good or ill fortune of any branch of the human family; and the land where one's kindred dwell, one's parents are buried, one's childhood was spent must be, to a man of ordinary sentiments, something more than a red or blue patch on the map. I have no quarrel with those who on the shores of New England, in the shadow of the Alleghenies, by the Mississippi or the Great Lakes or the far Pacific, remember to honor

St. Patrick or St. George or St. Andrew or St. Boniface or St. Wences-
laus—if the last is the saint I mean, and if I have his name aright. I
would put no prohibitory tariff on foreign sanctity; the production of
the domestic article will not be checked by its importation, nor will
the supply exceed the demand. As our country makes her own one
band of immigrants after another, she takes with them their traditions
and their ideals, their memories and their hopes, to blend these in the
moral and intellectual heritage of all her children. Neither do I stand
aghast at green flags or black, white and red flags flying once a year
beside the Stars and Stripes; or laws made public here and there in
the tongue of many thousands among those called to obey them. The
really sad and shameful feature of such incidents is the paltry dema-
gogism which too often inspires or magnifies them. But, whilst I think
only the better of a fellow-citizen because his birthplace or that of his
fathers yet claims his sympathies and shares his affections, I hold him
alike unworthy and dangerous if he has still to learn that here and
here only are all his interests and all his duties.

I say this especially to and of Catholics, because, as I have just
said, American Catholics have only gradually recognized its truth, and
other Americans have only recently and imperfectly come to see that
they recognized and acted on it. That the United States was and
would remain a Protestant country seemed, to many within no less
than to many without the Church, almost a matter of course seventy-
five or even fifty years ago; it was assumed, complacently or regretfully
as the cause might be, but generally assumed as certain. As to this,
we had no right to complain of public opinion: our fellow-citizens of
other faiths thought of us much as we thought of ourselves. If to some
of them, even now, an American Catholic seems in some sort a contradiction in terms, a few of both our clergy and our laity are still
rubbing their eyes to be sure that such a person is not in some sort an
impostor—that he is truly a Catholic while no less truly an American.

There is doubtless some measure of justification for this frame of
mind in both cases. In the immense mass of foreign matter absorbed
by the American body politic, certain Catholic elements have been,
perhaps, the least rapidly digested in the gastric juice of our free institutions, and are responsible for the most acute symptoms of our
political dyspepsia. To discuss all the reasons for this seeming fact
would tempt me into too wide a digression, but I may glance at one of

the most obvious and most potent; namely, the great disproportion in numbers between the Catholic population of the emancipated colonies and the multitudes of Catholic immigrants to be fashioned on its model. No Protestant communion native to the United States has had to transform from aliens into citizens so vast a number of its members; and I doubt if any, even the humblest, among these communions undertook the task so weak and so poor and so widely dispersed.

The foundation laid fourteen years after the Pilgrim Fathers landed at Plymouth, when a handful of exiles raised the cross at St. Mary's, has had to bear a gigantic super-structure, beneath whose weight it might well have crumbled had it been built by hands. When he reflects how vast has been the work of assimilation and inspiration imposed on the little body of Catholics who greeted their first bishop in 1789, and then recognizes how thoroughly and how rapidly, on the whole, bearing in mind all the circumstances, that work has been and is done, far from marveling at its present incompleteness, any fair-minded man will find his faith revived and strengthened in the boundless potency for good stored in our orderly freedom; any man believing as I do will see a further and greater cause for thankfulness and hope; he will feel assured for the future, as he has known in the past, the proven and abiding guidance of Almighty God.

I must not forget that I now speak first of all to laymen and more particularly to young laymen, soon to be charged with all the varied burdens of life resting upon Americans and upon Catholics. At the American Catholic Congress, to which I have already referred, an interesting and carefully prepared paper was devoted to "Lay Action in the Church"; it may be well this evening, not to discuss or criticize the views of its author, but briefly to consider some aspects of his subject.

Let me first note what was implied in the title itself; namely, that *action* is required by the Church of its laity. I strongly suspect that to a good many worthy people, clergymen and laymen, within the Church and without, this idea is at least unfamiliar. Their conception of the normal Catholic layman is of something essentially passive. To their minds he seems, first of all, one of a flock well guarded by shepherds and collies; docile enough in the main, and grazing now here now there as these point the way, but subject to fits of waywardness and very prone to nibble a little forbidden herbage on the sly. Yet it needs no serious argument to show that this view is fundamentally erroneous. Nothing could be less Catholic than to regard any class of Christians as less than fully responsible for the growth of Christ's kingdom on earth. We know no such distinctions as those recognized in some other communions between church members and men and women who, although in the Church, are yet not of it; between Christians who have and Christians who have not experienced "a change of heart." For the Church every baptized man is a Catholic; no doubt he may be a bad as well as a good Catholic, a rebellious no less than a loyal son of the Church, a useless and harmful just as he may be a useful member of the Christian body; but, whether he wishes it or not, whether he deserves it or not, he belongs to the Church. And he belongs to her body and soul. He cannot justly refuse her anything which he has; his time, his skill, his labor, his strength of arm or brain are hers no less than his means. He cannot compound for any ransom, no matter how costly, his obligation of personal service in her army.

It is a common but wholly unjustifiable error to confuse the order of disciplined labor with the indolence of slavery: to think that because a man knows his work and does it, knows his proper place and keeps it, knows whom he should obey and acts on the knowledge, he is without energy and will. A number of years ago in a reunion of clergymen belonging to one of the more recent among Protestant denominations, a proposal to agree upon some symbol of faith was resisted by one gentleman, himself a convert from another sect, on the ground that "having got one bit out of his mouth he didn't wish to put another in." A critic remarked, to my mind very justly, that this was all very well if his ideal was to be a colt running wild on a common; but that if he intended to draw a load or plow a field he would find the bit an indispensable part of the harness. We wear our bits just because we know we have a hard pull before us and we would pull to good purpose. If, therefore, the Catholic laity are sheep, they are not, or ought not to be, sheep of a breed pampered and protected into chronic helplessness. When a fleecy brother or sister gets into a hole, they should know better than to stand by and "baa" for the shepherd: each one of them must then turn in and lend a fore-hoof to get the victim out.

And in another respect they ought, as I think, to differ from most sheep as we know them. When I was a good deal younger, and per-

haps seemed to be more innocent than I am now, a plausible gentleman once asked me to lend him some money upon a mortgage on a
flock of sheep in Texas, and urged that my security would become one
hundred and forty percent better annually, since this was the usual
rate of natural increase in that prolific clime. On my asking whether
this form of the unearned increment, so odious to disciples of Mr.
Henry George, might not perhaps inure less to my benefit than to that
of the wolves, whose taste for mutton *au naturel* I supposed to be
as pronounced in Texas as elsewhere, he assured me that the Texan
wolf was a gentle and mild-mannered animal and very respectful to
the flocks; and if he was occasionally tempted to take compromising
liberties with the young lambs, the older sheep were bold and vigi-
lant chaperones and always promptly chased him away. I did not
make the loan, and I am harassed by doubts whether such wolves as
the would-be borrower described exist elsewhere than in his vivid
imagination; but his real or pretended sheep would be good exemplars
for us. Those we know have usually lost their natural weapons, since
for man's purposes these are useless; but the typical Christian sheep,
as I picture him, should have a strong pair of horns and know how to
use them effectively. A hard butt at some popular but mischievous
sophism, at some prevalent but unjust and uncharitable prejudice, at
the undeserved prosperity and credit of some wicked man, seems to
me precisely in his line of duty.

If then Catholic laymen are to act, what is the rightful sphere and
what are the just limits of their action? I see no need to answer this
question. The work God gives a man to do he is not forced to seek: it
will seek him. He requires no telescope to look for it in Mars or the
Milky Way, no microscope to find it among germs or bacilli. The fussy
people who are always mistaking their vocations and getting into each
other's way, meddle in everybody else's business precisely because
they will not attend to their own. There is certainly and always work
for each one of them to do, and it is certainly and always right before
his eyes. But it may, it probably will be, or at least, look hard and small
and uninviting; and so he tries not to see it where it is, and searches
for it painfully where he knows well it is not. To every suggested field
of energy and effort I would apply the Gospel test: judge of the tree by
its fruits—not by its branches or leaves or flowers; not by outward
bulk and show of foliage or promise of pleasure to the eye, but by the

plain practical consideration: will its products be good to eat? Will your labors make your fellowmen stronger and braver and happier and more useful? If you are sure they will, no matter in how small a measure and after how long a time, you have found your appointed task. It may be a little thing at first; but if it deserves to live and grow it will live and grow. Only one acorn out of a thousand becomes an oak, but that one was once as small as any among its less fortunate fellows.

When a great and unmerited honor was conferred upon me by your *Alma Mater*, I ventured to point out how important, nay, how vital, it was to the success and credit of the Church to have her children truly believe, and show forth by their lives how truly they do believe, that no man can be a good Catholic who is not also a good citizen; that the obligations of loyal obedience to constituted civil authority, of faithful and zealous fulfillment of the several duties imposed on each member of society by the law of the land—obligations which have been ever and everywhere unequivocally recognized and emphatically proclaimed by the Church—rest sacredly upon every freeman in a self-governing republic, and forbid any surrender to selfishness or cowardice or sloth, any compromise with iniquity or dishonor, in the work which his country demands of him. It is not enough that this doctrine be affirmed in our catechisms or declared by our preachers: it must be recognized in our lives. When there shall be no unworthy citizen who is also in name a Catholic, the Catholic Church in America will have no enemy whom any good man would wish to be her friend.

Do not tell me that things such as these concern not the Church. A Christian cannot draw a sponge over his record as a member of civil society: that record will avail to fix his destiny; and if it does this, it concerns the Church. Even if she would, she cannot limit her mission, cannot escape dealing with evils by closing her eyes to their existence. For be well assured that if this field be given up to the enemy his tares will spread to those adjacent. You cannot abandon a heart to sordid passions in the forum and hope that it will be pure and honorable and generous at the fireside. Burke has well said: "There never yet was long a corrupt government of a virtuous people."

The Catholic Church knows, indeed, nothing about tariffs or currencies: it is for Caesar to say whether his tribute shall be heavy or light, be paid in gold or paid in silver. If "politics" means those matters of public concern regarding which honest men may honestly differ, then, as I have already said, she has no interest in politics. But she is vitally interested in politics when "politics" becomes a euphemism for systematic rascality. Macaulay claimed that to say of Charles I, "He was a good man but a bad king," involved a contradiction in terms. No man who, in any relation of life, persistently disregarded the dictates of conscience and honor, could be, he argued, fairly called "a good man." Surely this is no less true of an American citizen than of an English king: organized fraud, open or secret bribery, official perjury and breach of public trust—these things can never be trifling or indifferent to any agency that makes for righteousness.

And if the Church of Christ exists among men, she exists as such an agency. The votary of Baal or Zeus or Woden might consistently enough share with his deity the fruits of slaughter and pillage. There was in this, perhaps, less of gratitude for past favors than a lively sense of favors to come; for, if he failed to divide equitably, the god might serve him some shabby trick when next he tackled his enemy. This view of the matter has outlived both the establishment of Christianity and the advent of modern civilization. When medieval cattle-lifters sent tithes of their spoil to the nearest cathedral or abbey; when today Dives makes his millions by fraud and chicanery, and out of them gives his thousands to home charities and foreign missions, we saw and see the same human nature, threatened by the same dangers, using the same shifts. But they are no longer used consistently: a Christian has been told plainly, a Catholic Christian has been told more plainly still, that they are foolish and unavailing—nay, that they aggravate his guilt, that they heighten his peril. And for American Catholics, for the laity no less than for the clergy, it is an imperative, a sacred, duty to show—and show so plainly that no man in or out of the Church, can misread the showing—that as truly as she lives to point the way to Heaven, so truly she lives likewise that truth and justice, honor and patriotism, good faith and fair dealing may also live among men.

—◆—

JOSEPH CHARTRAND

—✳—

Born in St. Louis, Missouri, of French-Irish heritage, Joseph Chartrand (1870–1933) studied at St. Louis University, the University of Innsbruck, and St. Meinrad Seminary in Indiana before his ordination to the priesthood in 1892. Bishop Francis Silas Chatard appointed him secretary and assistant pastor of the cathedral in Indianapolis. Chartrand subsequently served as rector of the cathedral and vicar general of the diocese. In 1910 he was consecrated bishop and named coadjutor to Chatard. Upon the latter's death in 1918, Chartrand became the second bishop of Indianapolis— serving dutifully until his own death in 1933.

Chartrand took seriously the urgings of Pope Pius X and encouraged regular confession and daily communion. He was known as the "bishop of the Eucharist." In this regard he influenced the young Father John O'Hara, C.S.C., of Notre Dame (later cardinal-archbishop of Philadelphia), whom he ordained in 1917. Although he placed greater emphasis on matters of personal piety than on larger social issues, Chartrand held a deep commitment to Catholic education. He encouraged the construction of many elementary and secondary schools throughout his diocese, most notably Cathedral High School in Indianapolis. Chartrand held a deserved reputation as an orator, being especially known for his annual Lenten sermons.

Education's Grandest Work

(1917)

Everyone, be he an alumnus or a visitor, coming to this famous shrine of learning, fascinated by the magnificent array of buildings, the sumptuous equipment, the harmonious beauty of the place, the splendid body of teachers, will pronounce happy the portion of those to whom it is given here to dwell.

The Diamond Jubilee has brought vividly to our minds the early history of Notre Dame, the saintly character of her founder and his associates, the part they played as pioneers in our beloved State of Indiana, and in what was then the old historic diocese of Vincennes. Surely we have reason, after seventy-five years to give public thanks to Almighty God, and to revere the memory of men, the instruments of Divine Providence in founding this and contemporary institutions. Who can adequately estimate the wonderful works of these generous religious communities, in the early years of this great commonwealth, during the formative period and down to the present day; each educational, yet different in scope, typical of the unity amid the rich variety of gifts to be found in the Church of God?

Indiana has been singularly blessed in the number and excellence of her religious schools and teachers, and at the very apex stands the University of Notre Dame. No other ranks higher, no other equals her. After years of struggle, striving, and sacrifice, profiting by the experience of kindred universities, led on by the wisdom of those whose souls were ablaze with the love of God, she is enthroned, today, in the temple of national renown. Perfect in organization, single, yea, supernatural in purpose, high in the standard of her intellectual activity, strong in the unity of all her mental and moral forces, her position, her power, her permanency among universities is established. It is remarkable that here should have been accomplished in seventy-five years what elsewhere has required centuries of unremitting toil and sacrifice, and what, even in our own country, has not been attained by institutions endowed by material wealth, and encouraged and supported by men of worldly position and power.

There is a peculiar charm about every great school of learning, but the universities have a magic all their own. The past, with all its achievements of peace and its trophies of war, contains nothing more majestic and inspiring than the renowned shrines of learning. Founded, dowered, conducted, frequented by the best of men, the early universities became the most powerful agencies of Christianity and civilization, the greatest ornaments and the glory of nations. Depositories of all available treasures of knowledge, homes and haunts of elevating minds and noblest fellowship, intellectual centers where dwelt in unity harmonious founders, benefactors, masters, scholars— they live for us again tonight in pageant magnificent, glorifying the past, shedding light and luster upon the present, and giving luminous promise for the future.

Subtle and profound in influence, with age lending dignity and authority to their utterances, the universities, not only reflected but shaped the mental, the moral, the social, the religious, the political attitudes of their respective times and places. There is about their venerable buildings a cloistral calm, an air of sanctity, the enchanting presence of disembodied saints and sages, ready to speak to posterity whenever consulted. To live in such environment and amid such company, should beget depth of understanding and largeness of view, and a charming sense of humility and power combined. Let there be absolute and unswerving devotion to truth and justice, enlightened and unalterable love for God and man, loyal pursuit of ideals, the very highest in the realm of knowledge and action,—and a university is blessed, indeed, the nearest approach to a terrestrial paradise. However, should there be a spirit of compromise in these matters, should erroneous principles be inculcated and find general acceptance, untold evil is the result. It is a well-known fact that some of the world's leading universities, abandoning the solid and sacred rock of the past, have launched out into the sea of unsound doctrine, have openly defended principles in direct contravention to the dictates of religion and morality. This sort of infidelity to the tried and tested past has at last borne fruit. Literature, statesmanship, family life, individual character, have felt it. From the leaders it has descended to the led, and today blood and tears are drenching unhappy Europe—Europe which owes all its good, all its glory, to the past of which it had grown tired. The deplorable results might have been foreseen; they had been predicted; the people were permeated with the poison of intellectual pride and disregard for authority, human and divine. The poison spread more quickly than was expected; the storm broke suddenly and with a fury terrific.

The divorce of religion from morality, nation-cult, necessity and expediency paraded as laws, these and other high-sounding designations were to supplant the outgrown, unchangeable teachings of the Incarnate Son of God. Rationalism and Atheism have been enthroned in the old shrines of learning and sanctity, things material remain the only objects worth the while, and at the entrance of these once-hallowed haunts we read the great blasphemy of the age—*welcome to all, but to God no admittance.*

And who is this God whom the modern so-called great universities would exclude? It is He "who enlighteneth every man that cometh into this world." "To Him," says Cardinal Newman in his *Idea of a University*, "must be ascribed the rich endowments of the intellect, the irradiation of genius, the imagination of the poet, the sagacity of the politician, the wisdom (as Scripture calls it) which now rears and decorates the Temple, now manifests itself in proverb or in parable. The old saws of nations, the majestic precepts of philosophy, the luminous maxims of law, the oracles of individual wisdom, the traditional rules of truth, justice, and religion, even though imbedded in the corruption, or alloyed with the pride of the world, betoken His original agency and His long-suffering presence. Even where there is habitual rebellion against Him, or profound, far-spreading social depravity, still the undercurrent of the heroic outburst, of natural virtue, as well as the yearnings of the heart after what it has not, and its presentiment of its true remedies, are to be ascribed to the Author of all good. Anticipations or reminiscences of His glory haunt the mind of the self-sufficient sage and of the pagan devotee; His writing is upon the wall, whether of the Indian fane or of the porticoes of Greece. . . . He is with the heathen dramatist in his denunciations of injustice and tyranny and his auguries of divine vengeance upon crime. Even on the unseemly legends of a popular mythology He casts His shadow, and is dimly discerned in the ode or the epic, and in troubled water or in fantastic dreams. All that is good, all that is true, all that is beautiful, all that is beneficent, be it great or small, be it perfect or fragmentary, natural as well as supernatural, moral as well as material, comes from Him."

It becomes our solemn duty to exercise the utmost vigilance lest these pernicious teachings find favor with the children and the young people of our beloved country and precipitate a similar, a worse catastrophe. Just at this moment, we in the United States of America hesitate, and justly so, to send the flower of our young manhood untrained to the battlefields of Europe, for fear that lack of preparation in such a frightful conflict make them helpless victims. But what greater consideration, what more scrupulous solicitude, should we not show in preparing them and equipping them for another, even a greater, an inevitable conflict, the battle of life, the battle upon which hangs their happiness for time and for eternity.

Nothing is more sad than the myopic groping of the perversely educated, mistaking the most important issues of life, led on to the unspeakable tragedy of talent ruined, genius degraded, life made useless, eternity bankrupt. The highest purpose of true education is to unfold, to safeguard, to strengthen, and to beautify God's precious masterpiece here—human character. This, education's grandest work, cannot be done without a just appreciation, a vision of man at his best, and his best is as God, his Maker, intended him to be. And in this, our holy religion, and it only, absolutely it alone, is competent to give the all-important higher view. A system of religion that produced a Clement, a Basil, a Chrysostom, a Thomas Aquinas, a Dante, and a host of others, men of full-orbed personality, moral and intellectual giants, amidst every variety of social and political ideas and conditions, cannot be destitute of structural elements of permanent value. Our fountainheads of learning, therefore, must be kept pure and unadulterated, fully prepared to assist in every way the youth of the land, who come, not in quest of gold or pleasure, notoriety or sudden success, but of something infinitely more valuable and permanent:— knowledge, forever allied with its source, Truth Eternal; character, based on principles that have as their impregnable foundation the very moral beauty of the All-Holy One.

It has been well said: "Education is the apprenticeship of life," and as such is not completed in the university. However, student years are precious years, because mind and body then develop toward perfection, habits take on definite form, modes of thought crystallize, presaging the convictions, the conduct of the future. I need not tell the graduates of this evening that I hardly think they realize fully the blessings, the advantages, that have been theirs in the activity and the atmosphere of this noble university of the new world. "Without me," said Our Lord to His apostles, "you can do nothing." This is the very foundation, the continuance, the success of Notre Dame. So marvelous is the magnitude, the grandeur of the achievements of Father Sorin and his collaborators that the world is astounded. It understands that human power alone could never accomplish what we see at Notre Dame today. But Father Sorin and his companions well knew the words of the Blessed Master: "Without Me you can do nothing." They well knew the challenge of the world: "Without me you can do nothing." Yet they listened to the voice of Him with whom everything is possible, and like unto the original twelve, who went without scrip or purse, these heroic pioneers went forth with nothing of the world's goods. Their only treasure was their faith in God, the greatest of all treasures, that faith which has erected the most magnificent works this world has ever known. To this faith was added their confidence in His promise, "Seek ye first the kingdom of God and His justice and all things else shall be added unto you." Men of the world, when they inaugurate a great seat of learning, ask for money, large endowments, spacious buildings, the patronage of the rich and the powerful. Father Sorin and his successors, your beloved leaders along the pathway of learning and character, have had nothing of these worldly gifts. The foundation, the strength, the permanency of the work of seventy-five years was their faith, their self-sacrifice, their love of God and man. If their heroic faith, their heroic love, led them on to heroic work, in other words, if God has been with them, because they lived and labored for Him only, then will He be with you also. Upon you, your Alma Mater places the crown of approval tonight. Take with you the indomitable faith, take with you the heaven-born ideas that tonight place the diadem of glory on the brow of Notre Dame.

Your Alma Mater's affection will follow you. Full well she knows the trials, the tests of ability and character that await you. She has endeavored to prepare you for the ordeal; she has imparted to you the correct notion of success, and whilst you are struggling in the danger, the din and smoke of life's battle, her prayers will ascend to the Great Throne, that you may always be to Church and Country, an ornament, a glory—the special mark of loyal sons of Notre Dame.

To thee, O Notre Dame, thou salient Mother of valiant men, to thee, resplendent in the aureole of thy seventy-five years' achievements, to thee on this auspicious day of thy Diamond Jubilee, we address the words of the Inspired Poet: "Thou art beautiful, grace is poured forth on thy lips; therefore hath God blessed thee. In thy comeliness and thy beauty, go forth, proceed prosperously and reign, because of truth and meekness and justice, and God shall wonderfully lead thee on."

WILLIAM J. DONOVAN

—w—

*William J. Donovan (1883–1959) is best known as the dynamic
founding director of the Office of Strategic Services (OSS), America's
intelligence organization during World War II. Born in Buffalo, New
York, and educated as a lawyer at Columbia University, Donovan first
practiced law in his hometown before moving to a Wall Street firm.
Corporate law, however, did not suffice to channel this colorful
Irish-Catholic's restive energy and undoubted talents. Military service
and public life called him forth to greater things. He served as a
cavalry officer with General John J. Pershing during the Mexican
border episode of 1916, earning the sobriquet "Wild Bill." Although he
was wounded three times in World War I, he advanced to the
rank of colonel and earned the Congressional Medal of Honor
for his remarkable bravery. His character was portrayed by
George Brent in the 1940 Warner Brothers film*
The Fighting 69th.

*After the war Donovan entered politics. He ran twice for statewide
office on the Republican ticket and twice he lost. During the twenties
he also served as a U.S. district attorney, as assistant attorney
general of the United States, and as a U.S. delegate for a variety
of government commissions. He strongly supported U.S. intervention
in World War II, and in 1942 Franklin Roosevelt tapped him to
head the OSS. At once both charming and audacious, he
demonstrated imagination and energy in overseeing America's
"cloak and dagger" activities during the war.*

—w—

Science, Civilization, and the Individual

(1929)

It has been pointed out many times that modern civilization has developed a force that is radically different from that produced in any other civilization and that difference lies in the fact that our civilization is grounded on science and upon the machinery born from invention and science.

Before steam the world was dependent for its material development and the production of its goods upon human muscle. This was supplemented by the muscle of a few animals, mostly horses and oxen harnessed to rude treadmills and wagons. There was a limited use of wind and running water. But on the whole the labor of the world was done by a great number of human beings who were condemned to mechanical drudgery with no hope of release.

Today for our labor we look to mechanical power rather than to animal power. While the great proportion of mankind are not yet free from drudgery, there is a hope, that mechanical progress will ultimately free them.

Science has won for itself a place of tremendous importance in our modern life. It is only in recent years that that central factor has come to be recognized. You have learned that it was not until the early nineteenth century that science through its process of invention, began to realign the structure of civilization. The English people of 1850 who saw the first railway, the first steamboat, the illumination of towns by gas, and the use of machinery driven by power, saw only the starting point from which enduring work was to be done. Consider these facts: Any man who has lived over fifty years can say that before he was born no one had ever flown in the air, gone under the sea in a ship and come out alive, listened to a talking machine, spoken over a telephone, looked at a moving picture—much less a talking one, tuned in on a radio, run an automobile, or communicated by wireless.

In the early eighties there was no college in this country where one could take a course in electrical engineering. But today no university can equip its students to go out into the modern world that has not provided facilities not only for the specialist but for those who, if they are to maintain their place in modern organized society, must have some comprehension of machinery and its uses. And so science has won its way, not only in the perfection of new means of destruction in war, but in the more homely pursuits of agriculture and trade.

It is upon a kind of scientific self-discipline that the modern state depends and modern industrial organization rests. We, who are the beneficiaries of such an industrial system, in some degree at least become subject to the system itself. Our great problem is while making the fullest use of these new forces that we should not be dominated by them.

Economic life is only one phase of life and activity. Identified with every general economic system there are certain social and political conditions. Economic activities which are more or less directly concerned with production and consumption of material goods have an important bearing upon political activity, that is, those forces of government which determine on a large scale men's relations one to another, in the obtaining of social peace. Our political system was conceived in a period when we were an agricultural country. Now, in a highly industrialized society, it is subjected to strains never contemplated. Improved systems of communication and transportation have crowded us close together. This crowding tends to depersonalize men and make them as subject to taboos as the early tribes. It has made the position of man in the universe smaller and less significant than anything that has happened since first it was discovered that the position of the earth in the scheme of the universe was much less important than man had believed. The development of the last century has been to lessen the position of importance of the individual by standardizing him and merging him in the mass of humanity.

Throughout America, during the latter half of the nineteenth century, went on a process of little shops closing down, big factories growing bigger; little one-man businesses giving up, great corporations growing and expanding; rural communities becoming stagnant, big cities pulsing forward; farm districts thinning out, cities growing denser; fewer shopkeepers able to buy where they would; fewer crafts-men, more factory operatives; fewer workers known by name to their employers, more carried on big factory payrolls as numbers identified by brass checks. The process was essentially an adjustment of man to steam.

The sweeping industrial changes since the end of the eighties are suggested by the fact that the evolution of the iron and steel industry did not begin on a large scale until about 1887; the automobile indus-try did not live in the late eighties; the motion picture industry was non-existent; the chemical and electrical industries were in their in-fancy. Ninety percent of the total growth of the electrical industry as a whole has occurred during the past twenty-five years.

There is an ever-widening gap between the things that people do to get a living and the actual needs of living. New tools and tech-niques are being developed with stupendous celerity and in the wake of these technical developments come new ideas of culture and new habits of living. Radical changes in the conditions of work have driven the individual workman ever farther away from his farm and village background of the eighties. More and more muscle is supplanted by invention and technology. The skillful hand of the master craftsman surrenders to those batteries of tireless iron men doing narrowly spe-cialized things over and over and which need be only tended in their repetitive processes by the human worker. As the tools of industry become further elaborated, the business class becomes increasingly involved in that by which the product of the worker is made available to the consumer. The whole business institution is dominated by the necessity of keeping costly machines busy and, as someone has said, the businessman himself is subjected to almost as many restrictions as the machine dictates to the worker who manipulates its levers.

In every development there are gains; also, there are losses. Our gains have been in facility of intercourse, in industrial growth, in the easening and broadening of human life. The definite line in loss is the loss of personal leadership. We are too apt to subordinate ourselves to the spirit of the machine.

In this world of things that serve us the important thing is what kind of men we are. And if organization and invention and specializa-tion debilitate the character of human beings and eat into the fiber of their aspirations, then machines are not of real service. In an age when every American wears the same kind of clothes, reads the same comic strips, is indoctrinated with the same catch-words, it is difficult to find independence of judgment and the willingness to develop ideas and to assume leadership.

In his book *A Preface to Morals*, Walter Lippmann says that the American social system is migratory and revolutionary. He declared that "it provides no recognized leaders and no clear standards of conduct." The so-called leaders he says, "have been educated to achieve success, few of them have been educated to exercise power."

The great opportunity of the American university consists in giving to the individual a sense of duty, an ample consciousness of ability, an ideal of courage, and a sense of the importance of human beings in the midst of the multiplicity of the things that serve them. There can be no greater value through a university education than this development of the individual in the midst of the regimentation of human society. The primary function of an institution such as this, is not only to make men master of the material things of life, but to develop men free to make their own choice in this world and with courage and intelligence enough to make the right choice.

But for the individual who is willing to stand out apart from his fellows and yet be of them, there is need of courage. There is no finer human attribute than this. Dr. Johnson has said that "unless a man has that virtue, he has no security for preserving any other." It may be used for improper purposes, but whether moral or physical, it will compel the reluctant admiration of those who oppose the use to which it is put. Some Latin poet has said—perhaps it was Virgil—that the supreme test of physical courage was one who would stand unterrified even though the shattered earth came falling round his head.

We have obtained victory over the powers of nature; what we need now are men who are willing to vanquish themselves and with the confidence that victory engenders, assume positions of right leadership among their fellow men. Some years ago J. M. Barrie delivered an address on Courage at St. Andrews University in Scotland. He said: "Diligence-ambition; noble words, but only if 'touched to fine issues.' Prizes may be dross, learning lumber, unless they bring you into the arena with increased understanding. Hanker not so much after worldly prosperity—that corpulent cigar; if you became a millionaire you would probably go swimming around for more like a diseased goldfish. Look to it that what you are doing is not merely toddling to a competency. Perhaps that must be your fate, but fight it and then, though you fail, you may still be among the elect of whom we have spoken."

Today to men of that faith which this college teaches, there is particular need of that quality of courage which is guided by intelligence, and directed by honor, a courage that can be patient. You will be subjected to attacks and attempted discriminations by certain narrow and ignorant groups, but you men, with the training that you have had here, cannot surrender to bigotry. You cannot yourselves be guilty of that which you condemn in others.

"Catholic" ought not to be a label. It is a faith, not a profession. It should represent a sterling character built in Christian principles. We should be Catholic in the true sense, universal in our sympathy, broad in our interests, and tolerant in our judgment. To you of this university there should be especial inspiration in the name of your institution. Notre Dame signifies chivalry, and that is a true source of courage.

This is a young man's institution. It was founded by a young man, who was filled not only with missionary zeal, but with a fine loyalty to the country of his adoption.

The same resourcefulness that made possible the building of this institution has characterized it ever since. In your sports you have assumed the dominant position in that particular sport that requires an unusual degree of individual courage, resourcefulness and teamwork. These are the qualities that fit men for leadership, and these are the qualities which your college during your years here has endeavored to inculcate in you.

The years ahead for you are glorious if you will make them so. You cannot stand to one side, indifferent, or scornful, or cynical. You must go in and put your shoulder to the task. Insist that you have a right to go in and help on the job. You cannot be content to find an easy cushion for your limbs, weary of the conflict before it starts. Your great opportunity is to help to work out a happier world for all. And in doing that, the problems you must face while difficult, are not desperate. They call for straight thinking and sustained effort. In any immediate future our race does not seem doomed to extinction through failure of natural resources. The tasks that will be handed to you are not of this negative source. They are more constructive, more challenging to your leadership. Yours is the task to help build a civilization that will provide for health and well-being upon a level of comfort rather than upon a level of poverty. Before us there is great expectation that this can be accomplished. The task of youth is to make this a fact of accomplishment. Your practical problem is how to go forward, to raise the standards of life, to better the technique of production and distribution by a fairer apportionment of income, by a rationalization of the use of income, and by an intelligent consideration of plans that will make our political institutions resilient enough to be responsive to changing economic and social conditions. There can be such revision without a loss of principle, there can be a change in procedure without a sacrifice of substance. There may be many generations of graduating classes before we can see the effective result of a constructive impulse that will liberate us from distrust and prejudice; but this is the day when you enlist to push forward that kind of civilization and leave your college here a record of accomplishment that will inspire your brothers who are to come.

JOSEPH P. KENNEDY

—◈—

*Patriarch of America's most famous Irish-Catholic family,
Joseph P. Kennedy (1888–1969) personified energy, ambition, and the
quest for power. He graduated from Harvard and responded to
the discriminatory treatment of Boston's WASP establishment by
launching his own independent business career in banking, radio,
Wall Street speculation, and in (so legend has it) Prohibition-era
bootlegging. In 1914 he married Rose Fitzgerald, the daughter of
Boston's mayor, and together they had nine children.*

*Kennedy weathered the stock market crash and threw his support to
Franklin D. Roosevelt in 1932 believing him to be capitalism's best
hope against revolution. The new president appointed him to head
the Securities and Exchange Commission and to serve on the
U.S. Maritime Commission. Kennedy aspired to more prestigious
posts, however, and eventually Roosevelt rewarded him with the
ambassadorship to the Court of St. James. While ambassador to
Great Britain, Kennedy proved sympathetic to the appeasement policy
of Neville Chamberlain. Consequently, his relationship with
Roosevelt soured, and he resigned in the fall of 1940. He ended his
public career with noted bitterness and remained negative both to
Roosevelt and to the world war in which his eldest son was killed.*

*He devoted the next two decades to working feverishly behind the
scenes to advance the political interests of his family. He died having
forged successfully the political dynasty that saw one of
his sons elected president and two others elected to
the U.S. Senate.*

—◈—

Conscience, Patriotism,
and Freedom of Speech

(1941)

The fact that you receive your degree from Notre Dame in this the ninety-ninth year of her existence, gives to your commencement more than the conventional meaning. Indeed, your commencement acquires unique historical significance. The rare honor of being her youngest sons before the turn of her century binds you to her past and binds you to her future with a particular depth and meaning. For you, her sons of 1941, represent the culmination of her first century of noble efforts and give bright promise of her second century of Christian educational achievement.

FORCED TO QUICK BATTLE

Moreover, you leave the protection of her sanctuary and enter the hard conflicts of life at a time unique in American history and in the history of the world itself. No class of graduates within my memory will grapple with life so quickly or be forced to battle so valiantly to preserve the truths you have learned and the beliefs you have treasured. Nor has any class of graduates within my memory faced the many-sided hostile attacks, the neglect and the scorn of the Christian truth—the very core of your education here. However, I do not think that thoughts about the disordered world of today should occasion a note of sympathy for you men of Notre Dame. All of us are part of our time, and some of us are more fortunate than others. In a real sense you are deserving of congratulation because you enter a world in turmoil where uncertainty and despair abound, with a background of truth and justice which your whole education symbolizes, for here you have learned that *ideas and ideals* are the basic elements which must shape the pattern of individual and national character.

We are living in a period which all too readily scraps the old for the new. Many of the modern campus philosophers clutch at every passing whim of fashionable thought. As a nation we are in danger of forgetting that the new is not true because it is novel and that the old is not false because it is ancient. Here at Notre Dame your good teachers have tried to instill in you a great respect for the traditional that has proven its value. Your leaders, ever alive to growth, have not hesitated to welcome what is progressive in a real and not a shadowy sense. Times change but neither man nor truth changes.

Picture of the Times

Let me quote a picture of the times:

Men have torn up the road which led to Heaven and which all the world followed, now we have to make our own ladders. . . . Never was there a period when young Catholics . . . could count less upon public opinion and the force of good example, to keep them in the right path. We may doubt if at any time it has been true that men were not swept along in the crush and carried by their surroundings almost in spite of themselves. But if such days ever existed they are with us no longer. The broad road has grown broader with every new discovery, and the narrow way has grown narrower. Every new facility...has filled modern life with greater restlessness and with the craving for fresh emotional excitement. With desolation the world is laid desolate because no man thinketh in his heart. Nevertheless, we have to save ourselves in the surroundings in which God has placed us. Nothing is to be gained by looking only at the difficulties and discouragements.

A candid picture, you will agree, of the world as it is today: But that statement was written about an era thirty years ago. I mention it to indicate that life provides very little new under the sun. Certainly nothing new in sufferings, in perversities or in trials. Every age and every generation must have its crises. Yours seems most tragic of all, but for its burdens you come forth well equipped beyond your dreams.

I do not have to remind you—the bachelors of 1941—the products of a great university—that you must "Commence" your adult life in a war-torn world. Even if our beloved country should remain at peace, your destiny will be profoundly affected by a world in total war.

SAW WAR APPROACHING

At my post abroad I first sensed and then saw the awful holocaust approaching. Within my limited field I did my very best to prevent it, knowing only too well that another world war might well send civilization tumbling down the precipice of savagery.

But Catholics may find comfort even in a world in what our Holy Father recalled in his peace message last November—a message that one day an exhausted and disillusioned world must heed—the Pope recalled that Christ himself had told his apostles, "You will hear of wars and rumors of wars. See that ye be not troubled for these things must come to pass, but the end is not yet."

We can take comfort in the fact that Pius has been the constant and insistent voice for peace in a world that heeds him not. My own brief acquaintance with His Holiness confirms the judgment of friend and foe alike that peace for the nations of the world is a cause for which he would sacrifice even life itself.

It is not unnatural in these times of death and destruction, when the beasts of the apocalypse are loose upon the earth, that the Prince of Peace should be forgotten, that his voice of eternal truth should not be heard above the roar of war. However limited the influence of that great man may now seem to be, I confidently assert that he will grow in stature while the prestige of the warlords declines. It is not only because of treasured memories of my audience with him or the profound impression his grasp of worldly affairs made upon me, but because what he champions, we know in the fortitude of our faith, must and will prevail. Let us not forget this Prince of Peace even in time of war.

WAR FAMILIAR TO NOTRE DAME

But *war* is not new to this Catholic university. The plaque at the Memorial Doorway to Sacred Heart Church on your quadrangle gives a daily reminder of the men who have given their lives "For God, for Country and for Notre Dame." And the Congregation of Holy Cross whose priests run this university has given generously of its members that Catholic men might keep the Faith in time of war as well as in time of peace. Father Corby, after whom the hall on your campus is named, was an outstanding chaplain of the Civil War. His "Memoirs of a Chaplain's Life" gives a graphic description of the priest administering general absolution to the soldiers at Gettysburg. And today your own former president, the brilliant Bishop O'Hara, as Military Delegate, supervises the work of the Catholic chaplains with the armed forces, including four priests of the Holy Cross Congregation.

You men of the 1941 class of Notre Dame will have another reason for remembering this day. Within the week the President of the United States has issued a most historic, and most solemn pronouncement. Calling upon his enormous constitutional powers, President Roosevelt has proclaimed an unlimited national emergency. What the technical legal significance of this decree may be is for the moment unimportant. What is important to everybody even to all of us who feel strongly that our country should keep out of war is this—that your President and my President—the leader of this nation having consistently and repeatedly assured this nation that he does not intend to take us into war unless attacked—has announced that the threat to our national security demands from all of us an unlimited loyalty, a cessation of personal antagonism which the defense and protection of this nation require.

REFLECTS DOUBT AND CONFUSION

Doubtless this splendid gathering of young men coming from all parts of our nation reflects to some degree the doubt and confusion which has made even the wisest adult hesitant and perplexed. The spectacle of sudden death for nations many centuries old, the shock of this colossal machine war, the unparalleled threat of world domination by the new paganism—all these make difficult the attainment of that singleness of purpose and that faith in ourselves so necessary to a sound national life.

But when our chief has pronounced the solemn words, "I declare an unlimited national emergency," the duty of every American is plain. We pledge allegiance to our flag and to the Republic for which it stands.

But in this very act of allegiance, in this pledge of devotion which you and I and all loyal Americans make we state clearly that our constitutional rights of free speech, of free assembly and our freedom of religious worship shall be maintained in all respects.

The builders of our supreme law showed their most profound wisdom in those sweet words of liberty enshrined in our priceless Bill of Rights. If we lost those freedoms, the framework of our government would indeed become a skeleton. Only too well do we know from the history of modern Europe how the silencing of the voice of protest was a prelude to national disaster.

But in exercising that freedom of speech, which includes the right to criticize, we must each one of us try to approximate a formula of which conscience and patriotism must be the monitors. As best I can express it, the formula is: No criticism or complaint that primarily gives aid, comfort, or information to the enemy, actual or potential, only criticism or complaint when, by the standard of judgment or experience or both, the actions or inactions of government are imperiling the success of its defense. This decision was made by Churchill, Northcliff and Lloyd George in 1915. They were constructive patriots in that what they said and did averted disaster. Should we fail to meet this test of the monitors of our conscience and judgment, we are but copying our partisan critics intent upon a selfish purpose.

However, criticism of the past smacks too much of pure politics which is dead. The past disappeared from controversy when the pronouncement was made that the country was in danger. To keep it alive smacks of that human wish to say, "I told you so." But should the time come when our mind and our heart, our eyes and our ears, inform us that either the activities of our leaders or their inaction, their mistakes or bad judgments endanger our common cause, then our conscience must speak and our tongue cannot be silent, for cowardice is not the lot of Notre Dame.

Freedom is an act of the will based upon truth. We must have the truth and the whole truth if we are to be free. My dear young men, eternal vigilance was and is and always will be the price of liberty.

The real test of the democratic process comes with the stress and strain of crisis. The democratic way is a hard way, because essentially it is based upon the spiritual side of man. As Americans we are proud that the ship of state has sailed on no matter how troublesome the times. Not in vain did the poet sing "Humanity with all its fears is hanging breathless on thy fate."

THRILLING SIGHT IN LONDON

I shall never forget a thrilling sight in London when I witnessed the vigorous but fair and intelligent criticism of His Majesty's government in the important policies and administration of the war even as the air raid warning was sounding. The British well know that they could never deny at home what they claim to be fighting for abroad—the basic freedom of the individual. In the awful days ahead we must resolve to keep fighting that human rights be respected and our way of life be vindicated.

We have witnessed in our lifetime the growth of a theory of living which denies every principle America holds dear. In the name of a "New Order" a small coterie of despots proclaim that they have the secret for the world of tomorrow. Their formula is not new to our church or to our civilization. It but turns backward the clock of history. It espouses the view that man in himself is without dignity, that force in and of itself is the sole arbiter of right. On this false code have been based policies and programs which have laid waste a large part of the civilization of the world.

In America, however, our proclamation is clear. We believe that there are rights—the rights of the individual. We declare that they are absolute God-given rights which the majority and the state itself must respect. Never forget that democracy can be a much abused and misunderstood term. But that democracy to which we profess allegiance is far different from the arbitrary mass tyranny which looks upon the will of the majority as the only law. There is no magic *in* counting noses. Our democracy springs from "truths we hold eternal." These are the rights of the minority, of the individual himself, which cannot be frustrated. These, in essence, are based upon the moral law which, in the last analysis, will come to judge even the state itself.

Your studies here at Notre Dame have taught you much wisdom. You have learned that which the world forgets day after day, year after year, and century after century—that lessons of what are enduring values and what are passing fantasies. St. Augustine has told us that "wisdom is nothing but the knowledge of the relationship of things." The poet teaches:

> Only the actions of the just
> Smell sweet and blossom in the dust.

No mirage of novelty has been given to you young men, but rather a stern and manly sense of the *fortitude of faith*.

TRENDS OF DISCIPLINE

One would have to be a disciple of Pollyanna not to know that in modern education there are developing trends of indiscipline which bode evil for our nation's future. In the name of collectivism we are being taught that the qualities of the individual are unimportant as against the claims of the omnipotent state.

The shift of emphasis of responsibility from the individual to government is an example of a dangerous trend. The world is on the move, and against the tide of collectivism no one can raise an effective hand. But it is not against the mere growth of the state as a more effective agent for social justice that we protest; it is the spectacle of the state allocating to itself the exclusive right to judge the morality of its own conduct. This is like the heresies of old which started by the approval of some element of truth, but which finally led by exaggeration to error and finally to the complete denial of truth.

By this shift of responsibility the political end has come to justify the means. Occupants of public office in many parts of the world, easily convincing themselves that they are almost divinely selected to administer the state, have too often put aside ethics and the rooted moral standards because they believed that by so doing they advanced the interest of the state or a so-called liberal cause. From this viewpoint the transition is simple to the broken promises and aggressions which make up almost the entire public history of the dictator countries. The philosophy of Notre Dame, which has become part of you, insistently declares that no wrongful act changes its odious quality regardless of the cause in which it is enlisted. My dear young men, only by insistence on re-assertion of moral values and intellectual honesty among our public men can we maintain the important blessings and benefits of the democratic system.

Democracy in government has become nearly deified. By distortion, government has become a thing apart, as if government could be self-contained and self-functioning, apart from the character of its people. The exaggerated emphasis upon rights, upon the negative protection of individual personality, and this shifting of financial responsibility from the individual to the government, reveal a lack of understanding of the essence of democracy which is the protection of *the individual* personality from dictator or demagogue. People understand that phrase as an expression and proclaim it loudly, but they fail to understand that the true meaning of human personality is vital to an understanding of the history of democracy. That personality is, as you have been taught, a divine bestowal of dignity and worth and eternal destiny.

But perhaps you will find your generation not so hostile to your traditional beliefs as you fear, for they look for leadership from confusion of thought, from their despair of defeat, and their prostration by this deadly defeatism. Many American non-Catholics of today will admit that the Catholic Church stands as the only authoritative teacher amid chaos. Many people whom you meet will admit that they long for your certainty of belief in a divine destiny, of your possession of the peace "which the world cannot give." For their hunger for certainty you can bring them the spiritual bread of the fortitude of Catholic faith.

Today you will have to guard closely your treasured possession and fight valiantly to preserve your Christian heritage.

LIVES ARE INTERDEPENDENT

A commencement address is not the place to tell you of the economic dislocations that inevitably lie ahead. Nor is it the time to suggest to you the ways in which your duty of leadership must be squarely faced.

Perhaps no more hopeful sign for the future of America can be discerned than the ever-increasing recognition of Americans generally that their lives are inter-dependent one on another. The olden days of rugged individualism, for all their possible economic justification are happily a thing of the past. From many sources we hear and read of a similar transformation in the rigid class lines of old England. And fortunate it is that the dream of the brotherhood of man and the fatherhood of God is being given a fuller recognition. You young men, inheritors of all the mistakes of our yesterdays, will not subscribe to any tearful tone of pity, for you have youth, courage, ideals and truth at your command.

When, and I hope it may be soon, a war-torn world climbs the slow and painful trail of economic readjustment, I hope and pray that you will furnish the leadership which your University stamp symbolizes—not the counterfeit stamp of one who regards himself as favored beyond his fellowman, but the genuine stamp of one whom the Church and the University have honored with the faith that his life will be full of Christian meaning.

As your life flowers, in joy or in sorrow, in crisis or in peace, you will look back to these days with the fondest of memories, for here you have imbibed a heritage of accomplishment in the face of adversity.

Struggles of Notre Dame

Indeed, *if* physical trials and hardships had overcome the Fathers of Notre Dame, the little cabin on your campus would represent the limit of their missionary efforts in this great Mid-West.

If the struggle against poverty had broken the spirits of your parents and grandparents, there would never have been the resources to send you here to obtain the benefits of Catholic culture.

If seemingly overwhelming odds meant surrender, there never would have been the glorious tradition of Notre Dame's athletic prowess, for indeed it is the will to win regardless of the odds that stirred this nation with the symbol of "the fighting Irish."

If misfortune crushed Notre Dame, then the great fire of 1879 which wiped out every University building except the chapel and the theater would have written "Finis" to "Notre Dame." But in the two remaining buildings—the chapel and the stage of life upon which generations should perpetuate Catholic teaching—there was a symbolic and prophetic meaning for the Fathers of Notre Dame.

If the Fathers of the noble Congregation of Holy Cross had fastened their gaze upon earth alone and placed their prize upon the praise of men, there never would have been the grotto by the lake where stalwart generations of Notre Dame men have knelt reverently in deep devotion and prayer to God.

Those triumphs over adversities spell for you the lesson of afterlife. And my wish this day for you, my fellow alumni, is that the lives of all of you will be marked by a nobility of character which will bring honor to your families and glory to your university.

CHARLES H. MALIK

—ⱲⱤ—

*A distinguished Lebanese statesman and educator, Charles Habib
Malik (1906–1987) graduated from the American University of Beirut
in 1927 and obtained a doctorate from Harvard University
in 1937. He returned home to teach philosophy at his alma mater
in Beirut, after which he was appointed as minister (1945–53) and
then ambassador (1953–55) to the United States. In conjunction
with his duties in Washington, D.C., Malik served as Lebanon's
delegate to the United Nations from 1945 to 1955, where he
was a signatory to the original U.N. Charter (1945) and a
principal drafter of the United Nations Universal
Declaration of Human Rights (1948).*

*After his return to Lebanon he served as foreign minister (1956–58),
in which capacity he supported the American decision to commit
troops there in 1958. He served again as a delegate to the United
Nations soon after and held the office of president of the General
Assembly during its thirteenth session from 1958 to 1959. Upon his
return to Lebanon, he continued his political engagements and
resumed teaching philosophy. An Orthodox Christian, he
opposed the presence of both the Palestine Liberation
Organization guerrillas and Syrian troops
in his homeland.*

—ⱲⱤ—

The American Question

(1952)

The world faces many fundamental questions today. There is the question of war or peace, in the general sense of the term. If peace, there is then the question, what sort of peace. Both of these questions raise the issue of the place of Marxism as a doctrine and of the Soviet system as a political reality in the world of the future. Within each country there are great questions of social and economic adjustment: the masses, what you call the "common men" or the "ordinary people"—and this always means 80 to 90 percent of the population—are more articulate and insistent in their demands than ever before. The great peoples of Asia and Africa are awakening, baffling the world with enormous issues of accommodation. Then there is of course Europe, weakened and divided internally, and overshadowed and overwhelmed externally; but neither the pride and traditions of Europe, for thousands of years the mother of so much civilization and the center of so much history, nor the actual requirements of world peace, can accept an impotent Europe, playing from now on always second fiddle in the scale of things.

Those of us who face the future—those of us who have a future to face—must resign ourselves to wrestling with these issues all our life. The rising East, the Slavic world, Marxist Communism, the mighty social ferment, and the ordeals of Europe, are tremendous questions which—so far as we can now pierce the unknown—we are going to live with for a very long time to come. We are all plunged into a world not of our own choosing in which our existence is riddled through and through by these issues. And he today who seeks escape from the East, or from Russia, or from Europe, or from the din of the masses, into some kind of a placid and protected existence outside this world of danger and trouble, is literally seeking the impossible.

There is another issue that is just as great as these. In fact, there are some who consider it even greater. This is the issue of America: her destiny and her meaning to the rest of the world.

So crucial has America become for Asia, for Russia, and for Europe, that a European thinker has recently suggested that since the people in Europe seem just as interested in the forthcoming American presidential elections as Americans themselves, it might be instructive to conduct a Gallup poll in Europe concerning the man whom the Europeans would like to see the next President of the United States.

When people abroad wonder, therefore, about United States policy and intentions, when they inquire into how the mind of America is likely to develop, they are simply evincing a deep concern for their own fate. In one important sense, there are no more independent fates: we all sink or swim together.

It is not for me to determine the content of the American message; but while you may afford perhaps not to inquire into the total meaning of this or that country, say in Latin America or in the Middle East or in Europe, and while some Americans may perhaps afford not to be particularly concerned about the meaning of their own nation, there is no other country, there are no thinking people abroad, who are not constantly faced today with the basic American question: what does America, what must America, mean to the world? No responsible non-American today can afford not to meditate as deeply as possible upon this tremendous question. If to meditate on a similar question with respect to any other country may mean to meddle in the affairs of that country, certainly, since so much depends upon the United States, to meditate on this question is not to meddle at all.

America means freedom: no arbitrary compulsion from outside, the autonomous determination of idea and action from within. This is a great message, especially now as there is a real contest between freedom and slavery throughout the world, and especially as in many instances the frontiers of freedom, both geographical and intellectual, have had to recede. For years to come, the gospel of free self-determination will be one of the most potent weapons in the war of ideas, and nothing looms so clearly and decisively in the horizons of statesmanship as the sincere and active attempt at helping to liberate peoples and cultures from Communist bondage.

But freedom is not the end of human life. After I become free, the question remains: what should I strive after, what and whom can I believe, what may I hope for, what must I be? For it is possible to be "free" and yet to miss the end of life altogether.

The crying need, therefore, is for a deeper, a more grounded and more responsible elaboration of the content of the free life. One must be honest with the enslaved peoples—whether enslaved politically or spiritually—in telling them that freedom is not the end but the beginning of a life of effort and development whose general character can nevertheless be traced in advance. Freedom is the immediate goal, but the distant lure is nothing short of the full realization of all that properly belongs to man. Thus the promise must be made clear, that the end is a universal human fellowship in which nothing that is possible—materially, socially, spiritually—shall remain for long unrealized.

America means independence: that people need not be ruled by aliens, that diverse cultures can develop each according to its own inner genius. This is a great message, instilling hope and self-confidence in the heart of the weak and helpless, especially at a time when mighty new forces, both material and spiritual, are threatening the independence of peoples from every side.

But, first of all, independence may not mean peace, unless to start with it is founded upon principles of peace; for the independent units may either fall out with one another or combine against the rest of the world. Secondly, what if certain peoples or cultures cannot be really independent? Thirdly, in our amazingly shrunken world the need is as much for a declaration of interdependence as for one of independence. And fourthly, people crave as much for fellowship as for being alone, and the urge at community and love is no less real and good than any impulse at individualism.

The need, therefore, is to work out conditions of true fellowship under which people will gladly seek the company of the just. Let me only feel that I am included in truth and justice and on the basis of respect, and you can forget about my "independence." The cry for independence is fundamentally a protest because the right mutuality of dependence has not yet been realized. Whatever the impact of America might be, certainly independence must be rigorously tempered with the promotion of community, cooperation, the habit of subordinating the local and partial to the requirements of the larger good.

Because there has been some misunderstanding abroad of the content of American independence, it seems necessary to elucidate precisely how an act of independence in the 18th century is radically different from a similar act in the 20th, and to make it as plain as possible that political independence is one thing, and independence in the realm of culture and spirit is entirely another. So long as there is objective, given, cumulative truth, we cannot be spiritually independent of one another. If oceans and poles can for a time, physically separate America from the old world, the intellectual and spiritual roots of this land all go back to Europe and the Mediterranean. And the supreme question today is precisely to rediscover, reaffirm and reestablish this great spiritual community extending temporarily for thousands of years.

America means democracy: that the citizens of the commonwealth themselves elect and dismiss their own rulers, and that the laws have no respect for persons, precisely by equally respecting the inherent humanity of all persons. This is a great message stressing as it does the dignity of the individual, affirming the primacy of the people, providing a mechanism for the avoidance of tyranny, bracketing all people under the beneficent protection of the law.

But even the most perfect design of government is but a formal structure within which men may seek fullness of being. Nor is it certain that if the entire world were democratized, wars will cease. What if two peoples, each fully democratic in its form of government, keep on fundamentally hating each other or coveting each other's goods? What if two total outlooks fundamentally contradict each other? Democracy is a great thing, but it is neither the only nor the greatest thing for which man hungers. And there are peoples who, preferring to develop other values than the political, are not much bothered by who rules them provided they feel they are sufficiently cared for, loved and protected.

America can be justly proud of what its democracy has been able to achieve. The rest of the world, however, thirsts for something infinitely deeper than freedom, democracy and independence, and when it inquires into the American message, it wonders how America is going to blossom in these deeper things.

America means technology: the reasoned exploitation of the resources of nature for the benefit of man. This is indeed a great contribution, considering the millions and millions of people throughout the world who are helpless before the forces of nature, and for whom a slight improvement in technique will mean a more abundant life.

But technology may be bought at a high price: the attenuation of the spirit. The inordinate concentration upon material and economic conditions inevitably leads to the blurring of the original sources of the spirit; sources that are utterly independent of all things material. A man who spends all his life exploring and controlling nature may end by thinking of other human beings as just nature to be controlled. Nor is a technologically perfect world necessarily a good one; for it may still be full of hatred and fear and lust, and the stature of man may be considerably diminished in it.

In the positive American tradition there are deeper things than technology. There are adventure and self-confidence; there is the zest of discovery and the joy of creation; there is mutual helpfulness and self-giving; there is an implicit trust in reason and discussion; and there is a committing of one's self to the Providence of God. It is these things that made technology possible in the first place. And while, if I were an American, I would be justly proud of the infinite techniques that my civilization has created, I would nevertheless seek first to understand and love the original creative spirit itself, in its joy and in its unity.

America means action: a premium upon practical objective realization, the passage of idea into fact. This is a wonderful message, considering how much there is still to be done for the betterment of man's lot, and considering that whole cultures have been arrested precisely because either they could not discriminate between fantasy and fact or because even the true idea remained forever in the head. Boldness to decide, to act, to bring deliberations to an end—nothing can be more wonderful than all this.

But it is evident that action itself must have an end. Nor can we pass restlessly from action to action if we are to remain human. Action pursued for its own sake leads inevitably to the worship of power; and power corrupts. Thus where and how to rest—that is the question. The old world stands to learn infinitely from the active American life; but now and then it asks itself the question: where does it all lead to?

The real justification is not action, nor the accumulation of material things but the creation of supreme human character made perfect through suffering; and such character—mellowed, wise, deep, understanding, loving—is impossible without rest in truth and God. Nothing is more needful than to balance action by thought and wisdom, movement by being and by the pause that seems the eternal. The old world, while deeply grateful for American activism and pragmatism, must nevertheless assert that all action must conform to pre-established principles that are lucid through and through to reason, and that the greatest "use" of thought is not just to produce useful things, but to help develop men of wisdom and understanding and truth; men whose existence is its own justification and without whom no culture can live and prosper.

Freedom, independence, democracy, technology, action—these things belong to the wisdom of America; a real and positive wisdom. The rest of the world must understand that this is part of the total meaning hailing them from this side. It is a much-needed tonic, a fresh breeze of hope.

These things would have had a freer course of development if America had not had to come out into the world. As you assume greater and greater responsibilities and become more and more entangled abroad, it is inevitable that your values will be pondered, weighed, questioned. You will find yourself limited by other valuations and other points of view. Asia, Africa, the Middle East, the Slavic world, Europe, Latin America—all these cultures have also their own words to utter. And the question is how to listen to all these words, how to merge cooperatively and harmoniously with all these cultures, without either losing heart or compromising one's own soul.

Is there any doubt that both the deepest in the American tradition and the present desperate moment in history require that America, having solved the problem of nature and of government and having integrated a whole continent, should now rise, in all humility and truth, to the challenge of leadership, to the end that, drawing the sustenance of her leadership from her finest Christian traditions, and striking in her message the vein of the universal, she may stress, not so much the material and formal conditions of existence, as the intellectual, moral and spiritual perfections of man? What is needed is depth, respect for the law of nature, emphasis upon equality and being, trust in reason and in its absolute ability to grasp and articulate the truth, a divine sense of humor, and above all, strength through faith: faith in the real living God and in all that He has concretely and authentically meant in history. There is neither life nor meaning apart from Him, and I believe that America, having been so much blessed by God, and owing so much directly to Christ, cannot in the maturation of her meaning to the world possibly forget Him.

JOHN A. McCONE

John A. McCone (1902–1991) followed a successful career as an industrialist with a noteworthy career as a government official serving in various capacities from the administration of Harry Truman to that of Lyndon Johnson. Born in San Francisco, he graduated from the University of California-Berkeley in 1922 and pursued a successful career in construction, aircraft manufacturing, and shipbuilding. His collaboration with various government agencies during World War II led to his extensive government service in the postwar era. McCone began this service in the Truman administration as undersecretary of the air force. In 1958 President Eisenhower appointed him to head the Atomic Energy Commission. Here he implemented the Atoms for Peace program, which promoted civilian uses of nuclear power. In 1961 he replaced Allen Dulles as director of the Central Intelligence Agency and served in this capacity until 1965. During his tenure, McCone dealt with such consequential matters as the Cuban Missile Crisis and the Vietnam War.

The Atomic Energy Commission
and the University

(1959)

President Father Hesburgh, Your Eminence Cardinal Konig, Reverend Monsignors and Fathers, honored guests, graduates who are today receiving their prized diplomas from Notre Dame University, ladies and gentlemen. I deeply and sincerely appreciate the great honor that Notre Dame has today given me. I accept it as a trust. With God's help I shall try to be worthy of that trust.

This honor links me to the glorious tradition of Notre Dame. Through the tradition of great teaching and sound direction, young men are equipped, as few others in this country, to face with hope and faith the challenging and perplexing world of today.

Thus, when you leave these halls with your degree you start with the advantage of an unusual endowment in mind and in Christian spirit.

In this scientific era, many of you will enter fields of specialization. Some of you will find careers in sciences, others in the humanities. May I, as one who was trained as an engineer in a less exacting era, suggest that you do not overlook the rich rewards that come from enriching your minds through a knowledge of many areas of human concern. The life of the fully developed person, the truly cultured man, is marked by an understanding of the humanities and the social sciences, as well as technical and scientific matters. To that we add the requirement of a belief in God, and a trust in the Christian way of life.

Notre Dame, throughout its long history, has successfully cultivated in its students—the future leaders of our country—an appreciation of both the responsibilities and the benefits which come to them because they are Americans and because they are free. I am proud to congratulate you—each one of you—for having grasped the opportunity of this valued education and for the successful completion of your courses in this University. You now possess a foundation of knowledge and of spirit which will mark you with distinction throughout your life.

My concern, as you men know, and as Father Hesburgh has said, is the atom. The Atomic Energy Commission's responsibility in this new and exciting scientific field is all-encompassing.

Let me briefly discuss the scope of our activities. We are, on the one hand, our nation's nuclear armorer. On the other hand, we are charged by law with the challenge of bringing the atom into the daily lives of the people of our great country and, indeed, of the world.

We hope and we pray that understanding among men will improve as we pursue and succeed in the second of these two responsibilities—the use of the atom for peaceful purposes. Then we and all others will know that the atom will serve always for man's benefit and advancement, never for his destruction.

Some months ago at a meeting with the press I was asked what particular activity of the Atomic Energy Commission held my greatest interest. I replied that it was the application of the atom to medicine. I had just visited several of our laboratories and studied the advanced work being done. Progress was being made in combating diseases, such as brain tumors and thyroid disorders, which had resisted all other forms of treatment.

I talked with the doctors and the scientists of their immediate successes, but more particularly of their hopes for the future. They seemed possessed with the prospects of their work. Though cancer eludes their grasp, they earnestly feel that the atom, with its many new and promising uses in medical research will point the way toward the answers to this mysterious disease.

Few people know—and I did not until I took my present office—that the Atomic Energy Commission is spending in the biomedical field alone, fifty million dollars a year, or three times the annual budget of Notre Dame University. Twenty-five hundred doctors and scientists serve in our laboratories and hospitals and are supported by an equal number of technicians.

This fascinating research ranges over a broad scope. It is increasing our understanding of nature's magic: photosynthesis. Using the radiation of the isotope carbon-14, our scientists study a wide range of subtle life processes in plants and animals.

But before the atom can be put to work, the rare nuclear materials essential to all fission process, must be brought into useful form. In this pursuit our work starts with mining uranium ore—for uranium is the source material for the nuclear fission. This ore is then concentrated in mills located close to the mines. Private industry now does this entire job.

From the mills the uranium travels a long route of extremely difficult, advanced physical and chemical processing. In our massive gaseous diffusion plants, of which historic Oak Ridge, Tennessee is the oldest, we separate the isotope uranium-235 from this uranium. At Hanford, in the state of Washington, and at Savannah River in South Carolina, this uranium is transformed into plutonium which is not found in nature. Plutonium and uranium-235 are the basic ingredients of a nuclear weapon. But, these elements and other products of equally intricate physical processes are also the foundation of nuclear power and all other beneficial uses of the atom.

What then is done with this material?

Great laboratories, directed by such eminent scientists as Norris Bradbury and Edward Teller and supported by four thousand other scientists and engineers, are engaged continuously and almost exclusively in the development of weapons. They do the research, create the designs, build and test the models, and draw the plans and specifications from which our weapons are built. A complex of hundreds of manufacturing plants, most of them owned by private industry, fabricate, assemble, and finally ship the finished weapon to storage sites.

This, then, completes our role as the nation's armorer. The weapons are deployed to our military forces as needed. I pray they will never be used but will always stand as a guardian of peace and the protector of the freedom so dear to us.

Let us turn now to the Atomic Energy Commission's challenge to explore and develop uses of the atom for man's benefit. Twelve thousand scientists and engineers devote themselves to this work.

To complement this fascinating research that is under way in the biomedical field, our physical scientists explore the material world.

Our engineers develop the means of applying this new knowledge. Let me mention a few examples.

The most fundamental of scientific studies employs the giant accelerator to discover ever smaller particles and to understand their significance in the sub-atomic world. The Commission has caused several of these machines to be built. Two, the Cosmotron at Brookhaven and the Bevatron at Berkeley are well known. A few days ago President Eisenhower announced that we would construct a linear accelerator under the mountains behind Stanford University. Two miles long, it will be more advanced than any existing in the world or planned—it will assure our continued leadership in nuclear physics.

The search for economical and, therefore, competitive nuclear power presents a challenge. Today, this goal escapes us. Tomorrow, it will be achieved. The scientist and engineer will lead the way toward the development of less costly means of producing electric energy from the atom. Fortunately, America possesses abundant quantities of coal and oil. As a result, we have the lowest cost power of any nation. Therefore, our need for nuclear power is not urgent. However, this abundance, of which I speak, may not always last. One day our ever-increasing demand will diminish our sources of conventional fuels. Then the atom will prove the cheapest and the most dependable means of producing power. Hence, we are determined to perfect our processes for producing electricity from the atom, knowing fully that by finding the answer to this difficult problem today, we are providing for tomorrow's vital needs.

Finally, there is the development of new applications of radioisotopes to research techniques and industrial processes. Few realize that steel plate coming from giant rolling mills is measured to the nearest thousandth of an inch by a radioisotope.

Four great research laboratories are devoted to the peaceful uses of the atom. They are operated at an annual cost of about 300 million dollars per year. They are, Brookhaven, on Long Island, Oak Ridge in Tennessee, Lawrence Radiation Laboratory in Berkeley, and Argonne in which Notre Dame plays such a significant role. They have been built by the Atomic Energy Commission at great cost. Each year, new advanced and exciting equipment and tools for research are added to them.

Three of these laboratories are operated by great universities—the fourth, Oak Ridge, by private industry with university participation.

Through the operation of our laboratories and the management of our research programs, the universities' relationship with us is direct and, conversely, our dependence on the university is complete.

Universities from Maine to California devote substantial scientific effort to basic atomic research. There are more than one thousand research contracts between the Commission and educational institutions for this great scientific work. Sixty million dollars will be the cost this year alone. Six thousand teachers and graduate students devote substantial time to the necessary research. Special advanced facilities are often provided. The particle accelerator installed in your own Notre Dame laboratory is one example. This machine is an essential tool for your radiation chemistry project under the noted leadership of Professor Milton Burton.

Beyond our direct support of such vital research programs, we help universities acquire the specialized equipment needed for instruction in the advanced fields of our concern. Grants-in-aid have been made for the purchase of simple sub-critical assemblies to acquaint students with the nature and control of the fission process. Some universities have also been provided laboratory equipment for use in other instruction. By such means will this nation be ensured a supply of well-trained scientists and engineers so essential to its welfare and future development.

The management of our laboratories, the direction of our research effort, the performance of essential work in your own situations in cooperation with us represents the link between the University and the Atomic Energy Commission.

There exists a carefully designed and well-constructed bridge between the university and the Atomic Energy Commission in our relentless search for new knowledge in nuclear science.

Specific examples of this relationship are the advanced genetics program of the California Institute of Technology, the high energy physics research of Harvard and the Massachusetts Institute of Technology, and the basic materials research at Iowa State at Ames. But none, in my opinion, is of greater importance to us, and to the people of the world, than the basic research in radiology and radiation carried on year after year here in Notre Dame. In these fields you excel. We consider your efforts pillars of our research program, and I believe this work will expand substantially with time.

I can foresee a new, fine laboratory on this campus which will be devoted exclusively to basic research in radiation chemistry. Your faculty feels it essential. Ways will be found to provide it. Personally, I feel it is within the province of the government to help universities with their scientific work by providing facilities essential to both government and university needs. I am an advocate of these programs. I believe that our progress in atomic energy, in defense, and in the space age, require the best in the university. This is the starting point, as I have said, of the search for new scientific knowledge.

In these few minutes my purpose has been to present in the broadest terms a picture of our activities and the interrelationship of the university and the Atomic Energy Commission in the conduct of our affairs.

Without the university in its persistent drive for truth and basic knowledge, the atom might never have been split. The great plants at Oak Ridge, Paducah, and Hanford, might never have been built. Without the university our nation's progress in the application of the atom in the fields of biology, medicine, agriculture, and industry—and for the production of power—would, in my opinion, be at a standstill.

Early in World War II when the nation faced a desperate and powerful enemy, it was recognized that if we could release, at our command, an atomic chain reaction, and do it first, our security would be guaranteed. The men who arrived at this conclusion saw beyond the then tragic conflict. They saw unlimited future benefits to man from the same source of energy which they confidently felt would secure his freedom.

Therefore, they decided upon a courageous step. It has proven a very wise one. Equally wise was the decision to draw upon the great universities of our country in this enormous venture into an unknown scientific field. By so doing we accomplished a task that most men would regard as impossible because it brought to bear on this perplexing problem the vision and imagination of the best of our theoretical scientists. We can thank such men as Vannevar Bush, Ernest Lawrence, Enrico Fermi, and Albert Einstein for our success.

The atom will bear on the lives of all of you. It will change the world in which you live. Thus, it demands your thoughtful concern. Basic research now in progress will open new vistas for you. Theories being formulated and tested this very moment may give you new ways to obtain energy, food, transportation, water, and almost every material human need.

Present-day work of mathematicians and physicists—some no older than you—will provide new means to sustain and enrich men's lives. During your lifetime man will produce electricity on this earth by a means which heretofore the sun alone had used. Before that, however, the energy of your era will increasingly be supplied by the nuclear reactor. This in itself will change many things in our lifetime—the economics of industrial geography, the standards of engineering practice, the raw material needs of the giant utility manufacturing industry.

Lastly, you will be citizens of an age of change. Whatever you do—you will do in new ways with new tools and new products and new ideas.

Many of you young men have already been initiated into this scientific work. Scores, perhaps hundreds, will entrust your fate to this endeavor. Some will do so as scientists and as teachers, others as industrialists, and still others as lawyers or businessmen. Many of you, I hope, will find your future in the service of your government. Public service is a challenging and rewarding experience. Personal sacrifice is often involved, but you will find, as I have, that the privileges of serving your government far outweigh the sacrifice.

The President of your University is a wonderful example of a man who willingly responds to his Government's call and works with great energy and dedication on every task assigned to him. This I know from personal observation. The Argonne National Laboratory, with its vitally important International School of Nuclear Science, flourishes under his watchful eye. The International Atomic Energy Agency in Vienna, where 61 nations work together to plan and to promote the peaceful uses of the atom, respects Father Hesburgh for the great contribution he makes to the Agency's affairs as the delegate and representative of the Vatican. His frequent trips to Washington are made necessary because his wise counsel is both sought and respected. This, then, is an example of a man willing to sacrifice to serve his government and satisfied that the rewards warrant the sacrifice.

There is need in public life for men of your training; men who have had the privilege of Catholic education; men whose ideals and values of life have been molded by the dedicated Fathers in Notre

Dame as they have given you the instruction which you have this day completed.

I congratulate you sincerely and enthusiastically upon your graduation from Notre Dame. You have earned this badge of distinction that you will wear with honor for the remainder of your life. Many of you will find your future in the field of my principal concern, atomic energy. I hope this will be so, for I believe man's ability to survive on this earth hinges upon his success in developing ways to use the atom for the benefit of mankind—never for its destruction. Men with the training and the deep convictions which providentially have come to you are needed to undertake this task and to do it well.

DWIGHT D. EISENHOWER

—*m*—

The prepresidential achievements of Dwight D. Eisenhower
(1890–1969) are as significant as those that occurred after he took
the oath of office. One of the major figures of the twentieth century,
Eisenhower was born in Denison, Texas. He grew up in Abilene,
Kansas, from where he matriculated to West Point. Commissioned
an officer in 1915, he began a notable three-decade career in the
army. Although his advancement was slow in the interwar years,
he rose meteorically in rank during World War II. After successfully
commanding the American forces in North Africa, Eisenhower
became the supreme commander of all Allied forces in Europe.
He led the Allied invasion of Normandy and coordinated the defeat
of Hitler's forces in Western Europe. After the war he served briefly
as army chief of staff, as president of Columbia University,
and as commander of NATO forces in Europe.

In 1952 Eisenhower secured the Republican Party's nomination
for the presidency and easily defeated Adlai Stevenson to enter the
White House. He proved a capable president who continued the
internationalist direction of American foreign policy and pursued
a moderately conservative domestic agenda. He secured an armistice
to end the Korean War and generally presided over an era
characterized by peace and prosperity. He proved hesitant,
however, to use his immense personal and political popularity
to further the cause of civil rights and he left office
in 1961 warning of the power of the
"military-industrial complex."

—*m*—

Beyond the Campus

(1960)

At Commencement time in our country a generation ago, a well-known Englishman felt an urge to tell us something about ourselves. The theme he selected was, "Why don't young Americans care about politics?"

He felt that the attitude of our young people toward civil government, at all levels, was like that of "the audience at a play."

* * *

There may be a plausible, if not necessarily a valid, explanation for the American's traditional indifference to politics.

Historically, the 19th century in America was one of amazing growth. A wilderness needed conquering; vast resources had to be utilized; illiteracy had to be eliminated; a great economic machine, reaching to every corner of the world, had to be built. This unprecedented development commanded extraordinary talents in our private enterprise system. To people busy in productive life, government seemed not only remote but relatively unimportant. The demand for real skills in political pursuits was minimal.

Moreover, in that long period, a view developed that political life was somewhat degrading—that politics was primarily a contest, with the spoils to the victor and the public paying the bill. This belief had some justification at one period in our history, and may still persist in isolated local situations.

It has caused many of the most highly talented to refrain from offering themselves for public service.

But times and government have changed. The first major party platform drafted in 1840 required only 500 words; in the last national election each major party used over 15,000 words to deal with the highlights of the principle issues. This thirty-fold growth in political platforms is illustrative of the increase of governmental influence over all our lives.

The need for the best talent in positions of political responsibility is not only great, but mounts with each stroke of history's clock.

A few years ago, government represented only a small fraction of the total national activity. Today, to support our national, state and local governments, and to finance our international undertakings, almost one-fourth of the total national income is collected in taxes. In every phase of life, government increasingly affects us—our environment, our opportunities, our health, our education, our general welfare.

Government is, of course, necessary, but it is not the mainspring of progress. In the private sector of American life, commanding as it does the productive efforts of our citizens, is found the true source of our nation's vitality. Government is not of itself a part of our productive machinery. Consequently its size, its growth, its operations can be justified only by need. If too dominant, if too large, its effect is both burdensome and stifling.

Only an informed and alert citizenry can make the necessary judgments as to the character and degree of need.

We do not want a government with a philosophy of incessant meddling, which imposes a smothering mist on the sparks of initiative.

We do not want a government that permits every noisy group to force upon society an endless string of higher subsidies that solve nothing and undermine the collective good of the nation.

We do not want governmental programs which, advanced, often falsely, in the guise of promoting the general welfare destroy in the individual those priceless qualities of self-dependence, self-confidence, and a readiness to risk his judgment against the trends of the crowd.

We do want a government that assures the security and general welfare of the nation in concord with the philosophy of Abraham Lincoln, who insisted that government should do, and do only, the things which people cannot do for themselves.

This concept is particularly relevant to most activities encompassed by the phrase "the general welfare."

But even with devotion to the principle that governmental functions can be justified only by public need, government has become so pervasive that its decisions inescapably help shape the future of every individual, every group, every region, every institution.

Though we recognize this vast change—and though most persons in public office are selfless, devoted people—we are still plagued by yesterday's concept of politics and politicians.

Too many of our ablest citizens draw back, evidently fearful of being sullied in the broiling activity of partisan affairs.

This must change. We need intelligent, creative, steady political leadership as at no time before in our history. There must be more talent in government—the best our nation affords. We need it in county, state and Washington.

Surely we should look to the growing body of college-educated men and women to lift political life and activity to the high standards required in this free country. Here is a task for every individual; no one can excuse himself and yet claim the proud title of good citizen.

Human progress in freedom is not something inscribed upon a tablet—not a matter to be shrugged off as a worry to others. Progress in freedom demands from each citizen a daily exercise of the will and spirit, and a fierce faith; it must not be stagnated by a philosophy of collectivity that vainly seeks personal security as a prime objective.

Clearly, you who enjoy the blessings of higher education have a special responsibility to exercise leadership in helping others understand such questions.

And, by no means, does your responsibility stop there. To serve the nation well you must, for example, help seek out able candidates for office and persuade them to offer themselves to the electorate. To be most effective you should become active in a political party, and in civic and professional organizations. In short, you should undertake, according to your own intelligently formed convictions, a personal crusade to help the political life of the nation soar as high as human wisdom can make it.

Some of you will become doctors, lawyers, teachers, clergymen, businessmen. Each of you will contribute to the national welfare, as well as to personal and family welfare, by doing well and honorably whatever you undertake. But a specialist, regardless of professional skill and standing, cannot fulfill the exacting requirements of modern citizenship unless he dedicates himself also to raising the political standards of the body politic.

I hope that some of you will enter the public service, either in elective, career, or appointive office. Most of the top posts in government involve manifold questions of policy. In these positions we have a particular need for intelligent, educated, selfless persons from all walks of life.

I believe that each of you should, if called, be willing to devote one block of your life to government service.

This does not mean that you need become permanently implanted in government. Quite the contrary. In policy-forming positions we constantly need expert knowledge and fresh points of view. Some frequency of withdrawal and return to private life would help eliminate the dangerous concept that permanence in office is more important than the rightness of decision. Contrary-wise, such a tour should not be so brief as to minimize the value of the contribution and diminish the quality of public service. Normally, a four-year period in these policy posts would seem to be a minimum. Most leaders from private life who enter the public service do so at a substantial sacrifice in the earning power of their productive years.

Although these personal sacrifices are, by most individuals, accepted as a condition of service, yet when these sacrifices become so great as to be unendurable from the family standpoint, we find another cause for the loss of talent in government.

We ought not to make it inordinately difficult for a man to undertake a public post and then to return to his own vocation. In the public service, one must obviously have no selfish end to serve, but citizens should not, invariably, be required to divest themselves of investments accumulated over a lifetime in order to qualify for public office. The basic question is this—is such divestment necessary to remove any likelihood that the probity and objectivity of his governmental decisions will be affected? And the question is proper whether the individual holds either elective or appointive office. We need to review carefully the conflict-of-interest restrictions which have often prohibited the entry into government of men and women who had much to offer their country.

*   *   *

But let me return to the more broadly-based consideration: that thinking Americans in all walks of life must constantly add to their own knowledge and help build a more enlightened public opinion. For herein lies the success of all government policy and action in a free society.

Leaders in America must develop a keen understanding of current issues, foreign and domestic—and of political party organization, operation, and platform.

They must have critical judgments regarding actions being proposed or taken by legislatures and executives at all levels of government. They need to be knowledgeable enough not to be misled by catchwords or doctrinaire slogans.

Thus they can analyze objectively how such actions may affect them, their communities, and their country—and help others to a similar understanding.

Political understanding, widely fostered, will compel government to develop national and international programs truly for the general good, and to refrain from doing those things that unduly favor special groups or impinge upon the citizen's own responsibility, self-dependence, and opportunities.

*   *   *

Graduates of the Class of 1960: A half century ago, when I was about to enter West Point—and, incidentally, to meet soon thereafter and to know that gridiron genius, Knute Rockne—our country was in what now seems to have been a different era. The annual federal budget was below seven hundred million dollars. Today it has increased more than one hundred-fold, and organized groups demand more and more services, both expansive and costly. At the turn of the century there was a certain grace, calmness, and courtliness about human deportment and the movement of events.

Now we operate on a relentless timetable which we must race to keep events from overwhelming us.

Complicating the lives of all of us today we know that in the dimly-lit regions behind the Iron Curtain, eight hundred million people are denied the uncountable blessings of progress in freedom, and compelled to develop vast means of destructive power. Elsewhere, among the underdeveloped countries of the world, a billion people look to America as a beacon that confidently lights the path to human progress in freedom.

This is no time to whimper, complain, or fret about helping other peoples, if we really intend that freedom shall emerge triumphant over tyranny.

The enemies of human dignity lurk in a thousand places—in governments that have become spiritual wastelands, and in leaders that brandish angry epithets, slogans, and satellites. But equally certain it is that freedom is imperiled where peoples, worshipping material success, have become emptied of idealism. Peace with justice cannot be attained by peoples where opulence has dulled the spirit—where indifference has supplanted moral and political responsibility.

*   *   *

Too often there is, in politics as in religion, a familiar pattern of the few willing workers and the large number of passive observers. Our society can no longer tolerate such delinquency.

We must insist that our educated young men and women—our future leaders—willingly, joyously play a pivotal part in the endless adventure of free government. The vital issues of freedom or regimentation, public or private control of productive resources, a religiously-inspired or an atheistic society, a healthy economy or depression, peace or war—these are the substance of political decision and action. They must command the dedicated attention of all the people, and especially all who have so profoundly benefited from our vast educational system.

Thank you—and may God Bless You.

ROBERT SARGENT SHRIVER, JR.

*Born in Maryland and educated at Yale College and Law School,
Robert Sargent Shriver, Jr. (1915–) practiced briefly as a lawyer before
serving in the navy in World War II. After the war he helped run
the Kennedy family's business operations and managed the
Merchandise Mart in Chicago from 1948 to 1961. In 1953 he
married Eunice Kennedy, with whom he had four sons and a
daughter, Maria. Active in civic and religious affairs, Shriver served
as president of the Catholic Interracial Council in Chicago
from 1955 to 1960. With the election of his brother-in-law,
John F. Kennedy, Shriver accepted responsibility to found and direct
the Peace Corps. This effort sent American volunteers abroad to serve
developmental needs of Third World countries and, it was hoped,
to build goodwill towards the United States. Shriver commendably
led the Peace Corps until 1966 and also ran the Office of Economic
Opportunity from 1964 to 1968, which had overall responsibility
for Lyndon Johnson's War on Poverty. After a stint as ambassador
to France he returned to the practice of law. He interrupted his
duties with his law firm to join George McGovern on the ill-fated
Democratic presidential ticket in 1972. With his wife he founded
the Special Olympics Organization. Notre Dame awarded the
Laetare Medal to Shriver in 1968 and twenty years later conferred
this honor, its highest, upon his wife.*

The Peace Corps
and Higher Education

(1961)

Today is Graduation Day at Notre Dame—your graduation day—the day you have longed for and worked hard to reach—the day your parents have saved and planned for. It is a day for congratulations and rejoicing. On this day every hope and dream and ambition seems attainable. The young can optimistically anticipate futures filled with happiness and success; parents and teachers can thank God for permitting them to share in the present triumphs and to indulge in happy foretastes of future achievements.

But today is an important day, not only in your lives, but in the history of higher education in our country. For on this day I am privileged to announce the first agreement of its kind ever reached between an agency of the U.S. Government, a consortium of American universities, and a foreign country.

The foreign country is Chile.

The agency of the U.S. Government is the Peace Corps.

The consortium of American universities is the Indiana Conference on Higher Education, with your own university, Notre Dame, taking the lead and serving as the principal agent in this new arrangement.

What's new about this agreement? Many things.

First: —there are 34 colleges and universities all cooperating in it. That's never happened before.

Second: —among these colleges are Catholic, Quaker, Methodist, Presbyterian and other religious institutions, all working *together* to achieve a *national* goal. And these *private*, educational groups have been joined by the *public* universities and colleges like Purdue, Indiana University, and Indiana College. This broad cooperation on a joint enterprise has never happened before.

Third: —this consortium of private, educational institutions has agreed to work with and through a private Chilean organization called the Instituto de Educacion Rural—and for the first time the Chilean government has put its blessing on such an undertaking.

Fourth: —the U.S. Government, represented by the Peace Corps, has entered an agreement with all these universities and colleges more flexible, simpler, easier to administer, and satisfying to the academic community than ever before.

And finally, of course, this is the first Peace Corps agreement ever negotiated with any university or group of universities.

So far as I am concerned, this is not just "news" in the transient sense of here today, gone tomorrow. Much more than that it is the fulfillment of a most important objective.

In his message to Congress on the Peace Corps, President Kennedy said that many of the most important Peace Corps projects would be carried out in partnership with American colleges and universities. Those of us in the Peace Corps have felt from the very beginning of this program that the academic institutions of our nation have the accumulation of overseas experience, the reservoir of trained leadership, and the inherent goal of intellectual and spiritual dynamism necessary to make a far-reaching contribution to international service. For example, in our new budget of $40,000,000, we have in fact proposed that $26,000,000—much more than one-half the total—be expended through universities and private, voluntary agencies.

But it hasn't been easy to work out this new marriage between government and education. At one point Father Hesburgh, Peter Fraenkal of Indiana University, and a Peace Corps staff member went all the way to Chile and worked there for two weeks straightening out details. Also, within the Federal Government there are many laws and regulations to observe in any attempt, no matter how well-intentioned, to open up new, more effective ways of doing business between private institutions and the public.

But success has come, and with it a great new chance for our universities, our government, and for our university professors and students. Under this new agreement, young men and women from the heartland of America will be recruited, trained, and sent abroad, to work in that part of Chile where the need and the opportunity are greatest. They will go there *not* for a summer vacation of fun or excitement, not to look-see like tourists, not to look down upon the ignorant and poor from a position of lofty, Yankee superiority. Instead they will be sent to work and work hard alongside other human beings in need of what we and we alone can give them—hope, skill, and a knowledge of the dignity of man under the Fatherhood of God.

Peace Corps Volunteers will work in horticulture, animal vaccination, carpentry, family education and recreation, home economics, health education, first aid, and child care. They will work with Chilean experts and with Chilean students.

One of their most important tasks will be to develop more interest in radio educational programs designed to lift the standard of learning in the villages of Chile.

In our country, Peace Corps Volunteers will receive intensive training—in languages, in physical fitness, in the history, culture and customs of Chile. And in Chile they will get additional training from the Instituto de Educacion Rural, the private Chilean organization distinguished for its excellent program in fundamental education and community development in rural areas.

But you may say: —Why should we go to all this trouble for Chile? There are many problems here at home. The poor and the needy are here too.

The answer is easy and true even though you may not believe it. It's very simple.

First of all, there's nobody in this country as poverty-stricken and hopeless, no one as cut off from educational opportunity and medical assistance as the millions in southernmost Chile, in India, in Pakistan, in northeastern Brazil, and in many other countries. There is no comparison between the need abroad and the need here at home.

Second, and more important, is the fact that we as Christians must fulfill our obligations to our fellow men, or God may well permit others to crush us. Either we do these jobs or the Communists will. And if we don't meet the test, the days of the Catacombs will return sooner than many suspect. For as our Lord Himself said:

> Would that you were cold or hot; and so because you are luke-warm and neither cold nor hot, I am going to vomit you out of my mouth. You say 'I am rich and have become wealthy and have no need of anything.' But you do not know that you are wretched and pitiable and poor and blind and naked.
> (Apocalypse 3:15–17)

The shocking fact is that this is exactly what the Communists say about us.

The Communists say that Americans have gone soft. Only recently Khrushchev branded American young people as "dissident good-for-nothings." On my recent trip around the world I encountered serious doubts about the ability of Americans to make the sacrifices essential for the Peace Corps or any other program of voluntary service abroad. The one big question seems to be is America qualified to lead the free world?

I believe we are and I'll tell you why.

The Peace Corps has been in existence only three months, but I have talked to many would-be volunteers who have the faith and conviction to make the sacrifices necessary to serve under Peace Corps conditions and according to Peace Corps standards in various parts of the world.

They have been called the silent generation, these men and women who are volunteering to serve in the Peace Corps, as surveyors in Tanganyika, farm extension workers in Colombia, teachers in rural schools in the Philippines, and now as community development workers in Chile. They are coming quietly to enlist for two-year terms of hard work in Africa, Asia, and Latin America. I believe they will meet the great tests they will face abroad with calm humor and steady perseverance.

For inside the silence, contained by a tough shell of skepticism, is a core of idealism. The stirring words of Wilson and the radiant optimism of Roosevelt have been tempered by world wars and depressions and by the long winter of the cold war. But I am convinced that faith in democracy, the belief in a civilization based on the God-given dignity of the individual human being, the readiness to sacrifice to enable such a civilization to live and grow—this is there, this has been waiting to be tapped, this is what the Peace Corps is tapping.

Nikita Khrushchev is not alone in doubting the fibre of modern Americans. This is a question asked all around the world.

In India, Ashadevi, a spirited woman associate of Gandhi, was so stirred by the idea of the Peace Corps that she interrupted her pilgrimage in Assam, traveled three days and three nights on a train, to put one great question to me.

"Yours was the first revolution," she said. "Do you think young Americans possess the spiritual values they must have to bring the spirit of that revolution to our country?"

"There is a great valuelessness spreading in the world, and in India, too," she said. "Your Volunteers must not add to this. They must bring more than science and technology. They must be carriers of your best American values and ideals. Even the Russians have their values beyond science and technology. Your Peace Corps must touch the idealism of America and bring that to us."

This is our aim, I assured her. But how will we accomplish it?

First of all, by a very careful selection of the men and women who are accepted as Volunteers. The academic tests which each applicant takes, the personal interviews he will have, the medical and psychological examinations, and the screening that will go on during training are all designed to pick out volunteers who will represent the best of American life, thought, dedication, and skill. We want men and women who are fit, physically, mentally, and spiritually, who are ready to work with their heads, their hands, and their hearts; who are able to discuss the Declaration of Independence and the problems of modern democracy with a student in Ghana or a farmer in Colombia; and who are trained to do a job that is needed and desired in the host country. I believe we will find those men and women among the 10,000 who have already volunteered.

Second, we will provide intensive training in the language, history, current affairs, and customs of the country to which they are going; in the health care required; and in the work to be done. Intensive refresher courses in American history and government will help prepare Volunteers for some of the questions they will be asked. Training periods will also be conducted in some of the countries where the Volunteers will serve.

For men and women selected and trained in these ways, there is an abundance of jobs in the developing nations. The Peace Corps needs both college graduates and skilled workmen who have not been to college; we need both liberal arts graduates and graduates with specialized degrees; we need both men from business and men from labor unions; we need women as well as men. The list of requests already includes doctors, nurses, public health workers, lawyers, farmers, labor negotiators, management experts, engineers, plumbers, electricians, athletic coaches, and teachers of all kinds, including teachers of English, for primary and secondary schools, and in universities.

The eight countries I recently visited asked for more than 3,500 Americans immediately. Prime Minister Nehru of India, President Nkrumah of Ghana, Prime Minister U Nu of Burma, President Garcias of the Philippines all hailed the Peace Corps. Some of them, I do not have to remind you, have *not* been favorable to all American policies.

In the Punjab the chief of a village said: "If someone from the Peace Corps would come here, we would welcome him. Whatever poor facilities we have, we would share with him." In another country the governor of a province said: "We have the mind and heart to do things. Our people are ready to move. We need your skills to help us start."

The real question, then, is not one of demand, but supply. Can we really find, recruit, and train Americans who will meet this challenge?

I think we can. Almost 4,000 Americans have already taken the first Peace Corps tests. Applications are coming in at the rate of more than one hundred a day. These Volunteers are saying to the world: "You can count on us."

There is a world-wide struggle going on. A revolution. All men are trying to achieve human dignity and a common identity. You and I are part of that struggle, for no matter whether a man be Jew, Buddhist, Moslem, Hindu, Communist, or Christian, he has been born of woman like every other man alive, he is living on this small spinning planet like every other man alive; he needs food, shelter, and spiritual comfort like every other man alive; and he will die the death like every other man alive. And if there is a destiny after death, the community of our experience here on this earth indicates that any life hereafter will be common to all.

It is easy to see and even magnify the differences among men: color, education, genetical inheritance, religion. But the new generation is beginning to realize that whereas political rationalism and economic aggressiveness may divide men, the most important of all experiences unite them—birth, marriage, death, destiny.

Many people in our land and overseas may not yet even understand why they are so stirred within their deepest reaches, but, as President Kennedy said in his message to Congress on the Peace Corps: "Throughout the world people are struggling for economic and social progress which reflects their deepest desires. Our own freedom, and the future of freedom around the world, depend, in a very real sense, on the ability to build growing and independent nations where men can live in dignity, liberated from the bonds of hunger, ignorance, and poverty."

The purpose of the Peace Corps is to permit Americans to participate directly, personally and effectively, in this struggle for human dignity. A world community is struggling to be born. America must be present at that birth, helping to make it successful.

Our volunteers must go with a true spirit of humility, seeking to learn as well as to teach. If they go in this spirit, America will gain most. And our greatest gain will be measured in the lives of the volunteers. They will, as President Kennedy has said, "be enriched by the experience of living and working in foreign lands—they will return better able to assume the responsibilities of American citizenship and with greater understanding of our global responsibilities."

Notre Dame is famous for its Victory March. It's famous for its philosophy of playing the game to win. As General Douglas MacArthur said, and as Notre Dame practices—"There is no substitute for victory."

I hope and believe that in its program with the Peace Corps, Notre Dame will live up to its reputation for success.

McGEORGE BUNDY

*McGeorge Bundy (1919–1996) is best remembered for his
service from 1961 to 1966 as national security adviser to
Presidents John F. Kennedy and Lyndon B. Johnson. Bundy
participated in many crucial foreign policy issues during this period,
including the Bay of Pigs invasion, the Berlin Wall episode,
the Cuban Missile Crisis, as well as the escalation of U.S.
involvement in Southeast Asia. From an establishment Boston
family, Bundy was educated at Groton School, Yale College,
and Harvard University.*

*After service in the army in World War II, he joined the faculty at
Harvard and became dean of arts and sciences in 1953 at the age
of thirty-four. He was a leading figure in "the best and the brightest"
contingent recruited by Kennedy for his administration. Bundy is
identified with the policy of sustained reprisals against North Vietnam
that was adopted by Lyndon Johnson in 1965, a policy that deepened
U.S. involvement in the Indochina conflict. Subjected to much
criticism for his role in formulating policy toward Vietnam, Bundy
left government service in 1966 to become president of the
Ford Foundation. In later years, he devoted himself
to writing history.*

American Power and Responsibility
(1965)

Father Hesburgh, I would like to take a moment, if I may, presuming to speak for all of us who have become instant alumni of Notre Dame today, to say how much we value this honor.

The University of Notre Dame over a hundred and twenty years, but at an accelerated speed in the last twenty years, has taken its place in the forefront of learning, not only of America, but of the world. I will say also, that for me personally it is a great honor to appear in the company of men and women who have done so much toward the work to which they are committed as the company in which I come to you today.

I would like also to join, if I may, in offering the warmest congratulations to all who have earned their Notre Dame degrees from the doctors of philosophy to the graduates in business administration. And I observe that, as is true in other academic exercises of this Spring, those who are the least learned make the most noise.

We all know that this day belongs really to those who take the first degree in art, science, engineering. We are grateful to you for letting us share in your joys and lengthen your afternoon.

Now, in casting about for an appropriate topic which would edify you without giving any displeasure in Washington, I have had a very difficult time, but I have finally concluded that I might at least escape the wrath of my employer if I were to direct your attention not to the events of your commencement year, but to those of my own, which happens to be 1940, and this is not a wholly egotistical exercise because it does happen that the Spring of 1940 marks the great modern turning point in the international affairs of the United States. It was in that month that what had been a phony war reached a terrible climax in the fall of France, and it was in a month, therefore, as a direct result that the United States, its people and government together, came face to face with the fact that choices of international affairs were real.

There is a sense in which the foreign affairs of the United States before 1940 are episodic, intermittent, unsustained, and in a measure even unreal, but from that day forward it has not been so.

We have been called first in series, and then in combinations, to address ourselves continuously for a quarter of a century to the obligations of great power. Our first task in a year was to make the beginnings toward the achievement of the power which had been merely potential before. And there is truth in the thought that the first five years, until the end of the second war, were occupied overwhelmingly with the problems of gaining power itself, its application, its use to the end of military victory, but it was not long before it became clear that if only as an end objective of the war itself, and in a larger way for broader reasons too, we must be preoccupied not simply with the gaining and the use of this extraordinary power, but with the end to which it should be used, and that end beyond victory was peace.

To many of us who served in that war it seemed too easy that victory itself would mean world peace.

We did not foresee the complexities and hazards and the error of the postwar world. We thought that we were forward looking when we gave our new allegiance to the notion of a new world organization when we saw and cheered the work of Franklin Roosevelt and those about him as they organized the U.N.; as they framed the charter for that organization; as they brought together a rolling and almost unanimous consensus first within this country and then beyond the borders for the notion of organization for peace. And we supposed that after war there would come peace.

So, that made two steps, new for our generation: The acceptance of power. The objective of peace and the responsibility for action to achieve it. It became clear very soon after the war that you could not simply win a victory or sign a peace. You had to build and you had to build in a world which was torn apart by destruction and shaking with beginning hopes, and the United States of America in serving its own interests must give its attention to the interests of others.

Now, I always thought that our generation, and, indeed, our nation, were extraordinarily fortunate that the first president of this age of world power was Franklin Roosevelt, a man to whom the notion of the hopes and aspirations of others came naturally so that in the opening frames of this long motion picture it was the expectation of the land he led; that power and peace both imply concern for the needs and the hopes and the interests of others. But, that seemed in a sense a separate undertaking; relief, rehabilitation, reconstruction, the World

Bank, even the Marshall Plan, exercises which would be completed and after which again the world would take up its own movement.

And then we found ourselves confronting a fourth continuing reality, the reality that there are great centers of power now increasing, greater centers of power in the world committed to imperialism and an effort for constantly expanding power, influence and prestige of their own; that if they were not resisted they would have their way on an ever wider scale; and that if they were to be resisted the responsibility in the first instance must fall to the United States.

And so we find ourselves, through no desire of our own, in what by common consent we have come to call the Cold War, and that for a while seemed preoccupied, and many, perhaps too many, came to think that this was the only reality.

Now, I submit to you gentlemen that the world in which you come to graduate is a world in which these four great facts of American life are still all with us, and I submit to you also that the tribulations and difficulties of 1965 are not greater than those through which we have come in the last twenty-five years.

I think it is true that we have met in the main the responsibility of having and of holding and of using the great power which comes to us by our size and strength and our social, economic and political success. I think that we have been true in the main to a continuing purpose of peace and have been ready to accept the discipline of membership in an international society wider than our own. I think that we have given respect, not always in the perfect order, but always I think with basic national good will to the fact that there are interests, hopes and purposes not the same as ours, that we have conducted our affairs so as to permit and even to encourage the diversity which the world has by the nature of its peoples and its countries and its climates, and that we have not sought to make of this an American century; and I think that in the main we have met the challenge where we could and as we could, posed not for us alone, but for the hopes of all free men by the ambitions of the communist imperialists.

The record is by no means perfect. We have had to learn much. If we had been told in 1940, that we would have it all to learn before our fiftieth birthday, it would have staggered us. We might not then have left the mark. We have had moments of weariness and weakness, moments of division and doubt. We have had debates, greater debates I think than any that we face this spring. The most severe, perhaps, the one at the beginning, in 1940 and in 1941, over whether we should go this course at all. For what was said about the administration of 1940 by the isolationists in the colleges, at least in invertive and sometimes I think in also analytic strength was much more powerful than we had to endure this spring from our critics. These great debates continue.

In 1947 was it right to try to save the Greeks, a hopeless and a helpless group beyond our interests and our range? In 1948, should we throw good money after bad and try to rescue the shiftless peoples of Western Europe? In 1949 was it really right to sign away our power to decide for ourselves, to break the traditions set for us by Washington enjoined in the North Atlantic Treaty? And perhaps you gentlemen are old enough to remember the turmoil and the trauma which surrounded the Korean War, which remains, nevertheless, the most extraordinary exercise of presidential courage in the whole long quarter century.

So, there have been troubles along the way, and there will be more to come. They come increasingly, I think, because what began one step at a time, one problem at a time; first power used in war then building of a peaceful organization, then reconstruction, and then the communist threat, what began that was in single stranded problems each to be met anew as if it were separate and alone, has now become a mixed continuing exercise, so that when we look as we must at the hard problems of Santo Domingo and Saigon, we are looking at problems of power and of peace and of the interests of other men and also of the ambitions of the communists, and we must look at them all four at once, work upon them, try to serve our purposes; all of them, at once.

It is not surprising then if one stands back from the wisdom or error of individuals, or even of administrations; that as we try to go about our business in a world so wide, so complex, so dangerous, there are times when we have argument, times when we have uncertainty. What is much more remarkable is that we belong to a society to which this choice was offered such a very short time ago, as human time is measured; that in a quarter century we have been able to make the progress we have made in remaking our ways of thought and action in setting ourselves to the tasks to be done, and in holding ourselves together as the first example in history of a society which retains its internal freedom while meeting these extraordinary responsibilities of world power.

I do not mean to say that others have not come a great distance along the same road. One thinks particularly of the achievements of the British in the 19th century, but there is something unprecedented nonetheless about the work which our country has done, of which our countrymen have done, and to which you are now called.

—ɯ—

EUGENE McCARTHY

*Eugene McCarthy (1916–) quickly rose to national prominence
in 1968 when the then Minnesota senator challenged (and almost
defeated) Lyndon Johnson in the New Hampshire primary over the
issue of the Vietnam War. Born in Watkins, Minnesota, McCarthy
attended St. John's University, Collegeville, and the University
of Minnesota, where he developed a firm grasp of and commitment
to the principles of Catholic social thought. McCarthy taught at
St. John's before serving as a civilian military intelligence analyst
during World War II. Following a teaching stint at the College
of St. Thomas in St. Paul, he was elected to Congress as a member
of the Democratic Farmer Labor Party in 1948. A decade later he
entered the U.S. Senate and served two terms, earning a
reputation for integrity and erudition.*

*McCarthy's firm antiwar sentiments led to his seemingly quixotic
gesture of challenging the sitting president of his own party in 1968.
The demonstration of Johnson's vulnerability in New Hampshire
prompted Senator Robert F. Kennedy also to enter the race. McCarthy
continued his campaign and attracted many youthful supporters to
politics—all promising to "get clean for Gene"—but
the nomination eventually went to his fellow Minnesotan
Hubert H. Humphrey. McCarthy retired from the Senate in
1970 but continued to contribute to public life, primarily
through his commentary and writing.*

The Educated Person on Trial

(1967)

Giving a commencement address would be, if not for the protection given by tradition and by its place in the ritual of graduation, a dangerous if not a desperate venture.

This might seem like a good time for me to leave the platform, or if not to proceed to give a kind of "music-minus-one" speech with the melody left out, or to use the anti-commencement approach of Bob Hope who has been advising graduates not to leave college and come out into the world, which he describes as a harsh and rough place. I could choose the easier way of speaking on a subject of limited scope and current application.

I shall not take this easy way out, however. This is a time of special challenge. A commencement speaker, if he plays the game fairly, is expected to present the meaning and significance of all a student has learned in four years of college, and make a projection of the bearing of that learning on the life of each graduate and, in a more generalized and comprehensive way, on the society of the future.

Assuming the responsibility of such depth and breadth is not as difficult for members of the Senate as it might be for other persons. We are not unaccustomed to making rash judgments. Every civilization has of necessity developed a formally functioning body to give ultimate rash judgments—in some cases the medicine men are used, in others the witch doctors, oracles, or high priests. The contest of America today, in politics at least, is between members of the Senate and the columnists, who currently have a slight lead on the Senate but who are without the support of the Constitution which quite clearly directs the Senate to advise the President and, of course, by implication the country.

A commencement address, although it may have little significance to graduates on commencement day, should, if recalled thirty years later, seem in retrospect to have been worthwhile.

Forty-six years ago, a speaker at a Notre Dame commencement sent the graduates off into the world with these reassuring words:

> The line of demarcation between right and wrong in every situation that can confront us, whether in professional or business life, or civic and social action, or in the multitudinous details of domestic experience has been clearly and infallibly drawn for us.

Thirty years later, the graduates of that class must have been somewhat unsure of the applicability of this text, and forty years later even less sure as they attempt to deal with the problems of the new morality and of situational ethics, to say nothing of the multitudinous details of domestic experience.

Thirty-four years ago, in 1932 in the midst of the depression, the members of the graduating class of Notre Dame were told, among other things, that the later appraisal of the men of the Thirties would result in their being criticized not for having done too little but for having tried to do too much, and they were warned that the threat to government budgets was due to increased charges for health, educational and social betterment.

These warnings in the context of today's expanded welfare programs, new levels of production, slightly different views on balanced budgets, deficit financing and inflation are not wholly relevant.

Much of the text of an address given here only twenty-five years ago on the dignity of womanhood and on the contribution of the church to the definition, preservation, and advancement of that dignity does not quite fit the sociological, psychological, and theological context in which the role of women is being considered today.

Thirty years from now, or perhaps twenty years from now, and possibly within ten years what I say may be wholly out of date or irrelevant. If so, I will have this defense: that we are today not at a threshold but beyond it in an age in which we have more power and competence—physical and intellectual—than we have ever had before; in an age differing from previous ones in that the mass of problems—not just in politics but in every aspect of life—is greater than it has ever been before. It seems to us quite suddenly all of these press in upon us; all of them say, "We are here," and they demand from us some attention and some judgment and, following that, some commitment.

And secondly, in that the speed of change is more rapid than it has ever been, we are called upon today to respond not on a timetable of our own making, but on a schedule or a timetable made for the most part by the very movement of history itself.

The greatest problem today is not that of the dead hand of the past holding us back, but of the violent or the threatening hand of the future which reaches back for all of us—politicians, educators, students, theologians—everyone.

Consider how much simpler it was, let us say, for Leonardo da Vinci. In dealing with the problems of aerodynamics, he did not have to keep in mind the question of how what he discovered might be used in the design or development of intercontinental ballistic missiles. Or Descartes dealing in abstract mathematics, not having to take into account the fact that his mathematics would be applied through modern technology in the development of nuclear weapons, and not having to take into account the way in which computers and chain reactions can take an abstract or pure idea and give it magnified and terrible application. Or someone like the monk Gregory Mendel dealing with heredity in the patch of peas, not having to take into account the problems which the nuclear biologists today must face.

Decisions in all of these areas must be made in broad social context and, to some extent, through social organizations and formal institutions.

Despite the fact of change, we must not dismiss institutions and other storehouses of values and meanings, or discount their influence too quickly or too easily. On the other hand, we must be ready to accept change and to bring about change and to discard that which is no longer useful. Father Gregory Baum has written wisely in *The Ecumenist,* March–April, 1967:

> Since institutions are made to promote man's life in society, they inevitably reflect the understanding of man that is current at the time they are created. . . . What is happening today is that with a new self-understanding many Christians find that these institutions no longer adequately promote human life. . . . This does not mean that the men responsible for the institution were lacking in generosity and kindness. . . .
>
> It is the people living the life that must give shape to the institutional patterns that serve them, and it is in this very process of finding the best institutional forms that men are drawn into participation and begin to experience themselves in a new way.

More than ever these decisions must be made by individuals, facing new situations without clear formulas and without the protection of accepted rules and traditional practices.

The general call is for the emergence of the human person, for the intensification and personalization of life whether this be reflected in the call for the emergence of the bishops or the emergence of the laity in religious life, or the emergence of the Senate and the emergence of the more fully responsible citizen in political life, or the acceptance of a greater measure of responsibility on the part of corporate directors and also for the intellectual and moral involvement of stockholders and of employees in the determination of corporate policy.

Education, educators, and the educated are always on trial, but they are on trial in a very special and clear way today.

Forty years ago, Gilbert Chesterton wrote that every time problems arise someone gets up and says that what we need is a practical man to solve the problem. The difficulty, he said, was that there was usually one around or perhaps more than one. But today, in the face of new and complex problems, while the role of the practical man or the experienced is not wholly rejected, it is more common to ask for an educated man, a student, for one who has given study to the problem.

The educated person no longer has the excuse that he is rejected or unappreciated: an excuse which had some validity in the last century. He no longer has the opportunity to run far ahead of decisions; history somehow has caught up. The advanced position of the philosopher, of the scientist, of the historian, and of other scholars has been overrun in many instances.

Every intellectual discipline today is called upon to make some contribution to society, as is every educated person.

Each important judgment must be made within the context of history and in relation to moral judgment as to right and wrong.

Politicians and those responsible for government decision have throughout the history of mankind been concerned about what historians might say about them. They have worked out various devices to help with the record. Many carried their own scribes; some still do. Julius Caesar—a kind of do-it-yourself historian—used, I suppose, the safest method. He wrote his own history. In any case, not only politicians but people generally look today to history and historians, accepting both the poet Santayana's view that to ignore history is to repeat all the mistakes of the past, and that of the politician-historian Churchill that to depend only upon the past is the best way to lose the future. We are asking historians today, and everyone is more or less an historian, to pass judgment upon the past and to help explain the present and to make projections into the future.

And more and more people today are seeking moral guidance and direction, turning to the philosophers and the moralists for help and for suggestions. This is the most serious test of the educated person. Those who preferred to think of themselves as pilgrims of the absolute, in a detached and unrelated world which was not be to challenged, are now called upon to become pilgrims of the relative; to, as Jacques Maritain has urged, enter into the fabric of their own time to perfect the means by which men are perfected in time and perfected for eternity.

The wisdom that comes 25 or 30 years after graduation—somewhere between the ages of 40 and 50—is not in new knowledge, but in the realization that one must pretty well make it with what he already knows and with the powers he has been given or has developed. In part, it is in the realization that it is too late for speed reading to help very much—if it ever does—or for the *Readers' Digest* or the *Catholic Digest,* or a crash course in the "Great Ideas," even directed by Mortimer Adler, to do much good.

Whereas my positive advice to you has been limited and somewhat unclear, as you have noted, my negative counsel and suggestions are somewhat more certain.

Do not yield to the temptation to compromise methods in pursuit of acceptable purposes, to consider persons as expendable, or to what T. S. Eliot has described as the worst treason—to do the right thing for the wrong reason.

Many men have written and spoken on this point, but none better, at least in recent days, than Henry Steele Commager before the Senate Foreign Relations Committee, when he said that certain government activities "in the various realms which have been called to our attention of late violate two of the great Kantian categorical imperatives: the first is never use any human being as a means but always as an end; and the second is so to conduct yourself that you might generalize your every action into a universal rule. The danger," as he saw it was in substituting "the immediate advantage for the long-run disadvantage; that it uses great things like scholarship, science, the community of learning, truth, for immediate purposes, which it doubtless thinks are worthy, but which, in the long run, are not to be compared with the larger purposes of learning, scholarship, literature, art, and truth. And the reason that they are not to be compared in the long run is that that is what the short-run purposes are about."

Second, avoid the temptation of the "inner ring." It is a very special temptation in the midst of complexity if not of chaos, in times of institutional failure and flux. The "inner ring" comes in many sizes and serves many purposes. On a national and international scale, we have seen it in its broadest form in fascism and communism, but almost every day we find it present and operative among our friends and associates. C. S. Lewis has spoken best on this in his essay entitled *The Inner Ring:* "I am not going to say," he wrote, "that the existence of the inner ring is an evil. . . . The desire which draws us into Inner Rings is another matter. A thing can be morally neutral and yet the desire for that thing may be dangerous. . . . This desire is one of the great permanent mainsprings of human action. . . . Of all passions the passion for the Inner Ring is most skillful in making a man who is not yet a very bad man do very bad things."

Third, do not corrupt language and be attentive to protecting its integrity: first, as to the obvious obligation to speak the truth; and second, in the more subtle commitment to preserve and protect the meaning of words. As Allen Tate has written, man has an immediate responsibility, to other men no less than to himself, for the vitality of language. He must, said Tate, discriminate and defend the difference between mass communication, for the control of men, and the knowledge of man which must be offered us for human participation.

And finally, this is a kind of ultimate test, be not overly concerned as to what the record may have to say about you if to make that record you must be false. Seek that high state of secular humility which leaves man free to speak and act without fear and without concern for the judgment of his contemporaries or his biographers, or any judgment the world may pass upon him. I suggest two models: Harry Truman in politics, and Pope John XXIII in religion.

If one believes that man is the subject of history rather than simply the object controlled by economics and by common will or by some other irrational force, if one acknowledges that the period of half-civilization and half-knowledge of the 19th century has been shattered, if one accepts that we must be prepared to face the judgment of our own person and of our nation and of our age, then the need is for a full response, accepting the commitment of Teilhard de Chardin in confidence and hope in the future.

—ɯ—

DANIEL PATRICK
MOYNIHAN

—m—

The distinguished scholar and public intellectual Daniel Patrick Moynihan (1927–) served in four presidential administrations before being elected from the state of New York to four terms in the U.S. Senate (1977–2001). Born in poor circumstances, Moynihan attended CCNY, served in the U.S. Navy towards the end of World War II, and eventually graduated from Tufts University. He pursued advanced studies at the Fletcher School of Law and Diplomacy, earning a reputation as a specialist on urban policy and matters concerning race and ethnicity.

In the 1950s he assisted Governor Averell Harriman of New York, but he moved to Washington, D.C., to work in the Labor Department during the Kennedy and Johnson administrations. After briefly teaching at Harvard's Kennedy School of Government, Moynihan surprised some of his liberal colleagues by accepting President Richard Nixon's offer to serve as assistant for urban affairs, where he proved influential in shaping the administration's domestic agenda. From 1973 to 1975 he served as ambassador to India, after which he brought especial vigor to his duties as U.S. ambassador to the United Nations.

Moynihan's long service in the Senate was characterized by his independent thinking and innovative approaches on social policy. In addition to his duties as legislator and committee chair, Moynihan also found time to produce a steady stream of thoughtful books. In 1992 Notre Dame awarded him its Laetare Medal. Retirement from the Senate did not mean withdrawal from public life, and in 2001 Moynihan agreed to cochair the Social Security Commission established by President George W. Bush.

—m—

Politics as the Art of the Impossible

(1969)

I take for my theme a sentence from Georges Bernanos: "The worst, the most corrupting of lies are problems poorly stated."

My charge is similar. It is that much of the intense difficulty of our time is in nature conceptual, and that it arises from a massive misstatement of our problems. Intellectuals, if this view is correct, have done their work badly and there is little prospect that their mistakes will soon be undone. As ours was perhaps the first society consistently to expect the future to be better than the past, the apprehension that we may have profoundly mistaken the nature of our difficulties, so that we must expect years of effort to resolve the wrong problems and in presumably unavailing ways, strikes with special force. A certain nostalgia arises for a future that now appears lost. It becomes necessary to live much more in the present than has been the American mode.

If this be no great pleasure, it can, nonetheless, be stimulating. Here a sub-theme can be taken from another alert Frenchman—when asked what he had done during The Terror, the Abbé Sieyès answered, "I survived." This must now be a very great concern of those Americans whose lives, in Midge Decter's formulation, are devoted to the direction of their thought. Anyone old enough to have had any intellectual contact with the 1930s will take my meaning. The men of both the left and right who dominated, even terrorized, *that* time lived intense but brief lives. Their intellectual corpses are still stacked in the odd corners of universities, government departments, and the like where they do whatever it is they do. No one much cares, for they were subsequently judged to have been appallingly wrong about American society and, worse, were seen to have been unforgivably intolerant of any who hesitated to embrace their all-encompassing credos. Archibald MacLeish has remarked of his fellow poets that: "There is nothing worse for our trade than to be in style." The equivalent for those whose concern is government is submission to the noisiest problems of the moment to the exclusion of the most important ones.

What then are the "problems poorly stated" of our time? They are various but have, it seems to me, a unifying characteristic; namely, the rejection by those seeking a more just, more equal society of any indications that the society is in fact becoming more just and more equal. Society is seen in ahistorical terms: what is not altogether acceptable is altogether unacceptable; gradations are ignored and incremental movements are scorned. Those who by disposition are incrementalists, or for whom the contemplation of society has led to a conviction that incremental change is a necessity not a choice in human affairs, are baffled by this attitude and resentful of it. The exchanges that follow are bitter and unproductive. It is at all events my view that this is so because the problems at issue have so far been defined in fairly traditional *political* terms when what in fact is at issue is an immense stirring, little understood, if indeed understandable, of cultural dimensions. Fundamental ethical and moral issues—religious issues— are involved: issues which politics, especially the politics of a liberal democracy, are uniquely unable to resolve.

Two years ago, in the Phi Beta Kappa oration at Harvard, I argued that in fact we were witnessing the onset of the first heresies of liberalism. Heresy is an unloved term, especially in a liberal society, but it has real meaning: the rejection of beliefs fundamental to the dominant, pervasive world view of the society involved. Of necessity, the heresies of liberalism would be procedural in nature, for it is in process that a liberal society defines itself. In thinking about the subject, I have not been able to get much farther than this, but neither have events moved so as to cast greater doubt on the thesis than that which must attend any such large assertion. To the contrary, the rejection of the *authority* of liberal processes, the code that holds it is bad form to club the Dean, that civic statutes must be abided by, that rules of order and civility will be followed at meetings—all that—continues apace, and the pace if anything quickens. As Robert A. Nisbet continues to remind us, when authority relations collapse, power relations take their place; and this process, too, has advanced. Violence, which is the means by which power relations are maintained, is considerably more widespread now than it was two years ago, and surely vastly more common at the end of the decade of the 1960s than it was at the beginning of it.

Nothing suggests that the pattern of former times will quickly assert itself. To the contrary, the indications are that we rose to a new plateau of internal violence in the mid-1960s and that the most we can hope for is to keep from yet another escalation.

Such violence has, of course, made its way onto university campuses and this has led to great apprehension for the future of academic freedom. There are analogues, indeed precedents, for the violence of the streets, the poor, the police, and suchlike. But nothing like the present pattern of threats to and actual assault on university institutions and university members has ever yet occurred. Here, in particular, it would seem a future has been lost to us.

This has led to great despair among academic intellectuals: far greater than the news media have yet let on. For probably the first time in our history, professors speak of going into exile. Nor is the alarm simply that of Bourbons. A Marxist historian such as Eugene Genovese speaks with not a little alarm of the "pseudo-revolutionary middle-class totalitarians . . . of the left wing student movement," and one learns that even Professor Marcuse has suggested that professors ought to be treated differently from the oink-ish common swine.

The strongest view, from a notably unhysterical pen, is the recent assertion by Arnold Beichman, writing in *Encounter,* to the effect that university faculties

> have quietly decided that for the foreseeable future the university is no longer a place where truth is to be pursued. What has been tacitly ratified is a decision that the American university is primarily (not secondarily) the springboard for upward social mobility as the ascriptive right for ethnic minorities.

This can be overdone. Beichman accurately (but almost alone in the flood of commentary) notes that ethnic mobility has always been a prominent component of higher education—certainly so from the time Catholics began to establish competitive institutions with Protestants. One recalls Yeats' letter of 1904 to Lady Gregory: "I have been entirely delighted," he writes, "with the big, merry priests of Notre Dame, all Irish and proud as Lucifer of their success in getting Jews and non-conformists to come to their college and of the fact that they have no endowments." One recalls far more vividly growing up in New York City in the poverty-ridden 1930s, and yet possessing in that Notre Dame football team a symbol of tribal might and valor that can stir the blood atingle to this day. O, the golden Saturday afternoons when, in the name of every Irish kid caught in the social wreckage of the eastern slums, thunder indeed shook down from the skies and those mighty Polish tackles swamped the Navy!

If the demands of newer groups come as a shock to some, it is at least in part because this group function of higher education has tended to be ignored by those groups for which it has been functioning. Yet, the role was obvious enough; and it was not less clear that it would become, if anything, more pronounced to the degree that universities became more central institutions of the society. In the concluding paragraph of *Beyond the Melting Pot,* [Nathan] Glazer and I wrote that: "Religion and race define the next stage of American peoples." We were not wrong, and one is mystified still that the proposition was viewed at the time by such skepticism on the part of so many. (Not a few of whom, it may be added, having become committed to ethnic studies, pursue the matter with a single-minded zeal that is notoriously the accompaniment of sudden religious conversion.)

Simultaneously, if somewhat incompatibly, universities have been mini-bastions of class privilege. This phenomenon has been evident enough in the insistence by almost all parties to intramural disputes that those involved are exempt from punishment for deeds that would send lesser persons—without the walls—to court at very least and prison in all likelihood. But again, this is nothing new.

Indeed, some good could come of this if the excesses of the moment were to serve to restore some perspective on just what universities are and what they can do. They are institutions inhabited by younger and older persons of often very great abilities, but usually of very limited experience. With respect to their individual specialities, the judgment of the professors is singularly valuable. But their collective judgment is no better—could, indeed, be worse—than that of the common lot of men. This is not an incidental, random fact; it is a fundamental condition of human society, and the very basis of democratic government.

When William F. Buckley, Jr., wrote that he would far rather entrust his governance—by which he would include the preservation of his civil liberties and his intellectual freedom—to the first hundred persons listed in the Boston telephone directory than to the faculty of Harvard College, he was saying no more than what Thomas Jefferson or Henry Adams would have thought self-evident. The remark was greeted with considerable derision in Cambridge at the time, but it may be stated with certainty that more than one tenured professor of that ancient institution has come of late to see its truthfulness with excruciating clarity.

All this is to the good. What is bad is that the diffusion of violence to the intellectual life of our society is likely to lead to even greater failure to correctly state our problems than has been the case to date. This is so for the most elemental of reasons. Intellectual freedom in the American university has now been seriously diminished. It is past time for talking about what might happen; it has happened. We would do well to clear our minds of cant on that subject. Especially in the social sciences, there is today considerably less freedom than there was a decade ago; and we should expect that it will surely be ten to twenty years before what we would hope to be a normal state will be restored.

I deem it essential that this almost suddenly changed situation be more widely understood; otherwise, the sickness of the time will gradually come to be taken for a normal condition of health—and that would be a blow not merely to the age, but to the culture. But if we do perceive our circumstance for what it is, if we do come to accept that for reasons of prudence, or cowardice, or incompetence or whatever, faculties have been everywhere allowing principles and men to be sacrificed, we will at least retain the understanding that something has gone wrong, something that it may be possible someday to right.

It is important then to survive, with our faculties, as it were, as little diminished as possible, and to seek to understand the times—which is to say to state the problems of the time correctly.

Few individuals can hope to contribute more than a small increment to this effort; but more, then, is the reason as many as possible should seek to do so. Hence, with less hesitance than might otherwise attend the effort to make a simple abstraction about a hopelessly complex reality, I would offer, from the world of politics, the thought that the principal issues of the moment are not political. They are seen as such: that is the essential clue to their nature. But the crisis of the time is not political, it is in essence religious. It is a religious crisis of large numbers of intensely moral, even Godly, people who no longer hope for God. Hence, the quest for divinity assumes a secular form, but with an intensity of conviction that is genuinely new to our politics.

It is important to be clear whence this peculiar secular moral passion arises. It is from the very eighteenth century enlightenment from whence arose the American civilization that has so far followed so different a course. The rejection of Christian religion by the Enlightenment has obscured the fact, especially to Christians, that it did not constitute a rejection of Christian morality. To the contrary, it was more often in the name of that morality that the creed was attacked. It was Rousseau, as Michael Polanyi argues (although others would disagree) whose work widened the channels of Enlightenment thought so that in fact "they could be fraught eventually with all the supreme hopes of Christianity, the hopes which rationalism had released from their dogmatic framework." Wherewith, supreme of ironies, was loosed upon the world a moral fury that has wrought as much evil, in contrast with the mere brutality of the past, as mankind has ever known, an evil which may yet destroy us. The process arises from a sequence of promises which are logically unassailable, yet which in practice produce a society that is inherently unstable. Polanyi states the argument, which he correctly observes, no one has yet answered.

> If society is not a divine institution, it is made by man, and man is free to do with society what he likes. There is then no excuse for having a bad society, and we must make a good one without delay. For this purpose you must take power and you can take power over a bad society only by revolution. Moreover, to achieve a comprehensive improvement of society, you need comprehensive powers so you must regard all resistance to yourself as high treason and must put it down mercilessly.

Repeatedly, as this fervor becomes pathological, a kind of inversion takes place which transforms violence from a means to an end in itself. There are surprises but few mysteries to this process: the nineteenth century was able to read it in Russian novels; the twentieth to watch it on film. It has been the great disease of the committed intellectual of our time. Thirty years ago, Orwell wrote that: "The common man is still living in the mental world of Dickens, but nearly every modern intellectual has gone over to some or other form of totalitarianism." For that is the correct term. The total state; the politicization of all things. It would seem that Britain and America managed in the nineteenth century to escape any deep infestation of this view mostly by not thinking too closely about politics. But one result of this is that in political theory there is no serious counter argument: all one can say is that one does not like doing good by sending men "up against the wall" to use the apparent term of Che Guevara and the battle cry of the Barnard girls. For the disease is amongst us, and will spread. Incongruously, it appears to have taken roots within organized religion itself. The course of the coming generation is all but fixed: it will include a strong and possibly growing echelon that will challenge the authority of American institutions across the board, and will not be especially scrupulous as to how it does so. In this the extreme left is very likely to be joined by the extreme right, for to each the values and process of the present American democracy are the enemy to be destroyed.

All in all, there is cause enough for despair. As Midge Decter has put it: "When you are caught between left and right, the only way to go is down." But we are not yet down. We are a strong and competent people, increasingly, I think, aware of our troubles and dangers and shortcomings. The challenge to authority that is now upon us can strengthen and renew institutions as much as it can weaken them. And it can be fun. There is always room, as Orwell wrote, "for one more custard pie." We are not especially well equipped in conceptual terms to ride out the storm ahead, but there are things we know without fully understanding, and one of these is the ultimate value of privacy, and the final ruin when all things have become political.

Having through all my adult life worked to make the American national government larger, stronger, more active, I nonetheless plead that there are limits to what it may be asked to do. In the last weeks of his life, President Kennedy journeyed to Amherst to dedicate a library to Robert Frost and to speak to this point. "The powers of the Presidency," he remarked, "are often described. Its limitations should occasionally be remembered."

The matter comes to this. The stability of a democracy depends very much on the people making a careful distinction between what government can do and what it cannot do. To demand what can be done is altogether in order: some may wish such things accomplished, some may not, and the majority may decide. But to seek that which cannot be provided, especially to do so with the passionate but misinformed conviction that it can be, is to create the conditions of frustration and ruin.

What is it government cannot provide? It cannot provide values to persons who have none, or who have lost those they had. It cannot provide a meaning to life. It cannot provide inner peace. It can provide outlets for moral energies, but it cannot create those energies. In particular, government cannot cope with the crisis in values which is sweeping the western world. It cannot respond to the fact that so many of our young people do not believe what those before them have believed, do not accept the authority of institutions and customs whose authority has heretofore been accepted, do not embrace or even very much like the culture that they inherit.

The twentieth century is strewn with the wreckage of societies that did not understand or accept this fact of the human condition. Ours is not the first culture to encounter such a crisis in values. Others have done so, have given in to the seeming sensible solution of politicizing the crisis, have created the total state, and have destroyed themselves in the process. Irving Kristol has warned against it in terms at once cogent and urgent:

> The one way not to cope with this crisis in values is through organized political-ideological action. Most of the hysteria, much of the stupidity, and a good part of the bestiality of the twentieth century have arisen from efforts to do precisely this. Not only do such efforts fail; they fail in the costliest fashion. And if modern history can be said to teach anything, it is that, intolerable as a crisis in values may be, it invariably turns out to be far less intolerable than any kind of "final solution" imposed by direct political action.

I surely do not argue for a quietistic government acquiescing in whatever the tides of fortune or increments of miscalculation bring about: and in our time they have brought about hideous things. I do not prescribe for social scientists or government officials a future of contented apoplexy as they observe the mounting disaffection of the young. I certainly do not argue for iron resistance, as other societies have successfully resisted somewhat similar movements in the past.

I simply plead for the religious and ethical sensibility in the culture to more clearly what is at issue, and to do its work.

Sympathy is not enough. *Tout pardonner, c'est tout comprendre* is not a maxim that would pass muster with Bernanos or any who have helped us through the recent or distant past. If politics in America is not to become the art of the impossible, the limits of politics must be perceived, and the province of moral philosophy greatly expanded.

—ᴍ—

JIMMY CARTER

—◆—

James Earl (Jimmy) Carter, Jr. (1924–), the thirty-ninth president of the United States, was born in Plains, Georgia. A United States Naval Academy graduate, he served in the nuclear submarine corps before returning to Georgia, where he proved a successful farmer and businessman. He entered politics in the 1960s and was elected governor in 1970. Against all odds, he won the Democratic presidential nomination in 1976 and went on to defeat Gerald Ford in the general election. A born-again Baptist who emphasized his outsider status in light of the Watergate scandal, Carter promised honesty to the American people.

In office, Carter enjoyed some success, especially in foreign policy. He campaigned to protect human rights abroad, secured ratification of the Panama Canal Treaties, and mediated the Camp David Accords between Egypt and Israel. In 1979–80, however, Carter's presidency was disabled by deteriorating economic conditions, the collapse of Soviet-American détente following the Soviet invasion of Afghanistan, and the Iranian hostage crisis. Carter lost the 1980 election to Ronald Reagan and retreated home to Plains. But his postpresidential years restored his reputation. He has pursued diplomatic missions to resolve international disputes, supervised foreign elections, and volunteered with Habitat for Humanity as well as writing a number of books. Carter received the Nobel Peace Prize in 2002.

—◆—

Foreign Policy and Human Rights

(1977)

In his 25 years as President of Notre Dame, Father Hesburgh has spoken more consistently and effectively in support of the rights of human beings than any American I know.

His interest in the Notre Dame Center for Civil Rights has never wavered and he played an important role in broadening the scope of the center's work to include all people—as shown in last month's conference here on human rights and American foreign policy.

That concern has been demonstrated again today by the selection of Bishop Donal Lamont, Paul Cardinal Arns, and Stephen Cardinal Kim to receive honorary degrees. In their fight for human freedoms in Rhodesia, Brazil and South Korea, these three religious leaders typify all that is best in their countries and in their church. I am honored to join you in recognizing their dedication and personal sacrifice.

Last week I spoke in California about the domestic agenda for our nation. Our challenge in the next few years is to provide more efficiently for the needs of our people, to demonstrate—against the dark faith of the times—that our government can be both competent and humane.

I want to speak today about the strands that connect our actions overseas with our essential character as a nation.

I believe we can have a foreign policy that is democratic, that is based on our fundamental values, and that uses power and influence for humane purposes. We can also have a foreign policy that the American people both support and understand.

I have a quiet confidence in our own political system.

Because we know democracy works, we can reject the arguments of those rulers who deny human rights to their people.

We are confident that democracy's example will be compelling, and so we seek to bring that example closer to those from whom we have been separated and who are not yet convinced.

We are so confident that democratic methods are the most effective, and so we are not tempted to employ improper tactics at home or abroad.

We are confident of our own strength, so we can seek substantial mutual reductions in the nuclear arms race.

We are confident of the good sense of our own people, and so we let them share the process of making foreign policy decisions. We can thus speak with the voices of 215 million, not just of a handful.

Democracy's great recent successes—in India, Portugal, Greece, Spain—show that our confidence is not misplaced.

Being confident of our own future, we are now free of that inordinate fear of communism which once led us to embrace any dictator who joined us in our fear.

For too many years we have been willing to adopt the flawed principles and tactics of our adversaries, sometimes abandoning our values for theirs.

We fought fire with fire, never thinking that fire is better fought with water.

This approach failed—with Vietnam the best example of its intellectual and moral poverty.

But through failure we have found our way back to our own principles and values, and we have regained our lost confidence.

By measure of history, our nation's 200 years are brief; and our rise to world eminence is briefer still. It dates from 1945, when Europe and the old international order both lay in ruins. Before then, America was largely on the periphery of world affairs. Since then, we have inescapably been at the center.

We helped to build solid testaments to our faith and purpose—the United Nations, the North Atlantic Treaty Organization, the World Bank, the International Monetary Fund and other institutions. This international system has endured and worked well for a quarter of a century.

Our policy during this period was guided by two principles: a belief that Soviet expansion must be contained, and the corresponding belief in the importance of an almost exclusive alliance among non-Communist nations on both sides of the Atlantic.

That system could not last forever unchanged. Historical trends have weakened its foundation. The unifying threat of conflict with the Soviet Union has become less intensive even though the competition has become more extensive.

The Vietnamese war produced a profound moral crisis, sapping worldwide faith in our policy. The economic strains of the 1970s have weakened public confidence in the capacity of industrial democracy to provide sustained well-being for its citizens, a crisis of confidence made even more grave by the covert pessimism of some of our leaders.

It is a familiar truth that the world today is in the midst of the most profound and rapid transformation of its entire history. In less than a generation the daily lives and the aspirations of most human beings have been transformed. Colonialism has nearly gone; a new sense of national identity exists in almost 100 new countries; knowledge has become more widespread; aspirations are higher. As more people have been freed from traditional constraints, more have become determined to achieve social justice.

The world is still divided by ideological disputes, dominated by regional conflicts, and threatened by the danger that we will not resolve the differences of race and wealth without violence or without drawing into combat the major military powers. We can no longer separate the traditional issues of war and peace from the new global questions of justice, equity and human rights.

It is a new world—but America should not fear it. It is a new world—and we should help to shape it. It is a new world that calls for a new American foreign policy—a policy based on constant decency in its values, and on optimism in its historical vision.

We can no longer have a policy solely for the industrial nations as the foundation of global stability, but we must respond to the new reality of a politically awakening world.

We can no longer expect that the other 150 nations will follow the dictates of the powerful, but we must continue—confidently— our efforts to inspire, and to persuade, and to lead.

Our policy must reflect our belief that the world can hope for more than simple survival and our belief that dignity and freedom are man's fundamental spiritual requirements.

Our policy must shape an international system that will last longer than secret deals.

We cannot make this kind of policy by manipulation. Our policy must be open and candid; it must be one of constructive global involvement, resting on these five cardinal premises:

First, our policy should reflect our people's basic commitment to promote the case of human rights.

Next, our policy should be based on close cooperation among the industrial democracies of the world because we share the same values and because together we can help to shape a more decent life for all.

Based on a strong defense capability, our policy must also seek to improve relations with the Soviet Union and with China in ways that are both more comprehensive and more reciprocal. Even if we cannot heal ideological divisions, we must reach accommodations that reduce the risk of war.

Also, our policy must reach out to the developing nations to alleviate suffering and to reduce the chasm between the world's rich and poor.

Finally, our policy must encourage all countries to rise above narrow national interests and work together to solve such formidable global problems as the threat of nuclear war, racial hatred, the arms race, environmental damage, hunger and disease.

Since last January we have begun to define and to set in motion a foreign policy based on these premises—and I have tried to make these premises clear to the American people. Let me review what we have been doing and discuss what we intend to do.

First, we have reaffirmed America's commitment to human rights as a fundamental tenet of our foreign policy. In ancestry, religion, color, place of origin and cultural background, we Americans are as diverse a nation as the world has ever known. No common mystique of blood or soil unites us. What draws us together, perhaps more than anything else, is a belief in human freedom. We want the world to know that our nation stands for more than financial prosperity.

This does not mean that we can conduct our foreign policy by rigid moral maxims. We live in a world that is imperfect and will always be imperfect—a world that is complex and will always be complex.

I understand fully the limits of moral suasion. I have no illusion that changes will come easily or soon. But I also believe that it is a mistake to undervalue the power of words and of the ideas that words embody. In our own history that power has ranged from Thomas Paine's "Common Sense" to Martin Luther King, Jr.'s "I Have a Dream."

In the life of the human spirit, words *are* action—much more so than many of us may realize who live in countries where freedom of expression is taken for granted.

The leaders of totalitarian countries understand this very well. The proof is that words are precisely the action for which dissidents in those countries are being persecuted.

Nonetheless, we can already see dramatic worldwide advances in the protection of the individual from the arbitrary power of the state. For us to ignore this trend would be to lose influence and moral authority in the world. To lead it will be to regain the moral stature we once had.

All people will benefit from these advances. From free and open competition comes creative change—in politics, commerce, science, and the arts. From control comes conformity and despair.

The great democracies are not free because they are strong and prosperous. I believe they are strong and prosperous because they are free.

Second, we have moved deliberately to reinforce the bonds among our democracies. In our recent meetings in London we agreed to widen our economic cooperation; to promote free trade; to strengthen the world's monetary system; to seek ways to avoid nuclear proliferation; we prepared constructive proposals for the forthcoming meetings on North-South problems of poverty, development, and global well-being; and we agreed on joint efforts to reinforce and modernize our common defense.

Even more important, all of us reaffirmed our basic optimism in the future of the democratic system. Our spirit of confidence is spreading. Together, our democracies can help to shape the wider architecture of global cooperation, and the London meeting was a successful step toward this goal.

Third, we have moved to engage the Soviet Union in a joint effort to halt the strategic arms race. That race is not only dangerous, it is morally deplorable. We must put an end to it.

I know it will not be easy to reach agreements. The issues are extraordinarily complex, and American and Soviet interests, perceptions and aspirations vary. We need to be both patient and prudent.

Our goal is to be fair to both sides, to produce reciprocal stability, parity, and security. We desire a freeze on further modernization and continuing substantial reductions and strategic weapons. We want a comprehensive ban on nuclear testing, a prohibition against chemical warfare, no attack capability against space satellites, and arms limitations in the Indian Ocean.

I hope that we can take joint steps with all nations towards eliminating nuclear weapons completely from our arsenals of death. We will persist.

I believe in détente with the Soviet Union. To me it means progress towards peace. But that progress must be both comprehensive and reciprocal. We cannot have accommodation in one part of the world and the aggravation of conflicts in another.

Nor should the efforts of détente be limited to our two countries alone. We hope the Soviet leaders will join us in efforts to stop the spread of nuclear explosives and to reduce sales of conventional arms. We hope to persuade the Soviet Union that one country cannot impose its own social system upon another, either through direct military intervention or through the use of a client state's military force—as with the Cuban Intervention in Angola.

Cooperation also implies obligation. We hope that the Soviet Union will join in playing a larger role in aiding the developing world, for common aid efforts will help us build a bridge of mutual confidence.

Fourth, we are taking deliberate steps to improve the chances of lasting peace in the Middle East.

Through wide-ranging consultations with the leaders of the countries involved, we have found some areas of agreement and some movement towards consensus. The negotiations must continue.

Through my public comments, I have also tried to suggest a more flexible framework for the discussion of the three key issues which have so far been intractable: the nature of a comprehensive peace, the relationship between security and borders, and the issue of the Palestinian homeland.

The historic friendship between the United States and Israel is not dependent on domestic politics in either nation; it is derived from our common respect for human freedom and from our common search for permanent peace. We will continue to promote a settlement which all of us need. Our own policy will not be affected by changes in leadership in any of the countries in the Middle East. Therefore, we expect Israel and her neighbors to continue to be bound by UN Resolutions 242 and 338, which they have previously accepted.

This may be the most propitious time for a genuine settlement since the beginning of the Arab-Israeli conflict. To let this opportunity pass could mean disaster, not only for the Middle East, but perhaps for the international political and economic order as well.

Fifth, we are attempting, even at the risk of some friction with our friends, to reduce the danger of nuclear proliferation and the worldwide spread of conventional arms.

At the recent summit there was general agreement that proliferation of explosives from reprocessed nuclear wastes is a serious issue. We have now set in motion an international effort to determine the best ways of harnessing nuclear energy for peaceful use, while reducing the risks that its products will be diverted to the making of explosives.

We have also completed a comprehensive review of our own policy on arms transfers. Competition in arms sales is inimical to peace and destructive of the economic development of the poorer countries. We will, as a matter of national policy, seek to reduce the annual dollar volume of arms sales, to restrict the transfer of advanced weaponry, and to reduce the extent of our co-production arrangements with foreign states. Just as important, we are trying to get other nations to join us in this effort.

All of this is just the beginning. But it is a beginning aimed towards a clear goal; to create a wider framework of international cooperation suited to the new historical circumstances.

We will cooperate more closely with the newly influential countries in Latin America, Africa and Asia. We need their friendship and cooperation in a common effort as the structure of world power changes.

More than 100 years ago, Abraham Lincoln said that our nation could not exist half slave and half free. We know that a peaceful world cannot long exist one-third rich and two-thirds hungry.

Most nations share our faith that, in the long run, expanded and equitable trade will best help developing countries to help themselves. But the immediate problems of hunger, disease, illiteracy and repression are here now.

The western democracies, the OPEC nations, and the developed communist countries can cooperate through existing international institutions in providing more effective aid. This is an excellent alternative to war.

We have a special need for cooperation and consultation with other nations in this hemisphere. We do not need another slogan; although these are our close friends and neighbors; our links with them are the same links of equality that we forge with the rest of the world. We will be dealing with them as part of a new worldwide mosaic of global, regional and bilateral relations.

It is important that we make progress toward normalizing relations with the People's Republic of China. We see the American-Chinese relationship as a central element of our global policy, and China as a key force for global peace. We wish to cooperate closely with the creative Chinese people on the problems that confront all mankind. We hope to find a formula which can bridge some of the difficulties that still separate us.

Finally, let me say that we are committed to a peaceful resolution of the crisis in Southern Africa. The time has come for the principle of majority rule to be the basis for political order, recognizing that in a democratic system the rights of the minority must also be protected. To be peaceful, change must come promptly. The United States is determined to work together with our European allies and the concerned African states to shape a congenial international framework for the rapid and progressive transformation of Southern African society and to help protect it from unwarranted outside interference.

Let me conclude:

Our policy is based on an historical vision of America's role;

It is derived from a larger view of global change;

It is rooted in our moral values;

It is reinforced by our material wealth and by our military power;

It is designed to serve mankind;

And it is a policy that I hope will make you proud to be American.

RONALD REAGAN

The most influential president of the last quarter century, Ronald Wilson Reagan (1911–) shifted the direction of American politics firmly to the right during his two terms in the White House (1981–89). Born in Tampico, Illinois, Reagan graduated from Eureka College in 1932, becoming a sportscaster and then a film actor. When his movie career stalled he became a public spokesman for General Electric and adopted a more conservative political stance. He joined the Republican Party and served as governor of California from 1967 to 1975. After two failed attempts, he finally gained the Republican presidential nomination in 1980 and defeated Jimmy Carter in the general election.

In office, Reagan reduced taxes, controlled inflation, saw the federal deficit increase markedly, and sought to reduce the role of government. He also sponsored a huge military buildup as part of his effort to meet the Soviet challenge. Surprisingly to some, Reagan responded flexibly as the Soviet Union pursued rapprochement under President Mikhail Gorbachev. The end of the Cold War was on the horizon when Reagan left office with his popularity intact. Diagnosed with Alzheimer's disease in 1994, Reagan withdrew with dignity from public life.

Great Years Ahead
for Our Country

(1981)

Nancy and I are greatly honored to be here today sharing this day with you. Our pleasure is more than doubled because we also share this platform with a long-time good friend, Pat O'Brien.

I haven't had a chance to tell Pat that I've only recently learned of another something we hold in common. Until a few weeks ago, I've known very little about my ancestry on my father's side. He had been orphaned at age 6. Now I've learned my great-grandfather left the village of Ballyporeen in Ireland to come to America. Ballyporeen is also the ancestral home of Pat O'Brien.

If I don't watch myself, this could turn out to be less a commencement than a warm bath in nostalgic memories. During my growing-up years in nearby Illinois, I was greatly influenced by a sports legend so national in scope and so almost mystical, it is difficult to explain to any who did not live in those times. The legend was based on the combination of three elements—a game, football; a university, Notre Dame; and a man, Knute Rockne; there has been nothing like it before or since.

My first time to ever see Notre Dame was to come here as a sports announcer only two years out of college to broadcast a football game. You won or I wouldn't have mentioned that.

A number of years later I returned in the company of Pat O'Brien and a galaxy of Hollywood stars for the world premiere of "Knute Rockne—All American" in which I was privileged to play George Gipp. There were probably others in the motion picture industry who could have played the part better. There were none who could have wanted to play it as much as I did. And I was given the part because the star of the picture, Pat O'Brien, kindly and generously held out a helping hand to a beginning young actor.

Having come to Hollywood from the world of sports, I had been trying to write a story treatment based on the life of Knute Rockne. And I must confess, my main purpose was because I had someone in mind to play the Gipper. On one of my sports broadcasts before going to Hollywood, I had told the story of his career and tragic death. I didn't have many words down on paper when I learned the studio where I was employed was already preparing to film that story.

And that brings me to the theme of my remarks. I am the fifth President to address a Notre Dame commencement. The temptation is great to use this forum for address on some national or international issue having nothing to do with the occasion itself. Indeed this is somewhat traditional so I haven't been surprised to read in a number of reputable journals that I was going to deliver a major address on foreign policy. Others said it would be on the economy. It will be on neither.

By the same token I will not belabor you with some of the standard rhetoric beloved of graduation speakers over the years. I won't tell you that "You know more today than you have ever known or than you will ever know again," or that other standby—"When I was 14 I didn't think my father knew anything. By the time I was 21 I was amazed at how much the old gentleman had learned in 7 years."

You members of the graduating class of 1981 are what the behaviorists call "achievers." And while you will look back with warm pleasure on the years that led to this day, you are today also looking toward a future which for most of you seems uncertain but which I assure you offers great expectations.

Take pride in this day, thank your parents and those who over the last four years have been of help to you, and do a little celebrating. This is your day and whatever I say should take cognizance of that fact. This is a milestone in your life and a time of change.

Winston Churchill during the darkest period of the "Battle of Britain" in World War II said:

When great causes are on the move in the world . . . we learn we are spirits, not animals, and that something is going on in space and time, and beyond space and time, which, whether we like it or not, spells duty.

I'm going to mention again that movie Pat and I and Notre Dame were in for it says something about America. Knute Rockne as a boy came to this country with his parents from Norway. He became so American that here at Notre Dame he was an All American in a sport that is uniquely American.

As a coach he did more than teach young men how to play a game. He believed that the noblest work of man was molding the character of man. Maybe that's why he was a living legend. No man connected with football has ever achieved the stature or occupied the singular niche in our nation that he carved out for himself, not just in a sport, but in our entire social structure.

"Win one for the Gipper," has become a line usually spoken now in a humorous vein. I hear it from members of the Congress who are supportive of the economic program I've submitted. But let's look at the real significance of his story. Rockne could have used it any time just to win a game. But eight years would go by following the death of George Gipp before Rock ever revealed Gipp's deathbed wish.

Then he told the story at half time to one of the only teams he'd ever coached that was torn by dissension, jealousy, and factionalism. The seniors on that team were about to close out their football careers without ever learning or experiencing some of the real values the game has to impart.

None of them had ever known George Gipp. They were children when he played for Notre Dame. Yet it was to this team that Rockne told the story and so inspired them that they rose above their personal animosities. They joined together in a common cause and attained the unattainable.

We were told of one line spoken by a player during that game that we were afraid to put in the picture. The man who carried the ball over for the winning touchdown was injured on the play. We were told that as he was lifted on the stretcher and taken off the field he was heard to say, "That's the last one I can get for you, Gipper."

Yes, it was only a game and it might seem somewhat maudlin, but is there anything wrong with young men having the experience of feeling something so deeply that they can give so completely of themselves? There will come times in the lives of all of us when we'll be faced with causes bigger than ourselves and they won't be on a playing field.

This nation was born when a little band of men we call the founding fathers, a group so unique we've never seen their like since, rose to such selfless heights.

Lawyers, tradesmen, merchants, farmers—56 men in all—who had achieved security and some standing in life, but who valued freedom more. They pledged their lives, their fortunes and their sacred honor. Some gave their lives, most gave their fortunes, all preserved their sacred honor.

They gave us more than a nation. They brought to all mankind for the first time the concept that man was born free; that each of us has inalienable rights, ours by the grace of God, and that government is created by us for our convenience having only those powers which we choose to give it.

This is the heritage you are about to claim as you come out to join a society made up of those who have preceded you by a few years and some of us by many.

This experiment in man's relation to man is a few years into its third century. Saying it that way could make it sound quite old. But look at it from another perspective. A few years ago someone figured out that if we could condense the history of life on earth down to a film that would run 24 hours a day for one year, 365 days (on leap year we could have an intermission), this idea we call the United States would not appear on the screen until 3 1/2 seconds before midnight on December 31.

As you join us out there beyond the campus, you already know there are great unsolved problems. The careful structure of federalism with built-in checks and balances has become distorted. The Central Government has usurped powers that properly belong to state and local government; and in so doing has in many ways failed to do those things which are the responsibility of the Central Government.

All of this has led to a misuse of power and a preemption of the prerogatives of the people and their social institutions. You are graduating from one of our great private, or if you will, independent universities. Not many years ago such schools were relatively free of government interference. But in recent years as government spawned regulations covering virtually every facet of our lives, our independent and church-supported colleges and universities found themselves included in the network of regulations, and the costly blizzard of administrative paperwork government demanded. Today 34 congressional committees and almost 80 subcommittees have jurisdiction over 439 separate laws affecting education at the college level. Virtually every aspect of campus life is now regulated—hiring, firing, promotions, physical plant, construction, record keeping, fundraising and to some extent curriculum and educational programs.

I hope when you leave this campus you will do so with a feeling of obligation to this, your alma mater. She will need your help and support in the years to come. If ever the great independent colleges and universities like Notre Dame give way to and are replaced by tax-supported institutions, the struggle to preserve academic freedom will have been lost.

Yes, we are troubled today by economic stagnation, brought on by inflated currency, prohibitive taxes, and those burdensome regulations. The cost of that stagnation in human terms mostly among those who are least equipped to survive it, is cruel and inhuman.

Now don't decide to turn in your diplomas and spend another year on campus. I've just given you the bad news. The good news is that something is being done about all this—being done because the people of America have said "enough already." We just had gotten so busy, that for awhile we let things get out of hand, forgot we were the keeper of the power. We forgot to challenge the notion that the State is the principal vehicle of social change; forgot that millions of social interactions among free individuals and institutions can do more to foster economic and social progress than all the careful schemes of government planners.

Well, at last we are remembering: remembering that government has certain legitimate functions which it can perform very well; that it can be responsive to the people; that it can be humane and compassionate; but that when it undertakes tasks that are not its proper province, it can do none of them as well or as economically as the private sector.

For too long government has been fixing things that aren't broken and inventing miracle cures for which there are no known diseases.

We need you, we need your youth, your strength and your idealism to help us make right that which is wrong. I know you have been
critically looking at the mores and customs of the past and question-
ing their value. Every generation does that. But don't discard the
time-tested values upon which civilization is built just because they
are old.

More important, don't let the doom criers and the cynics persuade you that the best is past—that from here it's all downhill. Each
generation sees farther than the generation preceding it because it
stands on the shoulders of that generation. You will have opportunities
beyond anything we've ever known.

The people have made it plain they want an end to excessive government intervention in their lives and in the economy. They want an
end to burdensome and unnecessary regulations and to a punitive tax
policy that takes "from the mouth of labor the bread it has earned."

They also want a government that not only can continue to send
men through the far reaches of space but can guarantee the citizens they can walk through a park or in their neighborhoods after
dark without fear of violence. And finally they want to know that this
nation has the ability to defend itself against those who would try to
pull it down.

All of these things we can do. Indeed a start has already been
made. A task force under the leadership of Vice President George
Bush has identified hundreds of regulations which can be wiped out
with no harm whatsoever to the quality of life. Their cancellation will
leave billions of dollars for productive enterprise and research and development.

The years ahead will be great ones for our country, for the cause
of freedom and for the spread of civilization. The West will not contain communism; it will transcend communism. We will not bother to
denounce it; we'll dismiss it as a sad, bizarre chapter in human history
whose last pages are even now being written.

William Faulkner at a Nobel Prize ceremony some time back
said man "would not merely endure: he will prevail" against the
modern world because he will return to "the old verities and truths of
the heart." "He is immortal," Faulkner said of man, "because he alone
among creatures . . . has a soul, a spirit capable of compassion and
sacrifice and endurance."

One cannot say those words without thinking of the irony that one who so exemplifies them—Pope John Paul II, a man of peace and goodness, an inspiration to the world—would be struck by a bullet from a man towards whom he could only feel compassion and love.

It was Pope John Paul II who warned last year in his encyclical on mercy and justice, against certain economic theories that use the rhetoric of class struggle to justify injustice; that "in the name of an alleged justice the neighbor is sometimes destroyed, killed, deprived of liberty or stripped of fundamental human rights."

For the West, for America, the time has come to dare to show the world that our civilized ideas, our traditions, our values are not—like the ideology and war machine of totalitarian societies—a façade of strength. It is time the world knows that our intellectual and spiritual values are rooted in the source of all real strength—a belief in a Supreme Being, a law higher than our own.

When it is written, the history of our time will not dwell long on the hardships of our recent past. But history will ask—and our answer determines the face of freedom for a thousand years—did a nation born of hope lose hope? Did a people forged by courage find courage wanting? Did a generation steeled by a hard war and a harsh peace forsake honor at the moment of a great climactic struggle for the human spirit?

If history asks such questions, history also answers them. These answers are found in the heritage left by generations of Americans before us. They stand in silent witness to what the world will soon know and history someday record: that in its third century the American nation came of age—affirming its leadership of free men and women—serving selflessly a vision of man with God, government for people and humanity at peace.

This is a noble, rich heritage rooted in the great civilized ideas of the West—and it is yours.

My hope today is that when your time comes—and come it shall—to explain to another generation the meaning of the past and thereby hold out to them the promise of the future, you will recall some of the truths and traditions of which we have spoken. For it is these truths and traditions that define our civilization and make up our national heritage. Now, they are yours to protect and pass on.

I have just one more hope for you: that when you do speak to the next generation about these things, you will always be able to speak of an America that is strong and free, that you will always find in your hearts an unbounded pride in this much-loved country, this once and future land, this bright and hopeful nation whose generous spirit and great ideals the world still honors.

Congratulations and God bless you.

JOSEPH BERNARDIN

A native of Columbia, South Carolina, Joseph Louis Bernardin (1928–1996) studied at St. Mary's Seminary in Baltimore and at the Catholic University of America. He was ordained a priest for the diocese of Charleston in 1952. He served in his home diocese until he was named auxiliary bishop of Atlanta in 1966. In 1968 he was elected general secretary of the National Conference of Catholic Bishops (NCCB). After four years of service he was installed as archbishop of Cincinnati, where he served for a decade before being appointed archbishop of Chicago by Pope John Paul II. He was named a cardinal in 1983 and quickly emerged as a Catholic leader noted for his moderation and conciliation.

In the early 1980s, Cardinal Bernardin chaired the bishops' committee exploring issues of nuclear war and peace which eventually resulted in the pastoral letter The Challenge of Peace: God's Promise and Our Response. *Thereafter, Cardinal Bernardin advocated a consistent ethic of life across a range of issues including abortion, capital punishment, nuclear war, and poverty. He referred to his approach on these matters as a "seamless garment." In his final years Bernardin taught much about forgiveness, suffering with dignity, and Christian hope. He died of pancreatic cancer after ministering to fellow cancer patients until the eve of his own death.*

The Challenge of Peace

(1983)

I am honored to be with all of you to share the joy of this special day. I greatly appreciate this privilege of receiving the honorary degree of Doctor of Laws, for which I thank Father Hesburgh, the faculty and the entire University community.

In a particular way, I thank you graduates for accepting me, your most recently arrived classmate. I did not have to put in the long hours of study and preparation you did these past years, at least not in the same way. I did not have to make the financial sacrifices which you and your parents made. But, on the other hand, neither did I create any headaches, heartaches or gray hairs for the faculty and administration! Yet here I am, a member of the class of 1983 of Notre Dame University. In your name I thank your families, your teachers and the countless others who have been a part of your life during the past several years. And in their name, I thank you.

Another reason I am glad to be here this afternoon is that, because of our close geographic proximity and for many deeper, intangible reasons, there is a special affinity between Notre Dame and the Archdiocese of Chicago. I am happy to reaffirm and renew that relationship today.

Someone has pointed out that I am the first clergyman to address the graduating class in the past 83 years. I do not know what he said, but if I do no better, the next cleric is not due until the year 2066!

I come before you today as a pastor. I come as a believer. I come as one committed to the Lord, as one who struggles—like you, I am sure—to walk faithfully in His footsteps. It is that commitment that makes me eager to share with you some deeply held convictions about life—the life God has entrusted to us, the life He expects us to cherish and protect.

You are at an important juncture in your life. Now that you have completed college, you must take your place in society; you must help shape the world in which you will live; you must address the critical issues which confront us.

My topic today is the pastoral letter on war and peace recently approved by the United States Bishops after more than two years of research and consultation. Entitled "The Challenge of Peace: God's Promise and Our Response," the letter raises questions that you will have to deal with in the months and years ahead. There is no way in which you can responsibly avoid them.

To put the pastoral letter in perspective, I will first discuss the reason why we decided to issue the document. Then I will give a brief overview of what we actually said. I will next analyze, in a summary fashion, the public reaction to the pastoral. Finally, I will raise the question of where we go from here.

WHY THE BISHOPS ADDRESSED THE ISSUE

There is little doubt that, with the constant escalation of the arms race, and the development of ever more deadly weapons, the threat of nuclear war is greater today than ever before. Nearly everyone seems to agree that there is an urgent need to reduce the threat.

But, some ask, is this not the responsibility of the state, of our elected officials whose task it is to defend us from unjust aggressors? Why has the Church entered into this arena? In other words, is the issue not political rather than moral or religious?

At one level the question of nuclear war is surely an issue of politics or diplomacy. The policies of governments and public opinion within nations are central features of the nuclear question. But a purely political definition does not adequately identify the threat posed by modern warfare. Today the stakes involved in the nuclear issue make it a moral issue of compelling urgency.

Even the moral definition of the nuclear question fails to capture its deepest meaning. The very dimensions of the moral issue push toward a religious definition of the threat posed by nuclear warfare. Pope John Paul II vividly defined the problem at Hiroshima: "In the past," he said, "it was possible to destroy a village, a town, a region, even a country. Now it is the whole planet that has come under threat." As the pastoral states: "For people of faith this means we read the Book of Genesis with a new awareness; the moral issue at stake in nuclear war involves the meaning of sin in its most graphic dimensions. Every sinful act is a confrontation of the creature and the Creator. Today the destructive potential of the nuclear powers threatens the human person, the civilization we have slowly constructed."

Because the nuclear issue is not simply political, but also a profoundly moral and religious question, the Church must be a participant in the process of protecting the world and its people from the spectre of nuclear destruction. Silence in this instance would be a betrayal of its mission.

WHAT THE BISHOPS ACTUALLY SAID

The pastoral letter devotes over thirty pages to the challenge of constructing peace in an increasingly interdependent world. The political and moral challenge it poses for world politics may be the most significant long-term teaching of the pastoral. This positive section on peace shows why the nuclear issue does not exhaust the challenges of the moment; issues of human rights, economic justice and respect for rights of all nations, great and small, are unfinished tasks in the daily business of world affairs today.

The urgent need to build peace does not, however, dispense with the constant effort required to prevent any use of nuclear weapons and to limit other uses of force in international relations. It is this section of the letter which has attracted the most attention—the policy section containing an analysis of the moral problems related to the use of nuclear weapons and the strategy of nuclear deterrence.

The argument of the pastoral must be understood in a context of Catholic teaching which is clear about the duty of the state to defend society, the right of the state to use force as a last resort, and the need for state action to be assessed by moral criteria whenever force is used. It is those moral criteria that the pastoral addresses and the argument moves in three steps: first, a basic premise is established, then this premise is related to three cases of use and, finally, to an assessment of deterrence.

The premise of the letter is that nuclear weapons and nuclear strategy constitute a qualitatively new moral problem. The nuclear age is not simply an extension of the moral questions on warfare addressed by our ancestors. Albert Einstein, one of the fathers of the nuclear age, said that everything is changed except the way we think. We have experienced the meaning of this statement as we have struggled with nuclear issues in the development of the pastoral.

From a moral tradition like ours, which judges *some* but not all uses of force to be morally legitimate, the nuclear era poses a profound—indeed a revolutionary—challenge. The extreme skepticism of the pastoral regarding our ability to control any use of nuclear weapons is a pervasive influence throughout the policy analysis of use and deterrence.

The first case is "counter-population" warfare; directly intended attacks on civilian centers qualifies as murder in Catholic moral theology. It is not justified even in retaliation for an attack on our cities and no exceptions of the principle are admitted.

The second case is the "initiation of nuclear war." This case requires a different moral judgment. The pastoral opposes the first use of nuclear weapons and supports a "no first use" pledge in these words: "We do not perceive any situation in which the deliberate initiation of nuclear warfare, on however restricted a scale, can be morally justified. Non-nuclear attacks by another state must be resisted by other than nuclear means." The letter explicitly acknowledges that it will take time to implement such a policy. It also acknowledges certain objections to a "no first use" pledge. Hence this assessment does not have the same absolute character as the "counter-population" section; we have made prudential judgments, and we are aware that people can and will draw other conclusions based on a different reading of the factual data.

The third case, that of "limited nuclear war," involves an assessment of what the *real* as opposed to the *theoretical* meaning of "limited" is. Taking into account the long debate—both strategic and moral—which surrounds this question, the pastoral argues that the entire burden of proof rests on those who would hold that limited nuclear exchange can indeed be contained within moral limits. The skepticism of the letter about the possibility of control shows through clearly in this section.

On the question of deterrence, the judgment of the pastoral is based on Pope John Paul's statement to the United Nations in June, 1982. We have taken the Holy Father's judgment and applied it to the specific details of U.S. strategic policy. Such an application, of course, is done in our name. The judgment of the pastoral is "strictly conditioned moral acceptance" of deterrence. Devoid of all modifiers, the judgment is acceptance not condemnation. But we have used the term "strictly conditioned" to stress that deterrence must be seen as a transitional strategy. The pastoral highlights the meaning of transitional by attaching a series of conditions to the content of deterrence policy. The letter seeks to keep deterrence limited to a very specific function; it resists extending it to war-fighting strategies, and it calls for keeping a clear fire-break between conventional and nuclear weapons. Finally, we have called for an aggressive pursuit of arms control and disarmament objectives, including a halt to the testing, production and deployment of nuclear systems.

THE REACTION TO THE PASTORAL

Never before has a document of the American Bishops received more publicity, both within the Church and throughout the broader community. This is due to the timeliness of the topic, its sensitivity and the open process by which the pastoral letter was developed. In the few moments I have this afternoon, it is not possible for me to summarize all the reactions to the pastoral, many of which have been positive, and some negative. One highly significant point, however, has emerged which makes the whole project worthwhile: It has sensitized both the Church and the general public to the fact that the nuclear issue has a moral and religious dimension which cannot be ignored.

Ambassador George Kennan, Professor Emeritus at the Institute for Advanced Study, in an article which appeared in the *New*

York Times on May 1, stated it well. "The development of the nuclear weapon," he said, "bringing the power of existing arsenals to a point that made their use in warfare suicidal and threatening to the very intactness of civilization . . . (has presented) dilemmas to which the wisdom of the past provided no sure answers, and (has raised) the demand for a fundamental rethinking of the role of armed force in the strategy and the moral philosophy of the modern state." Those dilemmas must be squarely faced and he sees the pastoral "as the most profound and searching inquiry yet conducted by any responsible collective body into the relations of nuclear weaponry, and indeed of modern war in general, to moral philosophy, to politics and to the conscience of the national state." "The beauty of the pastoral letter," he concludes, "lies precisely in the limitations it defines–in the moral perimeters it established for the use of force in international affairs."

Our major goal in the pastoral was not to solve all the problems of the nuclear era but to give the moral dimension of those problems their rightful place in the public debate. The letter has accomplished this. It has both engendered and responded to a sense of expectation. On the basis of what I have heard and seen, I am convinced that the majority of people think that a clear moral voice is needed. While they may not agree with every conclusion, they are appreciative of the framework provided by the pastoral—a framework within which they can make their own moral analysis of the many questions posed by the nuclear age.

WHERE DO WE GO FROM HERE?

It took over two years for the Bishops to develop their pastoral. They have now made it their own by an overwhelming vote which indicates a significant degree of unity in their perception of the problem and the need to address it. The key question now is whether the pastoral will actually become a document of the whole Church. Our hope is that it will serve as the basis for further study and reflection; that it will motivate people to struggle, in the same way we did, with the critical issues of our day in the light of our moral tradition. This is the function of the Church in a democratic society: to provide a framework for and to stimulate discussion on moral issues in the broader community and, within the Church, to form a community of conscience which will witness to the values of the gospel as reflected in our Catholic tradition.

The shaping of this community of conscience will require many different agents in the Church. One is the Catholic university. The issues of war and peace are complex and they need to be pursued on a continuing basis. In his 1983 World Day of Peace message, Pope John Paul called for "scientific studies on war, its nature, causes, means, objectives and risks." Such studies, he said, have much to teach us on the conditions for peace. Echoing this sentiment, the pastoral calls on "universities, particularly Catholic universities, in our country to develop programs for rigorous, interdisciplinary research, education and training directed toward peacemaking expertise."

Whatever the specific instrumentality might be, I urge Notre Dame to be in the forefront of peacemaking studies. What better way would there be to take seriously Jesus' mandate: Blessed are the peacemakers! Addressing the contemporary questions of peace and war in a scholarly fashion and in the context of our Christian teaching and tradition would be a great service both to the Catholic community and the wider society. I would be pleased to collaborate with you in such an endeavor.

Another important agent in this task of shaping a community of conscience is you, the graduating class of 1983. The pastoral letter describes the present time as a "new moment." This "new moment" resides in the vivid awareness people have of the danger of our times and the public determination that governments be challenged to take decisive steps against the nuclear threat. There is an openness, as I said earlier, to allowing a strong, clear moral voice to enter the debate as to how we should meet this challenge. I urge you to take advantage of this "new moment" by lending your own voice to the discussion. You do this, of course, more by example than by word. The Church's witness is really your witness because the Church's witness is tied to the integrity and the quality of life of its members. So how you live your lives, the priority you give to the values of the gospel, will speak loudly and make a tremendous difference in the future. Witness flows from prayer and wisdom; witness is the fruit of both and it will be the measure of your success. Your witness, both now and in the future, will help to make peace a stable reality in our nuclear age.

May the Lord, the Prince of Peace, bless you in the months and years ahead. And may Our Lady, Notre Dame, the Queen of Peace, be always at your side.

JOSE NAPOLEON DUARTE

*Jose Napoleon Duarte (1925–1990) was born in San Salvador,
El Salvador, to a family of modest means. He attended Notre Dame,
where he had the young Fr. Theodore Hesburgh as a theology
professor. On returning home he pursued a successful career as a
civil engineer before being drawn into politics in the 1960s. The
Christian Democratic Party in El Salvador that Duarte helped found
sought to occupy the middle ground between communism and
the vicious military totalitarianism that had dominated his country
for decades. He was elected mayor of San Salvador, his nation's
capital, in the 1960s, but in the following decade he was
tortured and exiled as a consequence of his quest to bring
democracy to the national level.*

*After his return from exile in 1979, Duarte participated in
a civilian-military government and continued his efforts in support of
human rights and democratic government. In 1984 he became the first
elected civilian president of his country in half a century. In addition,
he was the first graduate of Notre Dame to become a head of state.
Supporters portrayed him as "the father of Salvadoran democracy,"
struggling to bring justice to his nation. Critics, on the other
hand, pointed out his failure not only to introduce effective social
and economic reform but also to counter the brutal human
rights abuses of the Salvadoran military. Duarte was diagnosed
with cancer in 1988 but he courageously served out his
presidential term with the same determination and tenacity
that had characterized his entire political career.*

The Struggle for Democracy

(1985)

It is indeed a genuine privilege to come to this University where such a diversity of human wisdom is taught, discussed and learned.

Let us reflect on the problems related to bringing peace, freedom and social justice to my country. I am sure these are issues which have caught the attention of all free men in America. We will talk about realities in El Salvador and about our democratic revolution. As President of El Salvador, I want to talk to you about our struggle to achieve the goals of democracy.

Throughout the last four years, the people of the United States have generously supported our efforts in El Salvador to divorce ourselves from the repression and cruelty of the past, and bring new life to democracy in this hemisphere. Today, I bring you good news: democracy has been born in El Salvador. It is healthy and growing stronger. In the last three years, Salvadoreans had the opportunity to decide between the policies of the past and those of the future; between governments controlled by a few, and a government controlled by the voters. On all occasions, the voters spoke with one voice and with one purpose, confirming their dedication to peace, to freedom, to social justice and democracy.

Ladies and gentlemen, I come in 1985 to express my thanks for the recognition the University is granting me. The conferral of a degree *Honoris Causa* means you have considered that I have tried to practice the lessons learned at Notre Dame. I am here as a representative of my country, of the millions of people of El Salvador who have suffered the tyranny of dictatorship for the past fifty years, who have suffered injustices and lack of freedom. I come as the Constitutional President of my country, freely elected, to carry out humane and Christian principles, and to mold social discipline based on justice, liberty and democracy. You have acknowledged my efforts in striving to reach the objective of social peace as dictated by the Church, and instilled in you and me by this University.

It is for me a great honor to be at Notre Dame, under the cloak of Notre Dame du Lac and the Golden Dome, symbols of our tradition at Notre Dame.

From the moment I entered the University as a student in 1944 I began to feel what would later serve as the basis for my conduct and guide the destiny of my life.

I left San Salvador at a time when my country was in crisis. The totalitarian government then in power had forced many young men such as me to consider going to Guatemala to join Dr. Arturo Romero, leader of the democratic movement of our country.

When my father sent me to study in the United States, I passed through Guatemala, and I too considered staying and fighting with the opposition. I might well have died, as many of them did, in the Battle of Ahuachapan if Dr. Romero had not insisted I come and study in the United States.

En route, a Salvadorean companion and I stopped in St. Louis, Missouri, and, young men that we were, decided to have a few beers at a bar. We were joined by some young Americans with whom we struck up a conversation. One of them asked us: "Where are you headed?" My friend, who spoke English, answered, "We are going to Notre Dame." The American smiled and responded: "Well, now Notre Dame is importing football players from South America so they can beat Army and Navy!"

I did not know that Notre Dame was a university famous for its football team, but I soon came to understand what the sports prestige of Notre Dame meant; that the meaning of the "Fighting Irish" transcended the mere sports dimension underlying Notre Dame's educational scientific tradition and its social values.

The day I arrived at the University and saw the great and beautiful fields and wonderful foliage, my first impulse was to run across the lovely grass. The then-Prefect of Discipline, Father Joseph Kehoe, saw me in the middle of the field and called to me. He stared intensely at me and scolded me, but all I heard was a torrent of words that did not mean a thing. I spoke not one word of English, but Father Kehoe's face, eyes and attitude all said one thing: "What kind of a person are you? Don't you understand that the University's beauty must be protected; that you may not step on the grass; that you must discipline yourself and respect the University's rules and principles? . . ." This was my first lesson at Notre Dame.

That was way back when. . . . I don't know how much things have changed. But now that we are co-ed, I would be delighted to look around. . . .

During my student days, I came to understand the need for a system of discipline that established the city limits open to us: the "in and out" hours, or what, in difficult English for me, you call "parietals," norms of conduct and daily inspections.

Another anecdote concerns my first religion class. The professor, a very young priest, spoke to us about Apologetics, Religion, Philosophy and Theology. Thanks to the language barrier, I didn't understand a word he was saying. In need of help, I asked a friend to translate. The young priest saw me speaking to my neighbor while he expounded on such important matters. He pointed to me and asked: "What's your name?" I answered: "Napoleon Duarte," and he said: "Nappy, if you continue talking in class, I'm going to throw you out the window." I have been "Nappy" to Father Hesburgh ever since that day.

When class was over, Father Ted motioned to me and asked: "Why were you talking in class?" In my best eight-day-old English, I answered: "To understand what you say, I need help." His expression changed, and he said: "Nappy, pay a lot of attention and learn English fast because you're going to need it."

Thus passed my years at Notre Dame, much like yours: learning, studying, worrying. The work-load seemed never-ending, and we managed to pull some all-nighters, quite a feat in those days when lights out was strictly enforced at 10 p.m. Otherwise, it would be a matter of getting up an hour before Mass to do some last-minute cramming.

Then, there was the other kind of work: the kind to make ends meet. I worked variously as a waiter in the dining room, washing dishes in the kitchen, ironing clothes in the laundry, washing windows in summer. . . .

Just as I am sure you have done, I spent a lot of time thinking about how demanding my professors were, but in retrospect, after nearly 40 years, I can tell you it was worth the hard work. The day I received my diploma, as you will today, I left the University full of enthusiasm, ready to show the world what I had learned in the technical field of engineering. At that point, I had not realized the importance of the "other" education received; the one that deals with values, and discipline, and the principles of tradition that had been given me at Notre Dame.

But the lessons did not end with my graduation. When Father Hesburgh arrived in Central America for the first time on August 12, 1960, he called together the alumni and spoke to us on the role which we as "Domers" were called on to play in society. He insisted on the responsibility we had in serving our community and asked me specifically: "Nappy, do you remember the values we spoke about in our religion class? Our discussions of social justice, the dignity of man, the social doctrine of the Church?" I remember that he said: "You cannot stand with your arms folded and believe you are acting patriotically if all you do is construct bridges, buildings, roads. . . . You have an ethical commitment with yourself, a moral commitment to Notre Dame, and an historical commitment to your country."

Today I stand here accountable before you. For 25 years I have sought to spread the message that when God created Man in His image and likeness, He did so because He wanted man to live in harmony with society, not isolated from it. For this reason He gave Man the gifts of love, understanding and charity with which to strengthen the good in the world and compensate for the evil. Selfishness, ambition, envy, the seven capital sins, have given rise to and occasioned the historical foundations not only of my people, but of humanity as well.

The social structure has left its imprint on my country, on Latin America and on the rest of the world. The new generation that today assumes leadership inherits a world in which "might makes right" and where violence rules rather than reason, thereby indicating that we have learned nothing from history.

Contemporary social dichotomy has divided humanity along ideological and economic lines; it has confronted nation against nation in the power struggle for world hegemony.

Today's world has produced widespread terrorism. The disrespect towards life and social discipline allows for the decomposition of the social process. Anarchy has reached every nation, injecting fear and hopelessness into the life of humanity.

From an economic point of view, the financial crisis we are undergoing affects nations, rich and poor. Economic dependency, however, has cast industrialized countries against those of the Third World which are forced to bear the consequences of their own dependency. This is what we are up against in the Central American region, and this, my fellow graduates of the University of Notre Dame, is an integral part of the world you inherit today.

As an individual, I place myself against the process of confrontation and violence. In all aspects of life, we must exercise our free will. We must rely on the values we have learned and we must choose compassion as a guide for our own destinies.

But the very nature of the world's problems determines the social dimension by which we are joined together, not only as individuals, but as a brotherhood of nations. Just as on a multinational scale what affects one nation has repercussions on another, so too, it happens on a personal level, that the sadness of one man lost in a corner of our universe is felt by the rest of mankind. In the words of John Fitzgerald Kennedy: "The rights of all men are diminished when the rights of one man are threatened."

I consider that the principles of Christianity are more than valid when it comes to asking the nations of the world to comport themselves in manners conducive to achieving world peace. Selfish behavior and a mentality of oppression lead us in the opposite direction.

If one were to apply Christian theory in promoting international social justice, we should all dedicate ourselves to will for each individual the vital space necessary so that the basic needs of security, liberty and justice can be satisfied in the pursuit of self-fulfillment.

Humanity is at a crossroads of misery, caught between North versus South, East versus West, one another. All suffer from economic and social crises. We are also suffering from a crisis of moral values.

Another problem we cannot ignore regards the population explosion. In Latin America we already suffer from a socioeconomic crisis as a result of injustice, misery, lack of social services, malnutrition, disease and unemployment. This reality has sharpened the conflict within each Latin American nation, but of even greater concern is the increase in population, which, when seen in all its dimensions, presents a truly terrifying picture.

Today there is hunger, misery and unemployment in Africa, America, El Salvador, Mexico, Colombia, Brazil. But demographic growth gives us an even more somber panorama of Latin America when statistics tell us that in terms of millions of new lives, there will be a new Brazil every two years, a new Colombia every six months, a new El Salvador every two weeks. . . . Can you imagine this? Stop and think about it! Latin America simply cannot meet the demands posed by this sea of humanity.

These are the problems Father Hesburgh perceived.

This is the reason he took up battle in all possible forums, from civil rights to nuclear disarmament.

Father Hesburgh's objective has been to invite reflection by world leaders regarding the depressing reality of the world.

His motivation in favor of humanity has given prestige to the University, and commits all of us, students and alumni, to take up that call as soldiers of the "Fighting Irish" battalion. As members of the Notre Dame family scattered throughout the world, we cannot remain impassive in the face of the challenge modern-day society presents to us. Our duty lies in becoming knights of human dignity, who, with our shields of "gold and blue" defend the humble of the world.

Now I would like to tell you of my efforts on behalf of the people of El Salvador, a lifelong task that began with the call from Father Hesburgh and my subsequent work in founding and organizing the Christian Democratic Party of El Salvador. For three consecutive terms I was elected Mayor of San Salvador, beginning in 1964.

In 1972 those of us who believed in the democratic system joined forces to combat the ruling dictatorship. The people responded to our message by electing me President of our country. Those in power did not accept the popular will and instead imposed their own president. Along with others, I was arrested and tortured. I am alive today only because Father Hesburgh interceded on my behalf before Pope Paul VI and the President of the United States, Richard Nixon. A court martial determined my fate, and for the next eight long years I lived in exile in Venezuela. In 1979, a coup d'etat led by the progressive military sector of El Salvador allowed my return to the country.

When I returned, I found the country in social turmoil; the people were suffering at the hands of a repressive dictatorship that defended the oligarchy's hegemony of power. The Marxist fronts increased the use of violence as a means of effecting a revolution that only worsened the situation. Never were the verses of the Irish poet, William Butler Yeats, more true than when applied to my country:

> Things fall apart: the center cannot hold,
> Mere anarchy is loosed upon the world.
> The blood-dimmed tide is loosed, and everywhere
> The ceremony of innocence is drowned;
> The best lack all conviction, while the worst
> Are full of passionate intensity.

Destiny moved me to show that the center could hold together the world that was falling apart.

In 1980, I was asked to accept the challenge of forming part of the Revolutionary Junta Government, and after reflecting a good deal, I took the great risk of integrating a *de facto* regime, full of internal contradictions. Great violence had caused total loss of credibility for El Salvador on the international front. However, I felt reassured that my democratic mission in that almost hopeless moment constituted the ideal of El Salvador's peoples. It was my most intimate conviction that my obligation lay in freeing my country from the two totalitarian extremes: the Marxists and the fascists.

I must confess that those thirty months were dramatic for my spirit. Each crisis brought waves of doubt, and many times, my lone support came from prayer and the unbreakable belief that my failure would also mean the failure of my people. My mind and spirit carried the unbearable burden of so much hate and violence.

Throughout the course of these politically active years, I have always been able to count on Father Ted's moral support, but especially so in the past five years. In 1982, he formed part of the official U.S. delegation that acted as observers for Constituent Assembly elections. At that time, Father Ted visited even the most remote villages as a witness to the huge effort the people of El Salvador were making towards achieving peace via democratic elections.

The Christian Democratic Party did not win a majority of seats in that election, and, faithful to my democratic convictions, I handed over power in accordance with the decision taken by the Constituent Assembly. At that point, in 1982, I declared to our Congress and the people of El Salvador:

> I did not arrive on the political scene by accident. For me, politics is an ethic and I was drawn to it through my vocation to serve. As a professional, I could have earned my living easily; as a politician, I could have easily earned my death. . . . If an historian tried to determine the climax of my political life, it would not have been when I was elected President in 1972, or when seven Latin American Presidents, gathered in Santa Marta, Colombia, accepted my commitment to fight for democracy. No, the most important moment of my political life up to this point comes now, when I step down from power and say, 'mission accomplished.' It means the culmination of a new democratic profession of faith. It means we kept our promise to hold free elections. Now we hand over power to my legitimate successor without deceit or fraud. This moment is important because we have had the guts to confront destiny. We have established the basis for democracy and initiated structural reforms. We have fulfilled our historical obligation with our country, our people and our conscience. . . .

But my task did not end with this step on the long road towards a truly democratic society, and I prepared myself for the 1984 presidential elections.

The moment of truth drew closer. The Marxist left denied all possibility of a popular referendum and continued with . . . violent revolution. The rightist reactionaries [increased] the actions of their infamous death squads. At the same time, they used and abused the democratic electoral system to impose once again their repressive and dictatorial methods. I had faith in the people, and, under the green banner of hope, I led the people towards their liberation, casting aside all schemes of violence.

In 1984, the people responded massively to my plea for Faith and Hope. Despite terrorist actions from the two extremes and against all odds, the people scored a victory and democratically elected me Constitutional President of the country.

This, fellow graduates, has been my homework for the last forty years. I learned that there is a difficult right choice and an easy wrong choice.

Along with the Executive power, I now count on the support of our Congress to aid me in developing the five vital political areas the country needs: one, to humanize the conflict; two, to pacify the nation; three, to democratize our society; four, to guarantee the participation of our people in all decisions; and five, to reactivate the economy. These five objectives will serve as the foundation for human development and social peace in El Salvador.

I will devote all my efforts so that these policies serve as instruments of peace, and I will propitiate the dialogue among all sectors. I firmly believe that God gave us the gift of speech in order that we might understand each other and lessen our differences.

And so, my dear friends, fellow alumni and graduates, the time has come for you and me to say farewell.

I thank Notre Dame for the many lessons it taught me and for the values it helped me understand. To the young men and women who leave today to meet their own opportunities and choices, I have this advice:

First, you *can* make a difference. If you accept your responsibilities and make wise choices, you will be contributing to the solution rather than the problem.

Second, never lose sight of the values you have been taught; they alone will remind you of your responsibilities and guide you in your choices.

Third, in the face of adversity, maintain faith in yourselves and the human spirit; enter the world with optimism.

The Department of Engineering at Notre Dame gave me the technical know-how necessary in my profession, and now, with this distinction *Honoris Causa,* the University converts me into a social engineer, giving me greater strength to serve my country.

I will return to my home stadium, El Salvador, where I will have to imitate George Gipp and score a victory for peace. George is up there, and through him, I want to invoke the power of God. We in El Salvador need the help and protection of God. I also want to invoke the blessing of Notre Dame du Lac, our Lady of the Lake, that she may help me to continue serving with optimism. I want to serve my people;

I want to fight for my people in favor of freedom and democracy and peace. This is my commitment!

This is why I feel that this moving ceremony is like a pep rally where we have come together to renew the spirit of the "Fighting Irish," the rah-rah spirit of the night before the big game. And now, remembering our Victory March, let us say:

"ONWARD TO VICTORY. . .

"CHEER, CHEER, FOR OLD NOTRE DAME. . . ."

Thank you all very much.

ANDREW YOUNG

*A renowned civil and human rights leader, Andrew Jackson Young
(1932–) grew up in New Orleans and was educated at Dillard and
Howard Universities and at Hartford Theological Seminary. An
ordained minister in the United Church of Christ, Young emerged
as a top aide to Martin Luther King, Jr., during the civil rights
movement when he served as vice-president of the Southern Christian
Leadership Conference. Thereafter, Young pursued a distinguished
career of government service as a congressman, as ambassador to
the United Nations, and as a two-term mayor of Atlanta. After his
retirement as mayor he cochaired the 1996 Centennial Olympic
Games and developed a new career as an international businessman
and thoughtful humanitarian. In addition to serving on the boards
of numerous businesses and organizations, Young teaches
courses at Georgia State University's School of Policy Studies,
which is named in his honor.*

Let God and History Take You

(1988)

This has been a moving experience for me. I share in your joy and
your exuberance. You remind me of a school that I once ran, a school
for civil rights workers in southwest Georgia. Those students would
come together from all over the South, and in one week's time we
would develop something of the kind of camaraderie that you have
developed here. We would teach them the little that we knew about
voter registration and about literacy skills and how to teach their
friends and neighbors to read and write in order to register to vote.
And the last night was almost always a joyous celebration. Yet even as
I shared in the joy and as we put them on the buses to go back to Alabama, Mississippi, Louisiana, and South Carolina, I would almost
always go off by myself. I would find myself reflecting on the life that
I knew they were going into, and I would end up praying and crying.

I don't want to put a damper on your experience just yet, but
Father Malloy said something about responsibility in the conferring of
these degrees. In the midst of your cheers you may have not heard
him, and yet it won't be long before that sense of responsibility begins
to grip you. You cannot go to a great university like this without recall-
ing the biblical admonition, "To them to whom much has been given,
of them will much be required." All of the thrill and joy that has gone
with your education and the social experience which accompanied
it will certainly require of you the very same kinds of achievements
you recognized with honorary degrees on the occasion of this commencement.

There has been here today a distinguished gathering of people
from almost every walk of life—from business, from clerical administration to pastoring in the streets, from science, both in academe and

in practical life, to politics. I doubt that any of them would have imagined that at the time of their commencement that their lives would have encompassed all of the blessings and all of the joys and all of the accomplishments for which they have been honored. I was like probably most of you, I did not graduate *summa cum laude* or *magna cum laude*. I graduated, "O Thank Your Lordie." And yet, that same Lord that saw me through, a Lord who was petitioned every day without fail by my mother, who, though we were not Catholic, went to Corpus Christi Church every morning before she went to work and lit a candle on my behalf. Most of you are getting through because of your mother's prayers, too.

And so there is a lot, a lot that will happen for us. That is almost impossible for us to imagine at this time. Believe it or not, I didn't have the slightest notion on leaving Howard University or Hartford Theological Seminary that I would in any way be involved in civil rights. If I would stop for a minute to think, it was only logical that I could not go back to the South with the kind of education and the kind of commitment that I had developed without running into trouble with somebody, and that encounter would inevitably lead to some kind of movement. But, few of us, not even Martin Luther King, knew what was in store. For Martin Luther King went from Boston University to Montgomery, Alabama, really to finish his Ph.D. dissertation, and when he was asked to join the leadership of the NAACP, he declined because he didn't want to get involved. It was only a few months after he completed his Ph.D. dissertation and mailed it back to Boston University that Rosa Parks sat down in a bus, and he found himself almost snatched up by the shoulders and pushed to the front of the leadership of one the most powerful, spiritual and political movements that this nation has ever known.

I say to you, Martin Luther King was an exceptional man, but no more exceptional than most of you. For when God grabs you by the collar or grabs you by the shoulders and pushes you, inevitably you go. And when you go, you find your life radically changed, and it's almost as though there is nothing much you can do about it. It's not just when you are in the clergy. It happens to teachers. It happens to nurses, to doctors, and even lawyers and business people get religion now and then. There could have been no civil rights movement without the lawyers. It was the law, it was one nation indivisible under God living by the law, that enabled our nation to undergo a radical social revolution with a very, very minimum of violence. And it was the men and women of business who moved to bring the community together, even before the politicians. Most of the South's desegregation was accomplished by men and women in the movement and in business even before the laws were changed. And now we see a Southland that is dramatically different. But, you know, I have to give the engineers a little credit, too. Because if it hadn't been for engineers devising a Tennessee Valley Authority and rural electrification and a beautiful system of man-made lakes and irrigation that made the Southland beautiful, without that engineering infrastructure, the social and spiritual difficulties would have been far more difficult. And so you represent the sum total of the potential of the human spirit. Having received the best education that is available in one of the best institutions of the world, we expect a lot of you—and God will demand a lot of you.

I would urge you to go into politics. I think everybody ought to go into politics. And you ought not wait, you ought not wait to run for something, you should start right this summer. We are going to make decisions about the future of the next century in the 1988 elections in November. And in November we will chart the course of this nation for the remainder of this century at the local level, at the congressional level, at the presidential level. And I don't even want to make it a partisan suggestion. It's important that you work for what you believe in, because we even need some good Republicans. But the ideals and values that essentially have made this a great university are nonpartisan or bipartisan, they really are universal ideals. And in the volunteering—in the simple writing of speeches, of position papers, of putting on bumper stickers—you get involved in the political process. And you will find that, regardless of what you learn here, if you can't deal with politics, it is very hard to translate it into action in a democracy. Democracy is the vehicle by which all of what you believe and want to maintain about this society can become a reality. And so I say volunteer, volunteer now and be a part of this day's history and shape our future in these elections.

America has always been led by volunteers, and they have not always been the older and most experienced. All of the movements of which I have been a part—the civil rights movement, the peace movement, the women's movement, the movement for justice and human rights all over the world—has had its energy, its vision and its vitality coming from young men and women who were employed in other fields, but who took social change as the cause and meaning of their lives. They found it necessary to try to do something to shape the environment in which they lived. And so I would hope that you would work for a national voluntary service, something that extends and expands the kind of thing that Sarge Shriver did in the Peace Corps, which has done more to preserve and protect our nation's foreign policy than perhaps much of the military action of the recent decade. I assure you that the Peace Corps is much less expensive than any of our military actions.

Then I would like to dare you to think big. For we are part of a nation that has really shaped the life of our planet. We did it in the South through Franklin Roosevelt's New Deal, and at the end of the Second World War, there were agreements, agreements that stabilized currencies, provided for free trade, free exchange of technology, free access to markets, agreements that basically created a global economic order that allowed Europe and Japan to develop in 25 years into full-fledged competitors. That kind of bold leadership is called for in terms of the rest of the world. By the year 2000, 79 percent of world's population will be the so-called Third World. I would like to translate that into business terms—79 percent of the world market will be outside of America, Europe and Asia. It will be in Latin America, in Africa, in the Middle East, in Southeast Asia. And if we are going to survive as an economic entity in the free world, there's going to have to be some interrelationship between the developed world and the developing world. I was very pleased to run across a very bold notion by the Mitsubishi Research Corporation in Japan, an idea if advanced by a "do-gooder" like myself would be laughed at. Mitsubishi Research talks about $500 billion in a global infrastructure fund, to promote all over the world the kinds of development that would make life more livable, that would feed the hungry, that would clothe the naked, that would heal the sick. They talk about the kinds of projects that essentially would make the world make sense, things that are possible financially, things that are feasible in terms of the macro-engineering skills that are available in our planet, things that require only the political will and the vision of people of many nations. We need to come together and provide the growth and development for the entire planet that we have been provided in the United States and in Europe and Japan.

And so I would say to you that you are going to have to make this planet make sense. And it's not as complicated as it sounds. It certainly is no more difficult than some of the kinds of changes that have occurred in our own country in the last 25 years. But, if you are going to do that, you have got to be very suspect of much of conventional wisdom. You have got to look at the world through your own eyes; preferably, look at the world through the eyes of the Church. Look at the world through the eyes of your Lord, these are children of God, who perhaps demand and want the same sorts of things that you and I want. It's very hard for us. In fact, when I was part of the Carter Administration, everybody was sure that there could be no peace between blacks and whites in Rhodesia. When I began to look into the situation, I found out that one of the leaders was a Roman Catholic school teacher for 17 years and that we were writing him off as a Marxist terrorist. And I realized that another was a Presbyterian lay preacher, another a minister of the United Church of Christ and a fourth a bishop in a Methodist church. I couldn't understand how we could consign these people to Marxism and just forget about them and ignore them. Once we began to talk to them and approach them in the context of their Judeo-Christian heritage and in the context of the democratic ideals that were a part of their tradition, we were able to provide a constitution that ended the civil war and that made it possible for blacks and whites to live together with majority rule while protecting minority rights. Ian Smith was the man who waged that unilateral declaration of independence and who fought a bloody war against his black citizens, who had guns, tanks and rockets. And in spite of 15 years of bloodshed, Ian Smith now walks the streets of Zimbabwe without a bodyguard. And blacks and whites live and work side-by-side in peace.

If it can happen in Rhodesia and Rhodesia could become an independent Zimbabwe, with a little effort from your generation and mine the same could happen in South Africa in our lifetime. P. W. Botha and Nelson Mandela would make a great team negotiating and working on a constitution. We have got to be very careful in looking at these sorts of things; it's very hard for us to look at Central America and explain our nation's policies. I don't know how you can dismiss a government as Marxist, Leninist, totalitarian when there are three priests, a novelist and a poet leading the government. There ought to be something there that would enable us to deal with that kind of situation, short of violence and short of military confrontation and subversion. The best of America should be able to bring out the best amongst the people of the world. It ought to be possible with all of technology at our disposal to see to it that the hungry are fed and that the naked are clothed and that people somehow learn to live in peace.

Now, I know this is the kind of thing that people always say at commencements. And yet, I say that if the things could happen in my lifetime that have happened, God working with you can make much more happen in your lifetime through you. I left college driving back to New Orleans, my home, and when I went through to Georgia, I stopped, and turned around and got gas in South Carolina. Georgia was the worst place in the world for somebody black to be driving at night, and I didn't even want to stop in Georgia to get gas. I drove down Peach Tree Street in Atlanta and a rat crossed the road. And I was driving so easy and was so nervous at 3 o'clock in the morning, I slowed down for the rat. The rat had more rights than black folks in Georgia in those days. And if anybody had said to me, "Son, you better slow down and look around Atlanta; you are going to be the mayor there one day," it was inconceivable. Blacks didn't vote in Georgia then. And yet, somehow, that very Georgia that I was so afraid of has become the home that I love, has been transformed into the place that my wife and children call home, and is, well, almost as close to the Kingdom of God as we think we'll ever get. (And if you want a good place to work, come on to Atlanta—we've got plenty of jobs for you.) But, there is nothing about my ability, there is nothing about my vision, nothing about my skills that made it possible for these things to happen in my life. But somehow God and history can take you as you are and can do with you what you will let him. I would say to you, in the fields which you have chosen and the tasks that are at hand, go with God and go in peace. May the blessings of God be yours all the days of your lives. Amen.

—ɯ—

CONDOLEEZZA RICE

Born into a middle-class African-American family in segregated Birmingham, Alabama, Condoleezza Rice (1954–) became an accomplished classical pianist and a talented ice skater before deciding to study international relations. She trained first at the University of Denver, took a master's degree from Notre Dame in 1975, and returned to Denver for her doctorate, emerging as a Soviet and Eastern European specialist. She joined the political science faculty at Stanford University in 1981 and taught effectively there for eight years until National Security Adviser Brent Scowcroft recruited her to advise President George H. W. Bush on Soviet and Eastern European affairs during the critical years from 1989 to 1991 as the Soviet bloc collapsed and disintegrated.

After two years, Rice returned to Stanford to eventually serve as provost—the youngest person, the first woman, and the first African-American to ever hold the position. She proved a capable administrator but resigned her position in 1999 to advise George W. Bush on foreign policy issues during his presidential campaign. He appointed her national security adviser, where she plays a key part in the formulation of the nation's foreign policy. Her strong performance in the tense period after the September 11, 2001, terrorist attacks won her deserved praise.

The Role of the Educated Person

(1995)

I want to thank you for this opportunity to return here to Notre Dame and to be with you on this splendid occasion. I was actually here last in the fall when Notre Dame played Stanford in football. It was my first trip back to campus in better than 10 years. I was reminded of the spirit, the excitement, the sights and the sounds of South Bend on a football Saturday. I was also able to reflect on how important this place has been to me.

When I came to Notre Dame as a 19-year-old I had never lived away from home. I learned a lot about myself here. Even though I had lived for a while in Denver I learned what winter really meant. I grew up here in a very short time to be sure. Notre Dame was a nurturing and caring environment and I have never forgotten that. And so on that Saturday last October I want to assure you that I was reminded by Father Joyce of a paraphrase that seemed just right to me. John Kennedy once said this about the Naval Academy/Notre Dame football game: "I want you to know that last October I pulled for Stanford but I prayed for Notre Dame."

The years that you have been here have been extraordinary ones in human history. This very month we have been commemorating the end of World War II, the sacrifice as well as the unifying experience of that great moral crusade. It was a transforming experience for an entire generation, a source of pride in the rightness of the cause. But in commemorating the war's end, we need to remember that the hard work had really just begun in 1945: the rebuilding of Europe and much of Asia, decolonization, the creation of stable democracies in Germany and Japan that would become firm pillars of a more stable and prosperous world.

Fifty years later we can see the success of that era. There is no doubt that the community of free nations grew and that old enemies joined in alliances and friendships never to fight again. Peace between them flowed from the common values and aspirations of a democratic way of life. The universities and the educated people of that generation played a role in that historic transformation. They did it by realizing that ideas and learning should not, indeed could not, be confined to within national boundaries if nations were to overcome their differences. They did it by sending Marshall and Fulbright fellows and scholars abroad and in turn accepting them here at home. They contributed ideas to the policy process and scholars to public service. And they kept the door open to peoples and knowledge from places that wished to quarantine their populations from the light of free exchange. At their very best universities were places where educated people were bound, at least for the moment, by the title scholar or student that transcended national differences.

Now, in 1995, we are in the midst of another great and challenging transition. The Cold War ended in euphoria and hope. Who can forget the images as German met German across the no-man's land that was the Berlin Wall? Who can forget the celebration of democracy's dawn in Poland or the velvet revolution in Czechoslovakia? Who can forget the peaceful death of the Soviet Union as on Christmas night in 1991 the hammer and sickle of the mighty Soviet empire came down from atop the Kremlin for the last time? Who can forget the pictures of the old and sick in South Africa voting for the first time, voting with enthusiasm and pride for a better future that they will personally never see? The images are not forgotten but they have certainly faded giving way to a kind of quiet despair about the hard work yet to be done. That work is indeed made harder because we have also turned inward to look at ourselves, at the state of democracy at home in America, and that is fitting. There is much at stake here at home and abroad because people still look to the United States of America to see if one can be forged from many, to see if multiethnic democracy can work.

During the Cold War I sometimes chuckled when U.S. presidents talked about America as a beacon for democracy. Sometimes I was just plain embarrassed. I chalked it up to hyperbole or bad speech writing or perhaps both. But I want to tell you that as I traveled throughout eastern Europe and the Soviet Union in 1989 and 1990, as the grip of totalitarian government slipped step by step, I had to admit to myself that what American presidents had been saying was indeed true. You cannot know the strength of democracy's pull until you see it in someone else's eyes. Throughout eastern Europe and the Soviet Union, in those days, I saw America reflected through the eyes of those who were still searching for the civil rights that we take for granted: the right to say what you think, to worship freely, to choose those who will rule. But I would protest, we have so much more to do. Ours is an imperfect democracy. It was imperfect at its birth. When the founding fathers said, "We the people," they did not mean me. To them my ancestors were property. But little by little we are a more inclusive society where "we the people" have come to mean more and more of us. Therein lies the lesson: Democracy is a work in progress. The hard work is begun again each and every day.

That, then, is the cycle of the human experience and the challenge for every generation. Great changes are accompanied by euphoria and hope but they give way to hard work, to heavy lifting, hopefully inching forward each time to include more and more of the human race in the community characterized by democracy, prosperity and peace. As before, this generation's universities and educated people have to do their part. But the role of the university itself and that of the educated person that it produces, those are very different roles. There is constant pressure for places of learning to lead the charge, to make judgments about the relative moral weight of one political position or another. It is usually put rather starkly: The university must stand up for what is right and against what is wrong. Clearly there are times when that is appropriate, when the moral choice is black and white and absolutely clear. But much of the time the issues are gray. Universities are not the venue in which the great issues of our time will or should be decided. They never have been. That is the role of the democratic institutions of governance and the free debate that takes place within them.

I have become convinced that most of the time the university's proper place is to uphold the right of reason, to encourage the search for the truth and to teach and enlighten those within it. As before, the university must insist that knowledge and ideas have no national boundaries, remaining open and welcoming to the best and brightest from across the globe. Universities must do this believing that the educated will contribute rather than detract from the slow evolution of human society toward one that is more just and free.

The role of the educated person, though, is something else altogether. And I can assure you that I remember at my own graduation and it was just about the time that the speaker got to this point, that I had to dedicate myself to solving the world's problems, that my own inclination was to stay in school a little bit longer because it seemed a daunting and overwhelming challenge. Let me reassure you that is not what I'm going to say. Rather, I am suggesting that if you bring to bear the central values of education on your daily life, in the choices you make and in the way that you approach your fellow human beings you will contribute to a better world. So I would ask you now, for a few moments, to reflect not on the specifics of what you have learned but the environment and the context in which you have learned it.

First, always remember that you have been exceedingly privileged here. You have had the opportunity to explore the state of human knowledge as it stands today. You have been able to try new things and to find out a great deal about your interests and your talents. You have learned what you are good at doing and what you do less well. You now know that talents are varied and distributed and perhaps you have come to respect the skills of those who do well that which you do not. You have learned that it takes many of us contributing from our own interests and talents to make progress forward. If you are very lucky you have found your passion here. That life's work that helps you face each day with vigor and excitement. It might be a field of studies, a set of problems, or a moral cause that you want to make your own. It is entirely possible that you came here expecting to be passionate about something and simply changed your mind. That is the prerogative of those who come to places like Notre Dame. That in fact, happened to me.

I was destined to be a concert musician. I could read music before I could read. But one day I realized that I was good but, alas, not great. The 11 year old that I encountered in summer music camp playing the Chopin Ballade from sight—that it had taken me all year to learn—convinced me that that was an accurate assessment. I was about to spend my life teaching 13 year olds to murder Beethoven. I started to look for something else to do.

Fortunately I found Russia, a country for which I had a passion, a mysterious connection that to this day I cannot explain. I'm honored to share this platform with all of the guests here, but Jim Billington wrote a book called *The Icon and the Axe* that was actually the first book that I encountered on Russia. And it was the twisting and turning of Russian history, the intertwining with the Soviet Union's presence and thoughts about Russia's future in that book that led me to understand that I had found something very special.

If you have not found your passion, I want to encourage you to keep looking. There is nothing like the day when you feel, quite literally, that there is something in this world that you were born to do.

Second, as an educated person you have lived in the midst of a place where belief in reason and the centrality of the search to know are defining principles. Today in America, the shouting has become so loud, the temptation to wrap one's own interest in the legitimacy of moral argument so great, that people have stopped trying to reason together. We no longer want to know what the other person thinks, we just want to win the argument. The educated are more guilty than others because we are armed with skills of argumentation and the ability to mobilize facts to our side. There is nothing wrong with holding a view and holding it passionately, but when you are sure that you are right it might be well to talk with one who disagrees. They might even have a point. Instead the tendency is to talk to those who are like-minded, to yell at those who disagree, and to gain strength from the Amens of those who share your point of view.

Here at Notre Dame you have been especially privileged to be in a place where the commitment to reason and the will to know exist side by side with faith and belief. The simultaneous right to question and the ability to accept on the basis of faith is at the core of this place. It is not always easy for the educated person to find the integration of faith and reason particularly in a world that often denies that which cannot be proven, that which cannot be seen. Yet the journey toward the integration of the spiritual and the rational is a part of the evolution of human society toward one that is both knowing and humane. Without faith, humankind would surely not have survived the hardest times and found the optimism to push forward.

Those who came west across the Rocky Mountains timing the trip to leave one day after winter ended and arrive one day before it began again had to be acting on faith that a better tomorrow could be built. Those who survived the holocaust in Europe or slavery in America relied on faith that the horrors would give way and end in a better day. Father Sorin and Notre Dame's founders rebuilt this University after it burnt to the ground on faith and optimism about the future. The class that graduates today as the Class of 1995 experienced the tragic loss of classmates, of friends, four years ago. The Notre Dame family wrapped itself in faith so that life could go on. When there is no answer and reason fails, faith remains. It is the only source of the peace, of [the] path of understanding, and of optimism about a future that is irrepressible.

Third, as an educated person you have had the chance to know people from different cultures and different nations. You have not just studied them as objects you have lived together and shared your life's experiences. You have no reason to fear the borderless world, the globalization that so many find threatening. Something very odd is happening to humankind: As the world gets smaller, human beings seem to be ever more intent on finding finer distinctions between we and they.

Today everyone is angry with someone else, every nation, every people, every ethnic group seems caught up holding onto old wounds to find the moral high ground of victimization and suffering. To the degree that I have suffered more than you, my demands and my interests take precedence. Surely it is important to identify bigotry and to confront it. But if you are always looking back you cannot move forward. Finding someone else to blame is a recipe for powerlessness. If I am not powerful enough to help myself then surely I can do nothing for anyone else. We are all victims and no one is responsible for moving ahead. If you ever find yourself angry about what has been done to you or what you have been denied, try to remember that it is deluding and dangerous to always ask why someone else has been given more. It is almost always uplifting to ask why you have been given so much.

Finally, as an educated person, you have an obligation to defend the very nature and importance of education itself. You came to Notre Dame not as a reward for what you had already acheived, but for the chance to get better, to make yourself over. Our age is no different than any other in attacking the educated and universities themselves as elitists, out of touch and irrelevant. And it is absolutely true that people without the privilege of education have done as much to make

America and the world great as have the educated. But anti-intellec-tualism has a cost. It obscures the truly transforming nature of higher education.

We all have our heroes. My parents and my grandparents are mine. They all valued education and passed that on to me. I am, in fact, the third generation of Rices to go to college because of my pa-ternal grandfather. He was a poor farmer's son in Utah, Alabama. Somehow he decided that he needed to get book learning. He saved cotton to pay for his education and he asked passersby where a col-ored man could go to college. They told him of Stilman College, a black Presbyterian school in Tuscaloosa about 60 miles away. When he had saved enough cotton he made his way to Tuscaloosa but upon arriving there he was told that he could not pay his way with cotton. "How," he said, "are those boys going to school?" They said, "Well, they have what's called a scholarship and if you wanted to be a Pres-byterian minister you could have a scholarship too." "That," Grand-father Rice said, "is exactly what I had in mind." He became a minis-ter and my family has been Presbyterian ever since.

I have often wondered what caused my grandfather in Utah, Ala-bama, to want to get book learning. What caused my grandparents to spend their last dollars during the depression on leather-bound books that I still have. You know, they were onto something. Many who are graduating here today are here because grandparents or parents or perhaps they themselves understood instinctively the transfiguring nature of higher education and were willing to sacrifice to win its ben-efit. In fact, higher education is one of the few truly transforming and transfiguring experiences that we have left in America. It matters not whether you came to this place from privilege or poverty, from an urban or rural setting, from an ethnic minority or the majority, from America or abroad. You will leave here a graduate of Notre Dame and that will matter. You will leave here with ways of thinking about the world that are different than when you came and that will matter.

As you prepare to go from this place, reflect, then, not on trans-forming the world, but on how truly transformed you are by the ex-perience and the privilege of higher education. Then you will be ready to contribute to the hard work, to the change that comes day by day, brick by brick, step by step. That is the only way that the human con-dition has ever gotten better. And it's the only way that we can hope to build a brighter future for this great and good country and for the world beyond our borders.

Thank you and God be with you and your loved ones on this special day.

MARY ANN GLENDON

A distinguished legal scholar, Mary Ann Glendon (1938–) was trained at the University of Chicago. She practiced law in Chicago before joining the law faculty at Boston College in 1968. In 1986 she accepted an appointment at Harvard Law School, where she now holds the Learned Hand Professorship. She is an acclaimed expert in the fields of comparative and international law and has authored important books on family law, the legal profession, and the Universal Declaration of Human Rights.

She is also, as Notre Dame's honorary degree citation pointed out, "one of the most forceful expositors of Catholic social teaching on the American scene." In 1995 she led the Vatican delegation to the United Nations' Beijing Conference on Women, becoming the first woman ever to represent the Vatican at a major international conference. In 2002, President George Bush appointed her to serve on the President's Council on Bioethics.

Religion and a Democratic Society

(1996)

Bishop D'Arcy, President Malloy, reverend clergy, honored guests, faculty. I am delighted to join you in offering congratulations to the families, friends, and most especially, the members of the Class of 1996! I can well imagine the happiness and pride that you parents are feeling today. And I am deeply grateful to have been invited to share this special occasion with you.

So as a token of my gratitude, I'm going to make you a gift of the most important lesson I have learned in all the graduations I have attended as a student, teacher and parent over 28 years. I can put it in the form of a beatitude: Blessed is the commencement speaker who keepeth it short, and delayeth not the party!

One of the reasons I'm so pleased to be here today is that it gives me a chance to acknowledge a gift that I received from Notre Dame. Many years ago, when I was a high school student in a small town in western Massachusetts, I was beginning to have difficulty putting together what I had been taught in Sunday school with the world of ideas I was encountering in the local public library. Then, one day, I came across an essay in our local newspaper by a Father Theodore Hesburgh. One sentence jumped out at me, and it's no exaggeration to say that it had a profound effect on my life from then on. "When you encounter a conflict between science and religion," Father Hesburgh wrote, "you're either dealing with a bad scientist or a bad theologian."

That characteristically blunt Hesburgh-ism not only helped me on the difficult journey from childhood beliefs to adult faith, but it helped to channel my adolescent rebellion toward a critical engagement with the natural and human sciences.

You members of the Class of 1996 have had the good fortune of being steeped in the tradition in which Father Ted's insight was grounded. As I read in *Domers,* you were initiated into it four years ago when Vice President Patty O'Hara welcomed you with the words: "We don't apologize for being different here. We proclaim it. . . . We believe a true education integrates faith and reason."

As you know, the Hesburgh-O'Hara approach to faith and reason isn't new. You are the heirs of what Chicago's Robert Maynard Hutchins enviously referred to as "the longest intellectual tradition of any institution in the world." You are the heirs of the same fearless approach to knowledge that enabled Thomas Aquinas to commune with the ancient Greeks without the slightest fear that his faith would be unsettled. Why not? Because he understood the intellect as a great gift from God: a gift that not only doesn't threaten faith, but advances the ability of each new generation to know, love, and serve God in this world.

A very different set of attitudes prevails in some other parts of the American educational landscape. There, one dogma holds that faith and reason are each other's enemies, and that science has made religion obsolete. Another accords a place to religion as a kind of leisure-time activity, but insists that religiously grounded viewpoints are out of bounds in discussions in the public square. In many institutions supposedly devoted to free inquiry, those views are held with fundamentalist fervor and propagated with missionary zeal.

The idea that religion ought to be kept private has even attracted a certain following among religious Americans, including Catholics. The reasons are understandable. Just as it's not easy for an individual to grow from childhood to adult faith, it wasn't easy for American Catholics to make the transition from the immigrant church to the position in American society they now enjoy. On that rocky road, many people chose to follow what we might call "the way of the turtle." The turtle keeps her religion inside her shell. She keeps silent on many issues of the day, lest she be accused of trying to "impose" her views on her fellow citizens.

Other Catholics, eager to make their way in the world, chose what one might call "the way of the chameleon." The chameleon tries to blend in with established patterns of secular culture. When parts of their heritage didn't lend themselves to blending, chameleon theologians appeared to help make doctrine fit more comfortably with the lifestyles and attitudes of the upwardly mobile. The turtle generation so feared rejection by mainstream American culture that it hid its light under a bushel. The chameleon generation so craved acceptance by the elite culture that it sold its own birthright.

Fortunately for our beloved republic, Americans of all persuasions are now beginning to reject those choices. They have begun to let their light shine, just as your valedictorian Theresa said they should. They're taking their rightful places in the public discussion of where we are as a society and where we're headed. And Americans of diverse faiths have begun to discover that they often have more in common with each other than they do with the secularized rank-and-file of what my fellow honoree Steven Carter calls the "Culture of Disbelief."

When this new generation of unapologetically religious Americans brings its own insights to bear on the issues of the day, they are not trying to *impose* their views on anyone, but they will no longer be denied their right to *propose* their views along with everyone else's. And just in time, because public deliberation has been greatly impoverished by the absence of this kind of diversity. At the recent U.N. conference on women in Beijing, for example, it was troubling to see how few voices other than religious voices were raised on behalf of the world's poorest and most marginalized women. It is alarming how many political decisions here at home are taken without a care for their long-term effects or indirect consequences. As the American founders well knew, a democratic society without the influence of religion can easily consume its own cultural foundations. It can fall into a brutish materialism and a careless indifference about the future. Now more than ever in that complicated world that Theresa described to you, *now more than ever*, the country needs all of its voices.

But here is a key point (and here I speak to you not as a teacher, not as a parent, but as a fellow citizen): Religious participants in public debates will not be effective unless they can speak in terms that are persuasive to men and women of good will—of all faiths, and of no faith. They'll get nowhere if they just preach to the converted. And they'll get nowhere if they behave like the Dublin man who went to

London one day and saw a terrible brawl in the street. He went up to one of the participants, tapped him on the shoulder and said, "Excuse me, is this a private fight or may I join in?" In the "politics of persuasion," it's intelligence and skill in dialogue that are going to count. And here's where the education that dares to be different can *make* a difference.

You perhaps have heard Father Hesburgh say that "the worst heresy is that one life cannot make a difference." But you may wonder: just how might a Domer education make a difference?

Well, first, don't be surprised if habits, ideas, ways of thinking that you picked up here come back to you, taking on deeper meanings, turning up in unexpected places—like Father Ted's throwaway line years ago about science and religion. Don't be surprised if one day you find yourself quoting Patty O'Hara to your own children. Yes, an education like yours tends to be a "gift that keeps on giving."

Then, too, unlike the chameleons who tend to blend into the dominant culture just where it needs to be challenged, you Domers are more likely to be the kinds of independent-minded citizens that the American founders counted on.

You'll have a head start on bridging differences in our pluralistic society, because you know tolerance does not consist merely in putting up with the people who disagree with us. It means engaging with them—because we know that they are creatures of God just as much as we are, and because we know, alas, that our own access to truth is imperfect.

And finally, since your parents and I are veterans of the 1960s, I cannot resist adding that you are also well equipped to be radicals—in the sense of knowing how to get to the root of things. Many people who take lofty moral positions on social and economic justice, have sloughed off many other moral teachings that are hard to follow in our permissive society. Novelist Saul Bellow calls such persons practitioners of the "easy virtues." He compares them to a man who rides into a ghost town and declares himself to be the sheriff. On the other hand, many staunch defenders of traditional personal morality falter when it comes to social justice. They can't quite wrap their minds around the preferential option for the poor. The only options they know about are on the stock market.

But there are good reasons why the Catholic Church consistently warns not only against putting "profits ahead of people," but also against putting self-indulgence ahead of our responsibilities to our families and the common good. There is a growing realization, across the political spectrum and among people of all faiths, that materialism, present-mindedness, carelessness about life at its frail beginnings and its fragile endings are creating a culture that corresponds to *nobody's* vision of the good life. There is a growing appreciation of the essential connection, the seamlessness, if you will, between the duty to respect every human being no matter where he or she is on life's journey, and the duty to respond with compassionate justice to all who are in need. And here is where Judaeo-Christian traditions of responsibility and solidarity intersect with the great American traditions of hospitality and generosity, of welcome to the stranger, and lending a helping hand to the person in need.

Now, speaking of hospitality reminds me of my promise not to delay the festivities. So let me speed you on your way with a blessing attributed to a woman who understood the radical nature of the message of the gospel in all of its fullness. She was St. Brigid of Kildare. Brigid's abbey in sixth century Ireland was a hospice for the dying and a haven for needy strangers. And Brigid seems to have loved a good party. At least that's the impression one gets from her blessing which begins with this line: "Lord, I would have a lake of the finest ale." Brigid goes on:

> I would welcome the poor to my feast
> For they are God's children
> I would welcome the sick to my feast
> For they are God's joy
> Let the poor sit with Jesus at the highest place
> And let the sick dance with the angels.
> God bless the poor
> God bless the sick
> And bless our human race
> God bless our food
> God bless our drink
> All homes, O God, embrace.

If Brigid were here today, I'm sure she would add, "God bless the Notre Dame Class of 1996."

KOFI A. ANNAN

—ɯ—

The seventh secretary general of the United Nations, Kofi A. Annan
(1938–) was born in Kumasi, Ghana, the son of a Ghanaian
businessman from a family of chiefs. He began his studies in Ghana
and completed his undergraduate degree at Macalester College in St.
Paul, Minnesota. He undertook graduate studies in economics and
joined the World Health Organization in Geneva as a budget officer
in 1962. Thereafter, he pursued his career within the United Nations
system until his appointment as secretary general in 1997. He was
elected unanimously to a second five-year term in 2001. At the U.N.,
Annan worked hard to reform the organization's management system
and brought new energy to its efforts in support of conflict resolution,
human rights advocacy, and international development. In 2001
Annan and the United Nations were named the winners of the one
hundredth annual Nobel Peace Prize. In a congratulatory message,
Pope John Paul II told the Nobel laureate that the award
"crowns a lifetime dedicated to serving peace and justice
and the well-being of the world's peoples."

—ɯ—

World Poverty and Our Common Humanity

(2000)

Father Malloy, members of the Class of 2000, ladies and gentlemen: Thank you for that most flattering introduction, and thank you
for this degree of Doctor of Laws. It is indeed a great honour for me to
share this special day of achievement with so many of you. This University is justly famous, and we can all be very proud to be associated
with it. It has built its reputation for learning on a solid link with the
Catholic Church—a body which even we who are not members of it
must admire for its message of the universal brotherhood and sister-
hood of men and women, of social justice and respect for human life.

Just six weeks ago I had the privilege, with my colleagues in the
United Nations system, of being received in Rome by His Holiness
Pope John Paul II. Once again I was struck by his acute sense of the
times we are all living in, and by his burning desire to see the benefits
of human progress more widely and equitably shared. He spoke of the
world's increasing interdependence. He rightly said that this requires
new ways of thinking and new types of international cooperation. And
he defined the challenge facing us, at the dawn of the twenty-first
century, as that of building a world in which individuals and peoples
fully and unequivocally accept responsibility for their fellow human
beings, for all the earth's inhabitants.

I was greatly encouraged by this message because it chimes exactly with one that I myself am trying to get across. In just over three
months' time, political leaders from all over the world will gather in
New York for the Millennium Summit. In preparation for that meeting
I have issued a report, which deals with issues of peace and security,
with environmental problems, and with the reform of the United Nations itself. The longest section in it, which I feel is specially close to
the Pope's message, is entitled "Freedom from Want." And it is that
theme that I should like to dwell on briefly this afternoon. One of the
aims of the United Nations is "to promote social progress and better
standards of life in larger freedom." The founders knew that this aim is

inseparable from the other aims—peace, human rights and respect for international law—which they listed alongside it.

Without doubt, in the past half century the world has made great economic gains. Since the 1960s, life expectancy in developing countries has increased from 46 to 64 years; infant mortality rates have halved; the proportion of children enrolled in primary school has increased by more than 80 percent; and access to safe drinking water and sanitation has doubled. Some parts of the world are now getting richer at almost vertiginous speed. But others are falling further and further behind. Sixty percent of the world's income is now earned by one billion people living in developed countries, while the 3.5 billion in the low-income countries earn less than 20 percent. Nearly half the world's population has to make do on less than $2 per day. And some 1.2 billion people—including 500 million in South Asia and 300 million in Africa—are struggling on less than $1. No doubt one dollar goes further in the villages of India than in the shopping malls of Indiana. Even so, just imagine what it is like to have only one dollar in your hand to provide for all your wants and needs each and every day of the year. Just one dollar for food, clothing, education, medicine or shelter. How do you start a family, or a business, with that kind of capital? How can you enjoy any kind of freedom? How can you escape from pain and despair?

This extreme poverty is an affront to our common humanity. It also makes many other problems worse. For instance, poor countries—especially those with significant inequality between ethnic and religious groups—are far more likely to be embroiled in conflicts than rich ones. It is in poor countries, particularly in Africa, that the worst effects of HIV/AIDS and other diseases are concentrated. And poor countries often lack the capacity and resources to implement policies that protect the environment. I do not mean to suggest that the poverty of the many is caused by the prosperity of the few, or vice versa. It is not that the poor are exploited. Their tragedy is that they are *excluded* from the world market.

What I *do* suggest is that the extraordinary success of the new global economy offers all of us a great example and a great opportunity. But at present perhaps half of humankind is missing out. We *must* find ways to enable the rest of the world to join in. We must put the great new global market within reach of the poor, so that they too can become producers and consumers.

My report suggests some ways of doing this. Many of the keys lie in the hands of the developing countries themselves, and especially their leaders.   But there is much that the more fortunate people in the world—a category that includes all of us here this afternoon—can do to help. The future of developing countries depends, above all on their ability to mobilize capital and attract investment. And that in turn depends on their goods and services being allowed to compete fairly in the markets of richer countries, such as the United States. In many cases it also depends on their governments being able to spend money on education and health instead of having to devote all their revenue to servicing external debts. And when a country *does* adopt sensible policies, it can benefit enormously from financial assistance.

And yet, over several decades during which the industrial world has been enjoying unprecedented prosperity, development assistance has steadily declined. It is particularly shameful that the United States, the most prosperous and successful country in the history of the world, should be one of the least generous in terms of the share of its gross national product it devotes to helping the world's poor. I am sure many of you share my feeling that this is unworthy of the traditions of this great country. So there are three areas—trade, debt relief and official development aid—where I hope you will use your privileged position, as citizens of a great democracy, to advocate the changes in public policy that are needed.

But you can also make a difference more directly, as individuals. One of the glories of this University is its emphasis on service learning and volunteerism. A large number of you, I am told, have done service work throughout your years as students here—not just occasional hours tutoring but major time commitments, here in the South Bend community and, during your vacations, further afield. Even more encouragingly, Notre Dame students have a tradition of taking a full-time volunteer job for the year after graduation, supported both by the University and by their parents. I hope many of you will follow that tradition, and make that year a year of real service to those who need it most—the poorest countries and the poorest people.

Let me mention one way in particular that some of you could do that, especially those of you who have acquired skills in information technology—which I suspect is most if not all of you, whatever subject you have majored in. Information technology, I am convinced, is one of the main keys to economic growth and development for all countries. At present, information technology is even more unequally divided than other forms of wealth. There are more computers in this country than in the rest of the world combined. But information technology is cheap compared to other forms of capital. It depends less and less on hardware or on major financial investments, and more and more on human brainpower—the one form of capital which, thank God, is fairly distributed among the world's people.

All that is needed is a relatively small investment in basic education, and in making things like computers and cell-phones available to groups of people, so that each individual does not have to buy their own. That investment can give many poor people access to the new technology. And that, in turn, will enable many poor countries to leapfrog some of the long and painful stages of development that others have had to go through. Already this is happening in parts of the developing world. Bangalore, an Indian city, has become a center of the world software industry. Costa Rica, by exporting microchips, achieved the highest growth rate in Latin America last year. Public telecentres have been established in places from Peru to Kazakhstan. In Egypt—to give just one example—the United Nations Development Programme has helped create Technology Access Community Centers to bring the Internet and fax services to poor and rural areas. This is where you come in. We are in the process of setting up a United Nations Technology Service—UNITeS for short. It is a consortium of high-tech volunteer corps, which will send people out to train groups in developing countries in the uses and opportunities of information technology. Net Corps America is a member of this consortium. I am sure many of you here could help, and I hope you will not hesitate to get in touch with them or with the UN Volunteer Programme.

Your year as a volunteer could bring enormous benefits to people in a developing country. It would also make a difference to your own lives, which I am sure you would never forget, and never regret. In any case, I hope all of you will take a commitment to the wider world, and to the cause of peace and development, into your future careers—whether they be in business, public service, or professions like teaching, medicine and the law. All of these can have an international dimension. And all offer opportunities to be of service to your fellow men and women.

I feel confident that you will seize those opportunities. I know that Notre Dame represents much that is best and most generous in the American tradition. I am proud, as all of you must be proud, that from this day forward we can call ourselves Notre Dame graduates. I wish you all a very happy day; and may you live lives of great benefit to others as well as fulfillment to yourselves! Thank you very much.

—ᴍ—

GEORGE W. BUSH

George W. Bush (1946–) is the forty-third president of the United States and formerly had served as the forty-sixth governor of Texas. He grew up in the Texan cities of Midland and Houston. He received a degree in history from Yale University and an MBA from Harvard. He worked in the oil and gas industry prior to becoming the managing general partner of the Texas Rangers baseball team from 1989 to 1994, when he was elected governor of the Lone Star State. He easily won a second four-year term in 1998. In his 2000 presidential campaign, Bush presented himself as a "compassionate conservative" committed to the principles of limited government, personal responsibility, and strong families.

The second son of a former president to win the presidency, Bush entered the White House with less experience in international affairs than any president since Harry S. Truman. Yet, since the terrorist attacks of September 11, 2001, his presidency has been occupied primarily by the war on terrorism and the demands of foreign policy issues.

A Caring Society

(2001)

It is a high privilege to receive this degree. I'm particularly pleased that it bears the great name of Notre Dame. My brother, Jeb, may be the Catholic in the family, but between us, I'm the only Domer.

I have spoken on this campus before. It was in 1980, the year my dad ran for Vice President with Ronald Reagan. I think I really won over the crowd that day. In fact, I'm sure of it because all six of them walked me to my car. That was back when Father Hesburgh was the president of this University during a tenure that in many ways defined the reputation and values of Notre Dame. It's a real honor to be here with Father Hesburgh and with Father Joyce. Between them, these two good priests have given nearly a century of service to Notre Dame. I'm told that Father Hesburgh now holds 146 honorary degrees. That's pretty darn impressive, Father, but I'm gaining on you. As of today, I'm only 140 behind.

Let me congratulate all the members of the class of 2001. You made it, and we're all proud of you on this big day. I also congratulate the parents who after these years are happy, proud, and broke. I commend this fine faculty for the years of work and instruction that produced this outstanding class. And I'm pleased to join my fellow honorees as well. I'm in incredibly distinguished company with authors, executives, educators, church officials, and eminent scientists. We're sharing a memorable day and a great honor, and I congratulate you all.

Notre Dame, as a Catholic university, carries forward a great tradition of social teaching. It calls on all of us, Catholic and non-Catholic, to honor family, to protect life in all its stages, to serve and uplift the poor. This University is more than a community of scholars. It is a community of conscience—and an ideal place to report on our nation's commitment to the poor, and how we're keeping it.

In 1964, the year I started college, another President from Texas delivered a commencement address talking about this national commitment. In that speech, President Lyndon Johnson issued a challenge. He said: "This is a time for decision. You are the generation that must decide. Will you decide to leave the future a society where a man is condemned to hopelessness because he was born poor? Or will you join to wipe out poverty in this land?" In that speech, Lyndon Johnson advocated a war on poverty, which had noble intentions and some enduring successes. Poor families got basic health care; disadvantaged children were given a head start in life. Yet, there were also some consequences that no one wanted or intended. The welfare entitlement became an enemy of personal effort and responsibility, turning many recipients into dependents. The War on Poverty also turned too many citizens into bystanders, convinced that compassion had become the work of government alone.

In 1996, welfare reform confronted the first of these problems with a five-year time limit on benefits and a work requirement to receive them. Instead of a way of life, welfare became an offer of temporary help—not an entitlement but a transition. Thanks in large part to this change, welfare rolls have been cut in half. Work and self-respect have been returned to many lives. That is a tribute to Democrats and Republicans who agreed on reform and to the President who signed it: President Bill Clinton.

Our nation has confronted welfare dependency, but our work is only half done. Now we must confront the second problem: to revive the spirit of citizenship—to marshal the compassion of our people to meet the continued needs of our nation. This is a challenge to my administration, and to each one of you. We must meet that challenge—because it is right and because it is urgent.

Welfare as we knew it has ended but poverty has not. When over 12 million children live below the poverty line, we are not a postpoverty America. Most states are seeing the first wave of welfare recipients who have reached the law's five-year time limit. The easy cases have already left the welfare rolls. The hardest problems remain—people with far fewer skills and greater barriers to work. People with complex human problems, like illiteracy and addiction, abuse, and mental illness. We do not yet know what will happen to these men and women or to their children. But we cannot sit and watch, leaving them to their own struggles and their own fate.

There is a great deal at stake. In our attitudes and our actions we are determining the character of our country. When poverty is considered hopeless, America is condemned to a permanent social division, becoming a nation of caste and class, divided by fences and gates and guards. Our task is clear, and it's difficult: we must build our country's unity by extending our country's blessings. We make that commitment because we're Americans. Aspiration is the essence of our country. We believe in social mobility, not social Darwinism. We are the country of the second chance, where failure is never final. And that dream has sometimes been deferred. It must never be abandoned. We are committed to compassion for practical reasons. When men and women are lost to themselves, they are also lost to our nation. When millions are hopeless, all of us are diminished by the loss of their gifts. And we're committed to compassion for moral reasons. Jewish prophets and Catholic teaching both speak of God's special concern for the poor. This is perhaps the most radical teaching of faith—that the value of life is not contingent on wealth or strength or skill. That value is a reflection of God's image. Much of today's poverty has more to do with troubled lives than a troubled economy. And often when a life is broken, it can only be restored by another caring, concerned human being. The answer for an abandoned child is not a job requirement—it is the loving presence of a mentor. The answer to addiction is not a demand for self-sufficiency—it is personal support on the hard road to recovery. The hope we seek is found in safe havens for battered women and children, in homeless shelters, in crisis pregnancy centers, in programs that tutor and conduct job training and help young people who may happen to be on parole. All these efforts provide not just the benefit, but attention and kindness, a touch of courtesy, a dose of grace.

Mother Teresa said that what the poor often need, even more than shelter and food—though these are desperately needed, as well—is to be wanted. And that sense of belonging is within the power of each of us to provide. Many in the community have shown what compassion can accomplish. Notre Dame's own Lou Nanni is the former director of South Bend's Center for the Homeless, an institution founded by two Notre Dame professors. It provides guests with everything from drug treatment to mental health service, to classes in the Great Books, to preschool for young children. Discipline is tough. Faith is encouraged, not required. Student volunteers are committed and consistent and central to its mission. Lou Nanni describes this mission as "re-pairing the fabric" of society by letting people see the inherent "worth and dignity and God-given potential" of every human being. Compassion often works best on a small and human scale. It is generally better when a call for help is local, not long distance. Here at this University you've heard that call and responded. It is part of what makes Notre Dame a great university.

This is my message today: There is no great society that is not a caring society. Any effective war on poverty must deploy what Dorothy Day call "the weapons of spirit." There's only one problem with groups like South Bend's Center for the Homeless—there aren't enough of them. It's not sufficient to praise charities and community groups; we must support them. And this is both a public obligation and a personal responsibility. The War on Poverty established a federal commitment to the poor. The welfare reform legislation of 1996 made that commitment more effective. For the task ahead, we must move to the third stage of combating poverty in America. Our society must enlist, equip, and empower idealistic Americans in the works of compassion that only they can provide.

Government has an important role. It will never be replaced by charities. My administration increases funding for major social welfare and poverty programs by 8 percent. Yet, government must also do more to take the side of charities and community healers, and support their work. We've had enough of the stale debate between big government and indifferent government. Government must be active enough to fund services for the poor—and humble enough to let good people in local communities provide those services.

So, I've created a White House Office of Faith-Based and Community Initiatives. Through that office we are working to ensure that local community helpers and healers receive more federal dollars, greater private support, and face fewer bureaucratic barriers. We have proposed a "compassion capital fund," that will match private giving with federal dollars. We have proposed allowing all taxpayers to deduct their charitable contributions, including non-itemizers. This could encourage almost $15 billion a year in new charitable giving. My attitude is, everyone in America—whether they are well-off or not—should have the same incentive and reward for giving. And we're in the process of implementing and expanding "charitable choice"—the principle, already established in federal law, that faith-based organizations should not suffer discrimination when they compete for contracts to provide social services. Government should never fund the teaching of faith, but it should support the good works of the faithful.

Some critics of this approach object to the idea of government funding going to any group motivated by faith. But they should take a look around them. Public money already goes to groups like the Center for the Homeless and, on a larger scale, to Catholic Charities. Do the critics really want to cut them off? Medicaid and Medicare money currently goes to religious hospitals. Should this practice be ended? Child-care vouchers for low-income families are redeemed every day at houses of worship across America. Should this be prevented? Government loans send countless students to religious colleges. Should this be banned? Of course not. America has a long tradition of accommodating and encouraging religious institutions when they pursue public goals. My administration did not create that tradition—but we will expand it to confront some urgent problems.

Today, I'm adding two initiatives to our agenda, in the areas of housing and drug treatment. Owning a home is a source of dignity for families and stability for communities—and organizations like Habitat for Humanity make that dream possible for many low-income Americans. Groups of this type currently receive some funding from the Department of Housing and Urban Development. The budget I submit to Congress next year will propose a threefold increase in this funding, which will expand home ownership, and the hope and pride that come with it. And nothing is more likely to perpetuate poverty than a life enslaved to drugs. So we propose $1.6 billion in new funds to close what I call the treatment gap—the gap between the 5 million Americans who need drug treatment and the 2 million who currently receive it. We will also propose that all these funds—all of them—be open to equal competition from faith-based and community groups. The federal government should do all these things, but others have responsibilities as well—including corporate America. Many corporations in America do good work, in good causes. But if we hope to substantially reduce poverty and suffering in our country, corporate America needs to give more—and to give better. Faith-based organizations receive only a tiny percentage of over-all corporate giving. Currently six of the 10 largest corporate givers in America explicitly rule out or restrict donations to faith-based groups, regardless of their effectiveness. The federal government will not discriminate against faith-based organizations and neither should corporate America.

In the same spirit, I hope America's foundations consider ways they may devote more of their money to our nation's neighborhoods and their helpers and their healers. I will convene a summit this fall asking corporate and philanthropic leaders throughout America to join me at the White House to discuss ways they can provide more support to community organizations—both secular and religious. Ultimately, your country is counting on each of you. Knute Rockne once said "I have found that prayers work best when you have big players." We can pray for the justice of our country, but you're the big players we need to achieve it. Government can promote compassion, corporations and foundations can fund it, but the citizens—it's the citizens who provide it. A determined assault on poverty will require both an active government and active citizens. There's more to citizenship than voting—though I urge you to do it. There's more to citizenship than paying your taxes—though I'd strongly advise you pay them. Citizenship is empty without concern for our fellow citizens, without the ties that bind us to one another and build a common good.

If you already realize this and you're acting on it, I thank you. If you haven't thought about it, I leave you with this challenge: serve a neighbor in need. Because a life of service is a life of significance. Because materialism, ultimately, is boring, and consumerism can build a prison of wants. Because a person who is not responsible for others is a person who is truly alone. Because there are few better ways to express our love for America than to care for other Americans. And because the same God who endows us with individual rights also calls us to social obligations. So let me return to Lyndon Johnson's charge. You're the generation that must decide. Will you ratify poverty and division with your apathy—or will you build a common good with your idealism? Will you be a spectator in the renewal of your country—or a citizen?

The methods of the past may have been flawed, but the idealism of the past was not an illusion. Your calling is not easy, because you must do the acting and the caring. But there is fulfillment in that sacrifice that creates hope for the rest of us. Every life you help proves that every life might be helped. The actual proves the possible, and hope is always the beginning of change. Thank you for having me, and God bless.

—ᴍ—

MOTHER TERESA
OF CALCUTTA

*The extraordinary woman known as Mother Teresa (1910–97)
was born Agnes Gonxha Bojaxhiu in Skopje, Macedonia.
She joined the Sisters of Loretto in Ireland at the age of seventeen,
and within a year was sent to teach in Calcutta, India. She left
the Loretto sisters in 1948 and soon formed a new order, the
Missionaries of Charity, dedicated to serving the sick and caring
for the dying of Calcutta's vast slums. Mother Teresa adopted Indian
citizenship in 1950 and provided the sari as the habit for her sisters.
The growth of her order has been extraordinary and its apostolic
foundations are now located in over thirty countries. Pope Paul VI
awarded her the first ever Pope John XXIII Peace Prize, and in
1979 she won the Nobel Peace Prize. Following her death,
the cause for her canonization was
quickly promoted.*

Letter to the Graduating Class of 1986

[The following letter from Mother Teresa to Michael Mazza, who on behalf of his classmates had invited her to address the 1986 commencement, was read by Father Hesburgh at the baccalaureate mass.]

Calcutta
April 3, 1986

Dear Michael Mazza and all the Graduating Class of 1986,

Thank you very much for your letter of March 8, 1986 and your invitation to me to be the 1986 Commencement speaker at Notre Dame University. My thanks also to each of the many students who have signed the attached sheets signifying their wish for me to come. And truly I would like very much to be with you on this very important day of your lives.

However, I cannot be present because at the time of your Commencement and graduation, 91 young girls will be making their first Vows in our Congregation of Missionaries of Charity. They will be giving themselves to God with undivided love in Chastity, through freedom of Poverty, in total surrender to Obedience, and whole hearted and free service to Him in the distressing disguise of the poorest of the poor.

My gratitude to you is my prayer that each one of you young men and women on your graduation day shine forth as a bright light—the light of Christ—to the world around you:

Feeding the hungry—not only with food but also with the Word of God,

Giving drink to the thirsty—not only for water, but for
  knowledge, peace, truth, justice and love,
Clothing the naked—not only with clothes, but also with human
  dignity,
Giving shelter to the homeless—not only a shelter made of
  bricks, but a heart that understands, that covers, that loves,
Nursing the sick and the dying—not only of the body, but also of
  mind and Spirit.

But to do this we need to be pure of heart for only the pure can
see and recognize Jesus in the distressing disguise and touch Him in
the poorest of the poor. We need to be humble like Mary to be able to
say "Yes" to God—to accept God's law, God's teaching as given to us
by His Vicar on earth—the Holy Father and the Magisterium of the
Church.

Be whole hearted, fully committed Christians, dedicated to
Truth, Integrity and Justice. Love the Gospel without compromise—
holiness is not the luxury of a few but our simple duty for you and for
me. Let Christ live His life in you—accept the challenges of life and
dare to be what Jesus has created and called you to be.

Keep the joy of loving Jesus in each other and in the poor and
share this joy with all whom you meet, especially your own families.

Let us pray—
God Bless You,
Mother Teresa, M.C.

THEODORE M.
HESBURGH, C.S.C.

*Holy Cross priest, legendary president of the University of
Notre Dame, leader in American higher education, adviser to
popes and presidents, Theodore M. Hesburgh (1917–) guided the
University of Notre Dame from 1952 to 1987. His dynamic leadership
transformed Notre Dame from a primarily undergraduate and somewhat provincial institution into the leading American Catholic
university. Beyond the campus, he ably served both
his church and his nation in areas such as civil and human rights,
economic development, world peace, and higher education.
He has received numerous awards and honors, including the
Medal of Freedom in 1964 and the Congressional Gold Medal
in 2000.*

Charge to the
Graduating Class of 1987

From the *Brothers Karamazov*:

> Let us agree that we shall never forget one another, and what-
> ever happens, remember how good it felt when we were all
> here together, united by a good and decent feeling which
> made us better people, better probably than we would other-
> wise have been.

I think that expresses as well as anything from literature can,
the feeling of this particular hour. Let me tell you as a kind of father
figure leaving you, or leaving with you, that the days ahead will have
all kinds of lessons for you. The lessons haven't stopped by your leaving here.

The time has come, at long last you may think, to say to all of you
who go forth a word of parting on behalf of all those who remain behind. That we wish you God's blessing in the days ahead goes almost
without saying, as indeed we do, from the heart.

The days ahead will also have their lessons, some easily and joy-
fully learned, and some that will etch your very souls in the strong
acid of sorrow and adversity. We trust that the values you have learned
here: the joy of truth, the exhilaration of beauty, the strength of goodness, the passion for justice, the quiet courage born of prayer, the
love and compassion we owe our fellow men, the modesty and humility that our human frailty dictates, the reverence for the inner dignity of all things truly human, for human life from its beginning to its
end—we trust that all of these intellectual and moral qualities will

take deeper root and grow in you throughout all the days ahead, to enrich you as a person and to add luminosity to your life in a world often dark.

And because you have been schooled in the moral, as well as the intellectual dimension of life's total meaning, I give you as a parting thought these brief words of Winston Churchill:

> The only guide to a man is his conscience; the only shield to his memory is the rectitude and sincerity of his actions. It is very imprudent to walk through life without this shield, because we are so mocked by the failure of our hopes; but with this shield, whatever our destiny may be, we always march in the ranks of honor.

May Our Blessed Lady, Notre Dame, bless you ever with Her Divine Son—and may each of you ever be a true son or daughter of Notre Dame.

APPENDIX

List of Commencement Speakers

1844–1869   Speakers can be identified only for certain of these years.

1861   Rev. Dr. John McMullen, Chicago priest and teacher

1865   William Tecumseh Sherman, Union General

1867   T. E. Corcoran, Editor, *The Cincinnati Telegraph*

1870   Paul Broder, Professor, Beloit College, Wisconsin

1871   Hon. A. C. Dodge, U.S. Senator from Iowa

1872   Rt. Rev. Joseph Dwenger, Bishop of Fort Wayne

1873   John J. Fitzgibbon, Editor, *The Western Catholic*

1874   Hon. S. S. Hayes, Comptroller, City of Chicago

1875   Hon. J. S. Morris, Vicksburg, Mississippi

1876   William J. Onahan, Chicago Catholic activist and businessman

1877   Hon. Frank H. Hurd, former U.S. Congressman

1878   Rt. Rev. John Lancaster Spalding, Bishop of Peoria

1879   No commencement exercises

1880   Hon. Edmund F. Dunne, former Chief Justice of Arizona

1881   Hon. W. W. Cleary, Covington, Kentucky

1882   Rt. Rev. Francis S. Chatard, Bishop of Vicennes

1883   Rt. Rev. John A. Watterson, Bishop of Columbus

1884   Rt. Rev. Ignacio Montes De Oca y Obregon, Bishop of Linares, Mexico

1885   The scheduled speaker, Major General William S. Rosecrans, canceled his commitment due to duties in Washington, D.C.

1886   Rt. Rev. John Lancaster Spalding, Bishop of Peoria

1887   Wm. H. Johnston, alumnus, East Townsend, Ohio

1888   Rev. P. F. Carr, Denver, Colorado

1889   William P. Breen, alumnus, Fort Wayne, Indiana

1890   Rt. Rev. John Lancaster Spalding, Bishop of Peoria

1891   Rt. Rev. John Lancaster Spalding, Bishop of Peoria

1892   Rt. Rev. J. S. Foley, Bishop of Detroit

1893   Rev. Msgr. Robert Seton, priest of diocese of Newark, N.J.

1894   Rt. Rev. John A. Watterson, Bishop of Columbus

1895   Rt. Rev. John Lancaster Spalding, Bishop of Peoria

1896   Hon. Thomas A. Moran, Judge, Chicago

1897   Rev. Msgr. Joseph F. Mooney, priest of archdiocese of New York

1898   Rt. Rev. Maurice F. Burke, Bishop of St. Joseph, Missouri

1899   Rt. Rev. John Lancaster Spalding, Bishop of Peoria

1900   Rt. Rev. John J. Glennon, Bishop of Kansas City, Missouri

1901   Rt. Rev. John Shanley, Bishop of Fargo, North Dakota

1902   Hon. William P. Breen, A.B. '77, A.M. '80, Fort Wayne

1903   Hon. John M. Gearin, Attorney, Portland, Oregon

1904   Hon. Charles Joseph Bonaparte, Attorney, Progressive reformer, member of the Board of Indian Commissioners

1905   Hon. Marcus A. Kavanagh, Judge, Chicago

1906   Rev. D. J. Stafford, priest and lecturer, Washington, D.C.

1907   Rev. John Talbot Smith, priest, author, lecturer, New York City

1908   Hon. Charles P. Neill, U.S. Commissioner of Labor

1909   Hon. Hannis Taylor, former U.S. Minister to Spain, authority on international law

1910   Hon. Thomas Riley Marshall, Governor of Indiana

1911   Sir Charles Fitzpatrick, Chief Justice of the Dominion of Canada

1912   Rt. Rev. Thomas F. Hickey, Bishop of Rochester, New York

1913   Hon. James M. Cox, Governor of Ohio

1914   Hon. Joseph E. Ransdell, U.S. Senator from Louisiana

1915   John F. Fitzgerald, formerly Mayor of Boston

1916   Hon. Martin Joseph Wade, Judge of the United States District Court of Iowa

1917   Rt. Rev. Joseph Chartrand, Coadjutor Bishop of Indianapolis

1918   Edward N. Hurley, Chairman of the U.S. Shipping Board

1919   Monsignor F. B. D. Bickerstaffe-Drew, English war chaplain and novelist

1920   Hon. Morgan Joseph O'Brien, New York City

1921   Hon. David I. Walsh, U.S. Senator from Massachusetts

1922   Kickham Scanlan, Chief Justice of the Criminal Court, Chicago

1923   Thomas Lindsey Blayney, Rice Institute, Houston

1924   Hon. Woodbridge Nathan Ferris, U.S. Senator from Michigan

1925   Edmond H. Moore, Democratic National Committee member from Ohio, attorney, Youngstown

1926   Judge Dudley G. Wooten, Professor of Law in Hoynes College of Law, Notre Dame

1927   Alfred J. Talley, Judge, New York City

1928   Francis O'Shaughnessy, Attorney, Chicago

1929   Col. William J. Donovan, Buffalo, New York, war hero, former Assistant Attorney General of the United States

1930   Claude G. Bowers, author, editor, orator

1931   Angus D. McDonald, Treasurer, United States Railroad Commission

1932 Owen D. Young, New York City financier

1933 Hon. Paul V. McNutt, Governor of Indiana

1934 Hon. Frank C. Walker, Chairman of the Council on Emergency Relief

1935 Shane Leslie, essayist, dramatist, lecturer

1936 Dr. William J. Mayo, cofounder of Mayo Clinic

1937 Dennis F. Kelly, President of The Fair, Chicago department store

1938 Hon. Terence Byrne Cosgrove, attorney, San Francisco

1939 William H. Harrison, Vice-President and chief engineer of AT&T

1940 Hon. David Worth Clark, U.S. Senator from Idaho

1941 Joseph P. Kennedy, former ambassador to Great Britain

1942 J. Edgar Hoover, Director of the F.B.I.

1943 Rev. Arthur J. Hope, C.S.C., author and editor

1943/4 Hon. Harry F. Kelly, '17, Governor of Michigan

1944 Rev. Thomas J. Brennan, C.S.C., Professor of Philosophy

1945 Rev. Phillip S. Moore, C.S.C., Dean of the Graduate School

1946 George Sokolsky, columnist

1947 General George C. Kenney, Chief of the Strategic Air Command

1948 Paul G. Hoffman, Director, Economic Cooperation Administration, Washington, D.C.

1949   John Stephen Burke, President, B. Allman & Company, New York City

1950   John J. Hearne, Ambassador of Ireland to the U.S.

1951   Hon. Francis Patrick Matthews, Secretary of the Navy

1952   Dr. Charles Malik, Minister of Lebanon to the U.S.

1953   Dr. Detlev W. Bronk, President of the Johns Hopkins University

1954   James R. Killian, Jr., President of M.I.T.

1955   Herbert Brownell, Jr., Attorney General of the United States

1956   Admiral Arleigh A. Burke, U.S.N., Chief of Naval Operations

1957   Hon. Earl Warren, Chief Justice of the United States Supreme Court

1958   Hon. James P. Mitchell, Secretary of Labor

1959   John A. McCone, Chairman, Atomic Energy Commission

1960   Dwight D. Eisenhower, President of the United States

1961   Robert Sargent Shriver, Jr., Director of the Peace Corps

1962   Henry Cabot Lodge, former ambassador to the United Nations

1963   Hon. Lester B. Pearson, Prime Minister of Canada

1964   Hon. Thomas C. Mann, Assistant Secretary of State for Inter-American affairs

1965   McGeorge Bundy, Special Assistant to the President for National Security Affairs

1966   Lady Jackson (Barbara Ward), economist, London, England

1967   Eugene J. McCarthy, U.S. Senator from Minnesota

1968   Dr. James A. Perkins, President of Cornell University

1969   Dr. Daniel P. Moynihan, Assistant to the President for Urban Affairs

1970   Hon. James E. Allen, Jr., U.S. Commissioner of Education

1971   Dr. Kenneth Keniston, Yale Medical School

1972   Dr. Kingman Brewster, Jr., President of Yale University

1973   Dr. Malcolm C. Moos, President of the University of Minnesota

1974   Dr. Rosemary Park, Professor of Education, UCLA

1975   Alan J. Pifer, President of the Carnegie Corporation of New York and the Carnegie Foundation for the Advancement of Teaching

1976   Vernon E. Jordan, Jr., Executive Director of the National Urban League

1977   Jimmy Carter, President of the United States

1978   William F. Buckley, Jr., Editor of *The National Review*

1979   Joseph A. Califano, Jr., Secretary of Health, Education, and Welfare

1980   Benjamin Civiletti, Attorney General of the United States

1981   Ronald Reagan, President of the United States

1982   Pierre Trudeau, Prime Minister of Canada

1983   Cardinal Joseph Bernardin, Archbishop of Chicago

1984   Loret Miller Ruppe, Director of the Peace Corps

1985   Jose Napoleon Duarte, President of El Salvador

1986   Bishop James Malone, Bishop of Youngstown and president, United States Catholic Conference

1987   Derek Bok, President of Harvard University

1988   Andrew Young, Mayor of Atlanta, Georgia

1989   Peter Ueberroth, businessman, Los Angeles

1990   Bill Cosby, actor and producer

1991   Margaret O'Brien Steinfels, Editor, *Commonweal*

1992   George H. W. Bush, President of the United States

1993   Tom Brokaw, journalist and broadcaster

1994   Albert Reynolds, Taoiseach [prime minister] of Ireland

1995   Condoleezza Rice, Provost, Stanford University

1996   Mary Ann Glendon, Learned Hand Professor of Law, Harvard University

1997   Mark Shields, political commentator and columnist

1998   Joseph F. Kernan, Lieutenant Governor of Indiana

1999   Elizabeth Dole, former president of the American Red Cross

2000   Kofi A. Annan, Secretary General, the United Nations

2001   George W. Bush, President of the United States

2002   Tim Russert, moderator, *Meet the Press*

CPSIA information can be obtained
at www.ICGtesting.com
Printed in the USA
LVHW012132200421
685034LV00016B/949